Touched by Adoption

Stories, Letters and Poems
Compiled and Edited by
Nancy A. Robinson

Green River Press
P.O. Box 6454
Santa Barbara, California 93160

Published by Green River Press
PO Box 6454
Santa Barbara, California 93160

Publisher's Cataloging-in-Publication
(Provided by Quality Books)

Touched by adoption : stories, letters and poems /
    compiled and edited by Nancy A. Robinson. — 1st ed.
      p. cm.
    ISBN: 0-9673363-0-9
      1. Adoption—Literary collections. 2. American
literature—20th century. 3. Adoptees—Literary
collections. I. Robinson, Nancy A.

PS509.A28T68 1999   810.8'0355
                          QBI99-1319

Cover design by: Steven Small; Meitzler Prepress
885 Auzerais Avenue; San Jose, California 95126

Typesetting by: Cirrus Design

First Printing 1999 in the United States of America

For Ehren

I Want to Thank

McDonald Robinson for the financial, emotional, and intellectual support.

Adam Robinson and Compass Computers in Goleta, California, for putting together the computer hardware to make this project possible.

Shannon Robinson for her creative ability in solving computer software problems, her networking in finding others to assist, and her proof-reading skills.

Ehren Robinson Tennant for asking me to write her story and thus planting the seed for this book.

Royal Phillips for encouraging and supporting me throughout the work, for rescuing me after too many long hours of concentration, and for brainstorming ideas.

Felice Karmen for proof-reading and for extending interest and encouragement.

Claire Douglas for her unconditional support and encouragement.

Steve Small for his cover design and technical support.

Mary Watkins, Fred Greenman, and Carol Biddle for reading and endorsing the text.

Dan Poynter for his generosity in pointing the way toward publishing.

The contributors who made this book possible by sharing their hearts and talents.

Nancy A. Robinson

Contents

Preface

In the beginning there is a child who for innumerable reasons cannot grow up with his birth parents. There are birth parents in unfathomable circumstances and unable to care for their children. And there are adults whose arms and hearts ache for and reach out for a child or children to embrace. Out of this triangle, adoption develops. Sometimes these joined lives are well matched; sometimes they are not. Regardless, life unfolds, moves on, and happens, bringing unpredictable events, revealing insights, and challenging everyone.

Each of us is changed by so many lives touched by adoption. The boundaries of kinship and love are broadened, and today families are being redefined to include those from all parts of the world. People are choosing to live with an unprecedented openness about adoption that moves the human heart and soul toward a new awareness.

Within the cover of this book are stories of the early Orphan Trains, closed adoptions, searches, reunions, older adoptions, single parent adoptions, and open adoptions. Expectant parents waiting to adopt share their fears and excitement. With wisdom and humor, seasoned adoptive parents reflect on the meaning of parenthood. Adoptees searching unveil their inner feelings and hopes as they wait. Birth parents reflect on their struggles in relinquishment and attitudes toward reunion. Siblings also write about their experiences.

Most speak for themselves. Occasionally a writer takes the guise of fiction to better illustrate a truth. The individual voices are as varied as life, and no two stories, poems or letters are alike. There are questions, discoveries, losses, insights, sorrows and joys—all products of living life fully.

It is my hope that *Touched by Adoption* will fuel the common fire connecting us, and in the imperfect situations of our lives, the sense of isolation and separateness will not feel so immense. May we discover the common blood that flows in our veins, that's always been there, that makes us one with one another.

The Mother and It

at sixteen
i aborted a life
swore i would never
do that again
but at twenty
found myself
alone and lonely
no desire or capability
to care for myself
or someone else

refused to see
it when it was born
didn't want to know
the sex either
if it was a girl
i might think of myself
if it was a boy
might long for its father
so it remained it
i never thought about the people
who adopted it
told the social worker
i didn't want to know
just signed away my rights

but i never forgot
i could never forget it
come every birthday
i would buy a candle
and make a wish for it

after i learned
to love myself
and stand on my own two feet
i constantly wondered about it
whether it was healthy
whether it looked like me
whether i would recognize it
if i bumped into it in the street

it became my obsession
it was my passion
it was my day dream

what was its name
how tall was it
did it like to caress its chin
like i did
did it walk on its heels
all slouched down
like its father
did it sing when cooking

was its hair fibrous and tight
like mine
did it like itself
did it wonder about its real parents
did it look out the window at nights
and dream on the moon

thinking about it caused me
to lose the only man
who loved me enough to marry me
thinking about it caused me
to gray early
thinking about it made the bottle
my intimate friend
thinking about it made me sit up
many nights thinking about what
it was doing
what it was feeling
how it was sleeping

now i ain't gonna
think about it no more
don't matter no how
the past can't be written
and my future is just about gone

but i want it to know
i've been loving you
all these forty years
ain't a day goes by
i don't think about you
because you're
my one sweet baby child
my very own baby

Opal Palmer Adisa

Who Am I?

I.

for twenty years
he knew who he thought
himself to be

for twenty years
he loved the people
who were the only parents he knew

for twenty years
he was contented
living an average life
in a safe nuclear family

then on the brink of adulthood
his mother told him
you're adopted

he laughed out loud
thinking
surely she's kidding
but her face was tight and stiff
his father's nod trapped his laughter

adopted
a bad word
other people were adopted
not him

II.

not me
instantly
feeling rejected
someone didn't want me
twenty odd years ago
someone abandoned me
twenty odd years ago
my face does not belong
to the parents whose features
i thought i saw in my eyes
the lines of my jaw
the turn of my mouth
whose image who am i
who am i

adopted
where is the face
that resembles mine
whose blood courses
through my veins
who has a habit
of tapping their left foot
when anxious

adopted
for twenty years
i thought i knew
myself

now i have
to begin my search

adopted

Opal Palmer Adisa

Aunty Mother

yesterday
i told my best friend
that my mother is
really my aunty

she said *what do you mean your aunty*
told her my mama died when i was five
and her sister—my aunty—adopted me
but i didn't tell her how my mama died
didn't tell her what she used to do with men
what i saw her do
pushing the needle in her arm
didn't tell her
how at four i had to take care of my mama
and my baby sister too
didn't tell her how for days
i didn't see my mama
and i was scared
left alone with my baby sister
with no diaper or milk

i don't tell many people
that my aunty is not really my mother
because she's the only mother
i've ever had
but latasha is my best friend
and i know she still likes me
even though i am adopted
and don't have a real mother and father
like she does

she promised not to tell anyone else
that my aunty is not my mother
because i'm her best friend
even though i am adopted

Opal Palmer Adisa

We Are a Family

kids at school ask
how comes
you don't look like your parents
you're black
and they are white

i tell them
my parents hand-picked me
saw me as a baby
and fell in love with me
said he's the one we want
and they took me home
because family has nothing
to do with color
family is a joining
of hearts

Opal Palmer Adisa

Jamaican born Opal Palmer Adisa, Ph.D. Ethnic Studies, is a literary critic, poet, prose writer and story teller. Her published works are numerous. To mention a few, they include: *It Begins With Tears,* 1997; *Tamarind and Mango Women,* 1992, won the PEN Oakland/Josephine Miles Award; *traveling women,* 1989; *Bake-Face and Other Guava Stories,* 1986; *Pina, They Many-Eyed Fruit,* 1985; and anthology of children's poems, *A Caribbean Dozen.* Eds. John Agard and Nicols, 1994; *Weather,* Wayland Publisher, London, 1995. A Recording: "Fierce/Love" with Devorah Major, 1992. She has taught at San Francisco State University and the University of California, Berkeley. Presently she is Professor at California College of Arts and Crafts. She lives in Oakland, California, with her three JA-Merican children, Shola, Jawara, and Teju.

One Boy

Lost son, last seen when he was two days old.
His minuscule fingers wrapped my thumb like tendrils,
fragile yet tightly twined.

Awakening eyes the color of sky,
somewhere between blue and dusk.
Faintest show of brown silk hair. Twenty inches tall.

Missing ever since I signed the papers
Surprising, so much power in a signature—
I was only sixteen years old.

My baby born on New Years Day,
already with the gaze of wisdom.
My baby born to be someone else's son.

Abigail Albrecht

Finding Joshua
Abigail Albrecht

Santa Barbara in winter, 1983. I drive to work along the storm-damaged shore. The beachfront park is a disaster of fallen palm fronds, broken boats strewn upside-down in the sand. A small blue hull lies capsized on the lawn. I am mystified by my deluge of tears at the sight.

Three blocks later I arrive at my office. By this time my shoulders are rocking, I am crying so hard. I dash through the gamut of co-workers, covering my face with a tissue and my open hands. The office manager appraises the situation; though I cannot account for my distress, she agrees I have to go home.

Twenty-five minutes later, front door shut to the world, I am silently weeping at my kitchen table, chamomile steeping in my cup. The phone rings. I pick it up. "This is Reuben Pannor, Director of Vista Del Mar. Is Abigail Albrecht home?"

I grip the teacup, grip the receiver. Rain roars outside as I tell him, "Yes, this is she." Vista Del Mar, the adoption agency where I relinquished my first-born when I was sixteen years old. Mr. Pannor's voice softly reminds me of my letter last month, how I wrote and asked to be reunited with my son, now he has turned eighteen. My mind feels empty as I recall the letter, which seems to hover just beyond the verge of my thoughts.

Mr. Pannor has something difficult to tell me, and I urge him on. I feel his words circling closer. Blasts of rain blow against the window. From a distance I hear him saying, "Your son is dead. Brain tumor. Twelve years old. Wonderful family, every advantage. Did everything they could." Reuben Pannor holds on tenderly and I sob. He tells me they named my baby Joshua. My newborn baby, who I held three times. The life force of his grip on my teenage thumb. His adoptive mother wants to meet me. I feel my hand write down time and place. More words fall like rain, and I don't understand.

How do I tell my fifteen-year-old daughter? She has never known about the adoption. Instead of telling her, I somehow conceal my grief when she is home. This is hard to do, as I am distraught and cannot eat for many days.

Two weeks later, I carefully drive the ninety miles to Los Angeles. Stop at my friend Tinika's house on the way. Her mother sits on the stairs, one step above me. My head is in her lap. She murmurs and strokes me while I cry.

It seems like I awaken at a conference table. Everyone reaching out to me. The social worker with her grandmotherly warmth, who placed my baby, stayed close throughout his life. Mr. Pannor, a source of comfort. The adoptive father isn't here, couldn't bear to revisit the sorrow. Joshua's compassionate adoptive mother, bringing anecdotes and photographs. Trying to give me a piece of my child to hold.

My shock at recognition of the photos. Such a close resemblance to my daughter. The disembodied feeling of déjà vu convinces me I have seen these pictures before. Kindness and hugs and stories about my son pervade me through layers of loss and disappointment. My disgraceful pregnancy transforms in this new light. The burden of shame begins to ease as I discover Joshua's birth was a sacred gift. One small son and the love he was given, one small son and the wisdom and love he gave.

Later at home I tell my daughter, stammering with tears as I show her the photos. She weeps as she sees herself mirrored in his face. She has always wanted a brother. Her arms hold tight around me, close and sad in our embrace. She tells me she is sorry and how hard it must have been—to carry so much weight alone—the secret of the adoption and Joshua's absence all these years.

Abigail Albrecht is a native Californian. Born in Los Angeles, she has lived in the beachside city of Carpinteria, on California's Central Coast, for twenty years and now resides in Salem, Oregon. A publicist and community event organizer as well as noted regional poet, she has developed and implemented readings and poetry festival events, judged contests and edited poetry journals. She is co-founder of the Santa Barbara Poetry Festival, which has hosted such distinguished American poets as Galway Kinnell, Philip Levine, Diane di Prima and the late William Stafford. Albrecht has taught poetry for many years through the Carpinteria Poetry Workshop. Her work has appeared in numerous journals and anthologies, including *Cafe Solo, Art/Life, Spectrum, Verve, Talus and Scree* and *Red Tiles, Blue Skies: More Tales of Santa Barbara*.

Turn my eyes away
from what my human weakness cannot as yet understand
and therefore cannot bear to think about.
Teilhard de Chardin, The Divine Milieu

Turn my eyes away
from what I cannot dare comprehend and I'll continue feeding
the spirit of the barefoot, little boy who clutches a chicken-wire gate
with his sore left hand.

His name was Tuan
and one day he returned to the orphanage at Phu My,
carrying his neatly packed belongings and waited to be invited back in.
At six years old, his adoptive parents were killed by Viet Cong rockets.
Turned and scattered.

After losing two sets of parents, his feelings toward life
clung to his eyelashes like two heavy-set moths.
The madness of war skinned his soft resolve down to a fresh
batch of nerves until he barely felt human anymore.

Tuan walks around in my thoughts with his lips slightly parted
and his eyes half-open and he whispers to me in Vietnamese.
He still wears his baby overalls and paces back and forth
on pebbled dirt from one chicken-wire gate to the other.
And I can feel the hardened soles of his child's feet deep behind my forehead.

He eats from my ripe ambition and life-long plans
so he can keep on whispering to me May 2, 1999, in Vietnamese.
Not a word of his I know, but he has nowhere else to go.
And I keep him happy by swearing to him that I'll never
turn my eyes away.

Kevin Allen

Listen to the sound of your brother's blood
crying out to me from the ground.
              Genesis 4:10

I.

and then train your ears to detect tiny footsteps
dragging past your doorway in the dark.
Through your eyes they want to see
how the world they were forced to leave has changed.
They need to know if the world
has yet burst into flames, since their time on earth
was filled with screaming, lost whimpering, then a piercing thud
and, finally, inhalation of fire.
In limbo they were left, clutching the air for their mother's hair,
stripped of burning clothes, jet fuel dripped on the road.
Today, with the people's revolution completed,
these babies are coming back up through the rich, heavy soil
to seek out the surviving generation in order to witness
the executions carried out, the blood
of ex-patriots rolling down proletarian steps and the wives
still kneeling in ditches crying for the lives of their husbands
to be returned, immediately.

II.

You lie in your bed
full of lice and dried shrimp, and I've come back.
I've come back to touch your face,
and to reclaim the blood you spilled from your womb.
I would like to remind you of the bundled namesake you abandoned.
I've come back speaking the same language your love spoke to you.
I've come to shield you from the bullets still hanging in the sky
and to show you that no one should die alone.
I've come back to lie with you at your breast.
There's no need to cry. You called me.

III.

When you look at your mother
you can see that you have her nose and her ears.
When you look at your father
you can see that you have his eyes and his chin.
When I look at my mother,
I see a woman I love like a mother;
I don't see my mother.
When I look at my father
I see a man I love like a father
I don't see my father.
When my grandmother tells stories about her parents and grandparents
I would only nod and smile.
She tells me they're my great-grandparents.
I can only nod and imagine what their reaction would be
if I told them exactly what she told me:
that I stemmed from the same family tree.
　　　　There is a bridge that I will never be able to cross.
There are relatives who will never bear any relation to me.
There are documents that I will never be able to erase.
There is a difference
and that difference is me.

Kevin Allen

Kevin Allen was born 5 December 1973, in S. Vietnam. He was in an orphanage until adopted by an American family in November 1974. He is half Vietnamese and half American and has no idea who his biological parents are. Most of his life he has lived in upstate New York. He went to school in Webster, New York, a suburb of Rochester. He graduated from St. John Fisher College (1992–1996) and continued to graduate school at the University of Buffalo (1996–1998), where he received a M.A. degree in German. He is currently employed at a market research firm. He has been writing poetry for six years. Tuan was an orphan at Phu My. His plight was showcased in *Turn My Eyes Away,* published in 1976. Mr. Allen's identification with Tuan comes from an understanding of the loss and desperate search for security Tuan felt while holding onto that gate.

Birthing Joshua, An Open Adoption
Patricia Alpert

After seven years of infertility, we finally became parents. Our story is like a million others, except the frustration and tears are uniquely ours. David and I were living a very active life. We desperately wanted a baby as part of our lives. We had three artificial inseminations, each resulting in a miscarriage, as well as an unsuccessful in-vitro fertilization.

David always wanted to adopt. I hesitated. I heard others say, "It's in the genes! You just don't know what kind of child you are going to get these days."

One day during my lunch break, I was sitting at a table enjoying a fashion magazine and eating a sandwich when along came a cute mom with her daughter. The mom was putting her little ten-month daughter into the car seat. My heart started to melt. That night at home I told David, "I have changed my mind. I want to adopt!" He was excited. We called friends who had adopted children and/or knew of families who had adopted. We talked with many people and decided to contact an attorney specializing in open adoptions.

In August we met Susan Romig. She took only a limited number of clients at a time and was very personable. We felt we could trust her, and so we hired her. She asked us to make a photo album about our life and home so the birth parents could see how wonderful we were. I took a roll of film and went out to show how beautiful Santa Barbara and its scenery can be. I took pictures of our home, our families, and our lives. David's sister Barbara, a writer, created a wonderful and true profile about us.

We delivered the album and story in August of 1996, and the wait began. Two weeks passed and we became impatient. I called the lawyer and asked why we weren't picked yet. She warned me this process is very complicated, and many times it took years to find the right parent/child contacts. She encouraged me to calm down and let her do her job. David and I decided to go La Costa Spa in Carlsbad for a vacation.

As we were packing to leave Carlsbad, the phone rang. David's brother called saying Susan wanted to talk with us immediately. I was so excited I could hardly stand it. Apparently while we were away, a birth couple saw our album and was interested in meeting with us and Susan. Susan faxed the couple's information to David's office. We liked their background. They were from New Jersey like David. Keith was tall, 6' 2", like my family. Cyndi had a B.A. in fine arts. We agreed to meet.

We met Susan early at the restaurant. She warned us that these two were very particular, had prepared pages of questions, and were going to be very selective. I watched them walk up the restaurant driveway. They were young. Cyndi was beautiful, blonde, and tan. Keith seemed very serious.

Introductions were made and the questions began. What kinds of magazines are on the coffee table they asked? Who did you learn your morals from? Do you go hiking or camping? I was silent. David was nervous but he answered all the questions, not letting me say a word. It felt like we were on a blind date. Do they like us? Do we like them? The lunch went on over four hours. It seemed like days. On the ride home, we were exhausted. I felt excited and afraid.

"We're expecting a boy in October," they said. In less than four months I could be a Mommy! Two days later Susan called. The birth couple wanted to meet me for lunch. They felt that they got to know David, but they wanted to meet with me again.

I drove to Hollywood to take Cyndi to lunch. We talked for more than four hours. I asked her to paint a picture for the baby's room, if they picked us to be his parents. During our talk, Cyndi called him "Butterfly," because she said he felt like a little flutter inside of her. As I drove home, I wondered if we'd be the ones.

Six days later they called. Would we meet them near their house for dinner? By this time I was very nervous and scared. Would they have us drive all the way to meet them and tell us they were not picking us for some specific reason? When they arrived, they had more questions. We discussed religion. I'm Catholic and David is Jewish. They were concerned about how the baby would be raised. We told them our feelings—our baby would have the best of both worlds. Then after much discussion, we decided to raise him as Jewish. We hoped this satisfied Cyndi and Keith.

Before we ordered dessert, Cyndi and Keith said, "We want you to be the baby's parents." We jumped up hugging and crying. Everyone in the entire restaurant sat and stared at us. I didn't care. Our prayers were finally going to be answered. I was going to be a mommy. Then Keith asked if we had a name for our son. We said, "Joshua Martin, after David's late grandfather." So from August 28th, Cyndi and Keith called him Joshua. He was due October 26th.

On October 1st, I quit my career. I started to prepare for a full-time career as a mommy! Everyone at work was surprised. I was a store manager with the same company for over nine years. After all the trouble we went through, day-care or a nanny would not raise Joshua. We wanted to change every dirty diaper and wipe away every tear.

While we were happier then ever about our news, we were in a unique dilemma. Our home was being remodeled. The plans were implemented before we knew about Joshua. We were installing a steam shower and Jacuzzi, and now we would have to change our plans to include Joshua's new room.

September 1st: We invited Cyndi and Keith to Santa Barbara to see our home. We wanted them to see the place where Joshua would be raised. They loved it. When they were here, I started a journal for Joshua. I wanted him to know how much his birth parents loved him and how much effort it took to bring him into our world.

September 7th: With twenty other very pregnant couples David and I started a "Baby Basic" class at St, Francis hospital. Everyone wondered why we were there and when I was due, I smiled and said, "In a month and a half." David joked, "She's keeping her girlish figure." He volunteered to bathe and try to put on the baby doll's diaper.

I started going with Cyndi to her doctor appointments. I heard Joshua's strong heartbeat and learned Cyndi had gained only 14 pounds so far. She told me how Joshua liked to move around, pushing his butt up to her right side.

September 16th: We visited my Mom and Dad. We took the ultra sound picture of Joshua. They were excited but scared. They felt we shouldn't get too excited in case Cyndi and Keith change their minds. I kept telling them everything was going to be fine, but they didn't believe me. While we were visiting, my brother and his wife gave us the crib their two boys used.

Since the beginning, I felt in my heart that if Cyndi decided she wanted to keep Joshua then that was meant to happen. I believed that someday we would get our baby, if not this baby then another one. I wanted Cyndi and Keith to feel they made the correct decision. David joked that for all my strong words he knew if something happened, he'd probably need to find a mental hospital to put me in!

September 26th: Cyndi and I toured the hospital and its nursery. We were nervous and anxious. All four of us decided to take a Lamaze class.

September 28th: We invited Cyndi to a baseball game. Cyndi is a big Dodger fan. We ate Dodger Dogs, Ice Cream, Pretzel and a soda. The Dodgers lost, but we enjoyed the game.

Oct 2nd: I drove to Hollywood to take Cyndi to her doctor appointment. The doctor was very understanding. I asked tons of questions. Cyndi looked beautiful. She took great care of herself, ate the right foods, exercised all the time, got enough sleep. Joshua was very active by this time. He moved around a lot and made it hard for her to sleep. Sharing these last few months with Cyndi, I began to feel so much admiration and love for her. She was going through so much having this baby. How could I ever thank her? How could I ever pay her for this incredible gift? My love for her was the most I have ever felt for another woman.

October 3rd: Cyndi and Keith came to Santa Barbara for our Lamaze class. We decided each of us would have a job during Joshua's birth. Cyndi wanted all of us to be in the birthing room. The hospital had no idea what they were in for! Our Lamaze instructor gave us all the tools to make Cyndi very comfortable. We were prepared.

October 13th: Family and friends from all over came for my baby shower. Cyndi came also. She wanted everything to be just as if I was giving birth to our son. We received so many incredible gifts, even a baby jogger! There was so much that we couldn't bring it all home in one day. Cyndi met my friends and family and saw all the great people Joshua would have in his life.

October 16th: I took Cyndi to her doctor appointment. When I pulled up to the front of their LA apartment house, Keith was waiting outside. He informed me that Cyndi was having contractions five minutes apart. I was dressed in a dress and hat; all my shower gifts were still at my sister-in-law's house. David was at work.

I drove with Cyndi and Keith to see the doctor. Cyndi was dilated three centimeters. I called David and told him to get the diaper bag, install the car seat, and buy some diapers, but not to rush, it would be awhile. He went into a frenzy and immediately came to the hospital. Our doctor wanted us at the hospital right away. All of us marched into the maternity ward. The head nurse yelled, "Only one other person can go in." Cyndi barked, "Everyone is coming. Call my social worker, if you have a problem." So we set up her birthing room. We brought a cassette player, her favorite candies to keep our breath fresh, the TV was playing the World Series and we were all in our positions. The time was about 4:00. I took pictures of Cyndi and Keith.

Cyndi didn't cry or complain at all. The nurse came in and said Joshua was starting to crown. All of a sudden I felt faint. Our nurse laughed and told Cyndi that she was doing much better than I. I was overcome with excitement. Also, I hadn't eaten much that day. In a few minutes I felt better.

The doctor came in and said, "Let's get her to the birthing room." We all raced down the hallway. At the entrance to the birthing room, the nurse said. "One of you will have to stay out." David decided he would. At 9:38 Cyndi pushed one final time and screamed, "Fly out Butterfly!" Joshua came flying out. Cyndi held him then gave him to me. I cut the umbilical cord. The emotion in the room was very intense. David and I went to watch the nurses measure and weigh Joshua. Then we left to find a motel and spend our last night together before bringing Joshua home. We had dinner and sat up all night talking and laughing.

The next morning I wanted to hurry to the hospital. Before the birth, we went to a psychologist. We knew the day after was going to be hard for Cyndi. When we arrived, Cyndi and Keith were getting dressed. The four of us went to the nursery. We stood in a circle. Cyndi and Keith presented Joshua to us and told him goodbye. We would see them again. They were welcome to come to see him when they wanted.

The next few days were a dream. At this writing, it has been eleven months. Joshua is about to walk. He has Cyndi's eyes and Keith's mouth. He has my smile and David's strong will.

 Partricia Alpert was a retail manager before she became a full-time mother. She and her family live in Santa Barbara, where for Joshua she started a support group for adoptive families and a play group of adopted children. She and her husband continue contact with Joshua's birth parents, who have now gone their separate ways.

Searching for Likeness
Anonymous

Dear Sister,

It was so great talking to you the other night. I was very nervous, though and don't remember a few things about our conversation. I thought I could detect some similarities in our voices and laughs—the most amazing thing to me. I was so nervous and, in trying to explain things, I hardly learned anything about you. I hope we're not reading from different pages.

Here's what I really want to know: Do you have big feet? I've had size ten feet since I was twelve. I always thought I would be tall, but I grew only to 5'4" I also have a weight problem. I go back and forth between healthy and fat, mostly forth, unfortunately. When I'm not carrying around too much extra weight, I have incredibly small wrists and fingers. When I was married, my wedding band was a size four. I have a long neck, and I had to have my canine teeth filed in junior high because they were so pointed. I have always had excellent health though— low blood pressure, low cholesterol, no serious illnesses. Knock on wood. Growing up I constantly had strep throat. I was supposed to have my tonsils taken out, but I didn't. When you can see it, I have a very small waist. Are your second toes longer than your big toes?

I realize this may sound a bit strange to you, but I grew up not looking, sounding, feeling, or expressing myself like anyone around me. I'm so curious to learn what is hereditary and what is environmental. Of course without my birth father's information, the picture will still be incomplete. I am a very emotional person. When I'm really happy, I am downright manic. When I'm sad, I am overly contemplative and lethargic. So whatever I feel, I feel with passion. I used to be uptight, and people would go out of their way not to make me angry. But I have slowly matured and lightened up a lot. I'm basically an open book and wear my heart on my sleeve at all times. I'm annoyingly idealistic and I've decided to stay that way.

I could list about one hundred questions for you, but I don't want to be too pushy. I'm afraid I'll scare you off. Please tell me as much, or as little, about yourself as you want. Though, for the record, you could write a novel about yourself and I would be overjoyed. I would love to hear about your childhood. How long have you known your husband? Where did you meet? And how did you wind up in Oklahoma? Oh, that reminds me, a friend of mine pointed out that Bartlesville is six miles from where that massive twister touched down. Did you see it? I hope there's no damage where you are or to anyone you know. That was the wildest tornado I have ever seen. We get them in Kansas too. The sky usually gets green first.

Since you are an elementary teacher, you must love children. Do you plan to have some soon? I'm glad my husband didn't leave me with a child, but I also regret not having a child. I really hear the biological clock ticking, but there's no way I want to get married again.

I'm genuinely sorry if my reappearance has caused your mother pain. That's the last thing I intended to do. When I was growing up, I was always told that my birth parents were too young to keep me, and that they gave me up unselfishly out of love. I thought that was the most noble act a parent could do. I felt so special that my mother cared about my welfare so much she sacrificed her own. When you are adopted, the most common myth your parents tell you is how you were especially picked, as if they went to the baby warehouse and chose you above the other babies. I realize they say this hoping you won't feel insecure and unwanted. But it's such a ridiculous idea.

I'm sorry to upset the balance of things in your family. I have no control over the fact that Martha kept my existence a secret all these years. That was her choice. I don't know how she did it. I probably would have had a nervous breakdown, or something. I need people around for support. I was devastated by her rejection again, but I'm going through the feelings with a lot of support and I'll be fine.

Trying to establish a relationship with her probably meant so much to me because my adopted mom left me when I was seven. She wanted a divorce and Dad didn't. So, she left my brother and me with Dad. Apparently being left by two mothers was too traumatic for me. It's amazing what the subconscious perceives. I blocked it out. I blocked her out. I have no memories of her ever being mommy-like. The next thing I know I'm on a train going to see her every other weekend. I knew she was my mom, but I didn't feel it. She only felt like a concerned family friend. We were OK with each other as adults, but we only talk to each other maybe once a month.

Anyway enough of that. I am considering writing to Irina, but I'm scared. I'm afraid of her reaction and of how she got out of Yugoslavia. She sounds like an amazing woman. I don't think it was common for a woman to have a masters degree back then. Boy am I an underachiever! I'm smart but I have no degrees. What was your (our) grandfather like? Sarah said she was much closer to her stepfather. Do Robert and Sarah share many qualities? Is your mom a lot like her mother? Did you marry someone like your father?

Gees, I'm inquisitive. Sorry. I love to study human nature and psychology. People fascinate me, and of course I'm always interested in finding out what type of things are handed down. I saw a PBS program about twins, who were separated at birth and grew up in different families. They didn't know they were a twin set. When they were reunited as adults, they were amaze at how many things they had in common. They smoked the same brand of cigarettes, married spouses with the same names, even gave their children the same names. Not all of them, of course.

I will leave the ball in your court. I would love to hear from you often and at anytime of the day or night. But I will totally respect whatever boundaries you want. I pray that you will be interested in forming a relationship with me. If not, I will be heavy-hearted but will tell you the same thing I told your mother: if you ever change your mind, even if it's twenty years from now, that's OK. I'll be there with open arms. I hope that you and your family are safe and healthy. And if you ever need a kidney, I've got you covered! I'm sending a photo with this. Please,

please, please send me one too—a photo of you, your mom, your grandma, granddad, husband, uncle, cat, neighbor's dog, whatever! If I can't give you an actual hug, I would be in heaven to be able to look into your eyes.

Bye,
Sara

June 5, 1997

Dear Sara,

I received your letter several days ago, but only today I decided to write back. I needed to think about the situation, and I needed to talk to my mom. After you called that night, I called her and told her you had contacted me. We talked about it for a while, and then I spoke with her again the next day. She told me she gave you the information you requested, but you wanted more than information. She did not. I respect that wish and you should too.

I cannot imagine not knowing your birth mother, but I believe things happen for a reason. I feel very unemotional about this, primarily because it doesn't involve me. Granted you and I are biological half-sisters, but there is so much more to being related.

I have included a picture of myself to satisfy your curiosity. As to your questions, I have long fingers and normal sized wrists. My wedding ring is a size 6 ½. I also wear size ten shoes, but I am 5' 6" I am healthy most of the time. I was born allergic to milk and with asthma, but I quickly grew out of those two ailments. I've always been heavy, but I've learned to deal with it and not let it control me. My middle name is Naomi. After all your research, I'm surprised you didn't know.

I know you have many more questions to ask, but it's like asking a stranger, and that's what we are—strangers to each other. I know that it doesn't have to be that way but, because of Mom's previous choices, that is the way it must be. I love my mom very much and, as I said before, she made a choice years ago that I respect. That choice was for a lifetime, not thirty-two years. I hope you can understand her feelings.

Please do not contact my grandmother. This would be very upsetting to her. I apologize if this is not the outcome you wanted, but our lives are settled and complete. I hope you can find your own happiness.

Sincerely,
Carol

Letter to My Son's Birth Mother
Rosemary Arden

Dear Kate,

This letter has taken nearly 18 years to write. My son will be 18 in two weeks, but you know this already. Unlike me, you were present at his birth. You are the biological mother he has never known, but without your love, I would not have known motherhood at all.

"God knew you couldn't have six, so he sent you Ben instead," a mother of five children once told me after watching my active two-year-old tear around. I nodded, feeling that this one child provided the challenges of a handful of kids and all the joy of motherhood I had imagined but had been denied because of infertility.

At 24, I married a man 17 years older than I. Stan had four children; two were teenagers. He had a vasectomy, but I was probably already sterile after suffering from endometriosis. (Despite hormone therapy and surgery, I had a hysterectomy later at the age of 30, when our son was three.)

Luckily, Stan and I were able to adopt a newborn through a private adoption. It was a stifling, hot summer in the San Fernando Valley as we waited for the call that would announce me a mother. On September 12, 1979, a healthy boy was born. Three days later we brought Ben home to a waiting family. Stan's other children had been excited about the prospect of a baby brother—even his youngest, once she got over her disappointment that our surprise wasn't a new swimming pool.

As perfect as my joy was, I never forgot you, the girl who had given birth and would not be going home with her baby. I was treated like a natural mother at the hospital and dressed my baby for the first time in the nursery. I received the customary gift pack for mothers and was wheeled out in a wheelchair, even though I was capable of walking. I knew you were still in the maternity ward, recovering from the C-section you had undergone, but I wasn't allowed to see you and thank you for relinquishing your child to us. Even though I took my baby from the hospital, I knew I was leaving a piece of his history behind. I would be taking you home with us, too.

I had worried about bonding immediately with my newborn, since we had received the phone call late at night and couldn't see our son until the next afternoon. The nurses at the small community hospital were nurturing and carried Ben around, showing him off (even though he was a "no-show" baby and wasn't supposed to be visible because of possible conflicts or legal problems). Because of his Cesarean delivery, Ben was unmarked, and his large head was beautifully shaped. He had jaundice, which made his skin golden-colored. The moment I saw him in the nursery window, I claimed him as my own.

The nurses had been impressed with your maturity for a 16-year-old. You had remarked that you knew you were doing the best thing for Ben, yourself, and for us. Later, I learned that you returned to high school after your recovery.

Another student had spray-painted your name and "slut" in red across the campus sidewalk. At night, your father quietly painted over the spiteful words. Already, I knew that I would love my child that much. I didn't know that 16 years later, I would be driving Ben to that high school and watching him walk across the same pavement on his way to class.

I quickly bonded with this sweet baby, who asked so little of me at first. At night, I'd awake for feedings and stay awake to play with him. Enchanted, I watched his eyelashes grow. His umbilical cord, his final physical connection to you, fell off and the site became infected. When it healed, I gave Ben his first bath. His eyes widened in a blissful expression, and it was the first real exchange of joy between us. Months later, a judge would sign the adoption decree that finalized our union. He said, "Love him as though you gave birth to him." He didn't know I already did.

An adoptive parent always worries that the birth mother will claim her child. The first few days, I prepared myself. I told myself that if I had to give him back, at least I could say I had a child, I held a baby I called my own, I nurtured an infant. After a couple of weeks, I felt this is my child. I would do anything to keep him.

Several months later, you and I met through arrangements with the social worker. I was eager to become acquainted with you and your mother, who drove you to the social services office. I felt guilty sitting in the lobby and hearing the receptionist tell prospective adoptive parents on the phone that there was approximately a seven-year wait for babies. I had waited about two months— hardly enough time to assemble a layette, decorate a nursery, or sew a baby quilt—and spent $150 for the lawyer's fee and another $75 for an ultrasound your father's medical insurance didn't cover.

My husband declined to join us. He protested that he didn't want to know who you were, and he was afraid that if you saw photographs of the beautiful child you had relinquished, you would change your mind and take him back. I brought three albums of pictures and gave you copies of some. You gave me your high school portrait and a Polaroid taken toward the end of your pregnancy. I wanted to know your face and not wonder if every woman peering into his baby carriage was the one who had given him up for adoption.

I wanted to know that face peering into the stroller, and I wanted you to know what the baby you never held looked like. I gave you portraits taken during his first six months, but I imagine you have seen his face since then without recognizing him. By chance, when Ben was nearly four, we moved to the city where you grew up. Now a teenager, Ben has worked at local fast-food places where you may have ordered hamburgers or tacos. He marched in the annual city parade one year. His photograph and Little League write-ups (he was a star pitcher) have appeared in the local newspaper. Ben was an extra in the movie Apollo 13, and if you watched it, you saw him magnified on screen for a few seconds and didn't realize you gave birth to the handsome young man.

Ben has asked about you sporadically through the years but seldom since he hit adolescence. I have saved the two photographs you gave me when we met. I clipped your sister's and brother's wedding announcements from the newspaper to give him later. Ben looks remarkably like you and especially your brother, who I met briefly and thought, "That's what my son will look like when he's 18."

I'm prepared for the day this won't be enough for either of you. When we met that day years ago, we discussed the possibility of my son searching for his birth mother. You said it would be acceptable once he was in his twenties. That seemed a long way off then. Now it looms alarmingly close as other milestones like menopause approach to age me. I imagine my son in college, married and raising children in the next decade. It was only yesterday he was eight and telling me, "Just think, Mom, in eight more years I can drive."

Raising Ben has been a challenge. The hyperactivity that manifested during his terrible two's never disappeared completely. Ben experienced the world differently than I would have. Once, when he was about 10, he raced a helicopter on his bike. The helicopter won, and Ben ran into a parked van with his mouth, knocking a triangular piece out of his front tooth. During the O.J. Simpson trial, he spent hours drawing elaborate renderings of the courtroom scenes he watched on TV.

He tested my patience as much as six children but brought me as much joy as half a dozen would have. When our cat had kittens, Ben insisted on acting as a birthing coach during delivery. Ben is extraordinarily tender with children, particularly with his half-brother's small son, who suffers from a rare liver disease. It's amazing to see a hulking, teenage boy tend competently to the baby's many tubes and medications.

Because I couldn't have children biologically, I considered it a blessing to receive this gift of motherhood, and I always vowed to be worthy of this honor. Like any biological mother, I succeeded at times and failed at others to give Ben exactly what he needed when he demanded it.

Now that he's nearly legally an adult, Ben is asserting his independence. What had seemed so natural and necessary when I was his age feels brutal to me now that I'm on the other side of the fence. I'm learning to balance on that tightrope of nurturing an adult who I once diapered. The toddler, who clung crying to my legs when I took him to preschool, seldom calls now. It's difficult to let go, but I'm learning from the example you set 18 years ago.

You relinquished him once, but every day I give him up again.

With gratitude,
Ben's Mom

A Picture of the Family
John Azrak

For George and Mary

My wife Lisa sat in the back seat, her place next to me taken by the infant car seat. The arrangement seemed oddly appropriate, since we talked little that week, even during the sleepless night before. The sun pierced the windshield of our Honda and reflected sharply off the metal arms of the car seat. We were on our way, five more exits on the LIE, to pick up our daughter, the baby you bore.

I glanced at Lisa in the rear-view mirror. Though she wore dark sunglasses, I knew her eyes were watering. Her long brown hair was tied back in a ponytail, and she wore the silver drop earrings she'd bought in Woodstock the summer of our fifth anniversary, when we first talked seriously about having a child. She looked like a schoolgirl then. She still does.

Lisa is a high school art teacher, as I'm sure the lawyer told you, but she also free-lances photography. She has a terrific eye and a pretty unique view of her subjects. Recently, in a double exposure of trees in the snow, she made the shadows multiply. She sold the photo to a New England quarterly. Her photos almost always show more than what's there.

After waving at her reflection in the mirror, I slid my hand over to the seat— I had done this several times already—to check that the buckle was fastened. I felt around the cushioned seat and then poked at the empty space with my fingers, sort of like a magician about to make something appear. No way, though, could I imagine a baby in there. No way did I see that space filled for the ride home. If someone had said, "Hey, don't forget you have to drop that seat off at so and so's," I would have agreed that's what I was doing. I imagine things were as unreal for you that morning.

We got off the expressway to go the four miles on Route 104. To ease our nerves, I popped in the Cat Stevens' tape, "Morning Has Broken," I had cued the day before. But the crystal clear March sky, the brightest that winter no doubt, gave the song too much bite. I was about to fast forward when Lisa started to sing along. (She once sang harmony with a friend of ours in Village clubs.) And at the chorus, just as we passed Bob's Big Boy and I knew we were close, I let loose, which is rare for me. "Blackbird has spoken," I yelped.

When we pulled into the lawyer's parking lot, I shut off the tape and said, "Holy shit, we're here." Lisa slid her hand up the back of my neck, and we breathed deeply and opened our doors. We still didn't speak and that felt strange but good. We talk to each other a lot. Always have. But there were times during the years we were trying to have a child when we seemed to talk ourselves dizzy. You see, you try to make sense out of things. Then, trying to adopt, enlisting at agencies, putting your life onto forms and your home on display, answering questions, waiting, always waiting, the talk got even dizzier . . . dizzier still when we found out about you, the stranger who would carry our fate for the next six months, the mother who might yet change her mind at any time.

We talked over, under, around your decision, knowing full well our words, the hopes and fears that filled our scenarios were as removed from you as you, the stranger, were from us. In that dizziness, though, I took comfort. You were apart from us and that's where I wanted you to be, no matter how things worked out. Only recently has Lisa convinced me to eclipse gently (her words) the fear I have of you by working out for myself how you fit into our lives. She wants me to deal with the impossible silence (her words again), and I decided the best way was to let you know what happened that March morning.

I'll continue here even if, as Lisa suspects, at first you might not want to hear. I do understand. Like us, you know pain. The words, our daughter, your daughter, speak it. Is there a worse sounding kinship? And many times I've imagined what you went through making your decision. Our shared pain is our unhealthy alliance, that which binds us. But there has to be more than that link. I've begun to say your name, Lorraine.

In the attorney's foyer I wanted to close my eyes. I was scared to look around, like when you want to see something too much—your first bike at Christmas, or not at all—the figure in the dark alley. I clutched Lisa's hand, and then the secretary greeted us with a motherly smile and led us into the lawyer's office. I looked straight ahead at him and at the hook of his cane balancing on the desk—polio from birth, you probably know. I glanced at Lisa, who tilted toward my shoulder, her hazel eyes wide, lips slightly parted, composed, as if she were summoning a vow, like on the altar fourteen years ago. The secretary stood as a witness on Lisa's right.

"Here we are," the lawyer smiled. The sound and mystery of *we* froze any response I might have made.

"Glad to see you, Paul and Lisa." His voice hoarse but gentle, his eyes bright in an otherwise sad, drawn face, used to hardship—his own and his clients. "You look well." He seemed to savor the moment, as he fiddled with the hook of his cane, shuffled the papers he said were for later, commented on the weather. He took Lisa's tweed overcoat and then told us something we hadn't known—that he was an adoptive parent.

"Why didn't you tell us?" Lisa asked.

"It was a different route in my time. Easier. Children to spare. Uncomplicated agency work. Little need for private adoptions, for overseas babies, for expensive lawyers or expensive arrangements." He looked apologetically at us. "And if a woman changed her mind, a child became unavailable, some other problem arose, you weren't out thousands of dollars and you weren't faced with more years of waiting. Some of what goes on today."

He shook his head. "There's a group in Chicago that for thirty thousand will try to match you with the specifications you submit for a child. Boy, blue eyes, educated procreators, etcetera . . . Any camaraderie on my part seems unfair, or at least misleading—like what comes from our friends who have children and say they understand what we've been through."

"You're a sweet man," Lisa said.

I wondered about the exact number of his clients hurt by loss and about how hard he had taken each.

"You won't mind that I won't be getting up," he said.

A surge of adrenaline shook my balance, the rigid posture I had been holding. I squeezed Lisa's hand to hold on.

The lawyer gestured to his secretary, who grabbed Lisa's other hand. I let go. We turned around and there—unbelievably—on the couch at the far end of the long room, in an infant seat, slept our child, your child, alone, yet with us the entire time.

"My God," I gushed, as I stood over her and stared.

Lisa began to cry. She turned to me and we held onto each other. "She's beautiful, she's beautiful," Lisa repeated a litany of beautifuls, and I nodded, quivering from head to toe, trying to believe she was ours, not wanting to disturb her, afraid to pick her up, afraid I'd have no idea how to get her from this seat, to the car seat, to our home safely.

The baby stirred, her tiniest ripple turning waves in us. The secretary, beaming, bent over and removed her from the infant seat. "She's angelic," she said. "She's barely fussed all morning."

Then she put the baby in Lisa's arms. Lisa rocked her gently, quieting her whimpers. A glow enveloped them and the ease with which they coupled. I was overcome by Lisa's joy. My fears melted. I put out my arms.

I swear the baby smiled at me when I took her. I made fun of her little sprouts of reddish hair. She dribbled. I put my finger under her lower lip, wiped it, and was ready to carry her confidently. I felt love, so strange, so immediate, yet so natural.

I can tell you that now. As hard as it's been to share this joy with you, it's harder still, I'm sure, for you to receive it. But I want you to know the peace, the sanctity, the softness of it. You made it happen. Three and a half years later, I can say that unconditionally.

I began to move easier, like a tennis player getting his legs back after a nervous opening set. I carried the baby over to the lawyer's desk, even swung her in my arms, handed her to Lisa, completed the paperwork and said goodbye and thanks. Lisa kissed the lawyer, who blushed like a proud grandparent. "Please send a picture of the family," he said as we left.

I had no trouble with the car seat. I drove with one eye on the expressway and one eye on the baby. I talked with Lisa faster than I drove, about what I can't remember. A reception awaited us at home.

Our families were there and there were flowers and gifts from all over. Many gifts were from our students, two with letters from Lisa's students who were adopted. We played music and sang, and the baby cried and cooed and was swamped with attention. I learned how to give her a bottle and how to burp her. During our walks, I told her everything about Lisa and me. When everyone left, she sat with me and watched a college basketball game. I gave her a running play-by-play account Lisa rested. When the game was over, Lisa came in and we had our last cry of the day, cradling the baby between us. Lisa put the baby in the bassinet and curled up on the couch next to her, on call for the night.

I went up to bed, and during the night, I fought thinking about you, what you looked like (I had a sketchy portrait from the lawyer—petite, blonde, pretty), what you might be thinking that night, what you would mean to our lives. But I didn't get too hung up analyzing. That's not my way. It is Lisa's. I'm pretty good at keeping things at bay. A couple of tosses and turns, and I'm usually tuned out.

I remained pretty much undistracted by you. And when I learned you were moving back to Ireland for good, I thought distance and time were on my side. But Lisa didn't feel that way. She sees the whole picture, and from the outset, she said you should be in it. From the day the lawyer called to tell us you'd arrived in America three months pregnant, Lisa carried your presence.

We fought.

"What do you want me to do, call her?"

Our child was growing wonderfully healthy, and the lawyer had told us how conscientious you were with your diet and exercise during the pregnancy, and how even during periods of stress, you wouldn't take anything that might affect the baby. "Not so much as aspirin," we were told. Lisa reminded me of the girls we had each known at school who had used their pregnancies as another excuse to party.

"No," she said. "I want you to accept her. Accept that she is the birth mother. Accept that she is part of us." Then, leaning forward, she added, "Of course, you could always write her or yourself about us and her. It might help to see what you're thinking."

"I can't do that," I said. "I can't accept her." I felt threatened. It wasn't easy to say, but it was painfully obvious even to me. "We're so happy as we are. Why do you have to make more of it?" *Ruin it* is what I was implying whenever I felt challenged.

"There is more to us," she'd say.

Early, even as I was making out checks for your medical expenses, balancing this strange record of figures for a child yet to be born, yet to be ours, for a girl and her doctors too distant to be real, I can remember Lisa leaning over me, rubbing the kink out of my neck and initiating talk about our souls and how they unified this extended family of ours.

If you are trying to picture us, that's the way it's always been—Lisa up there on the observation deck and me grounded in the lobby. I'm more than a little convinced that our opposing natures have helped keep us together

Can you imagine a more difficult test than not being able to make your own children? We have friends who have split because they couldn't make ends meet. Be assured, we get along. And our struggle brought us even closer. All I said then was, "Yeah, souls. Sure, souls," as I tried to estimate just how much we'd exceeded the lawyer's projection.

Lisa was patient. She left it up to me to question her. I didn't for a long time. I didn't until I was frustrated enough by my feelings of gratitude to you that I began to take seriously her suggestion to write down something.

"That's terrific," she said when I told her.

She was less enthusiastic, though, when I asked to be let in on her soul talk. She began tentatively. "The transcendence of soul is what I'm really talking about, Paul," she said, waiting for a cue from me.

"Hmm," I said, vaguely recollecting the word transmigration from a course

I'd had on world religions.

"It's not so far-fetched. I believe love changes us all. It's changed you and me. We've talked about that, haven't we?"

"Sure," I said.

"Love develops our existence, changes it into essence, into soul. That's its real power. That is how we say as a couple we are going to last forever, isn't it? What's so different?"

"But that's us," I said. "We're dealing with a girl we don't even know. I love her baby, not her."

"She loves her baby, that's the important thing you're leaving out," Lisa said. And with a rueful smile, added, "Unlike the manly father who took off."

I nodded.

"She chose to have the child. That's love. She could have gone to England for an abortion. She could have done some damaging things during her pregnancy. She didn't. That's love. She hasn't severed the spirit that connects her to our child and I think connects us all."

I don't know where you are when it comes to matters of the spirit. Catholic and reared in Ireland, I assume you have a leg up on me, lapsed several denominations Protestant. Lisa is Catholic with a Zen bent (I tease her) and believes in her Church's Eucharist. Believes that the body and blood of Christ transubstantiates into the thin wafer she regularly receives. That's always been a leap for me.

"We're in communion with this girl," she continued. "Isn't that a beautiful, nonthreatening thought, Paul?"

"Well, it is. But maybe it's too easy, I don't know."

"Too easy? Why does it have to be hard? It seems to me that the hardest questions, after the most difficult searches, wind up having the simplest, clearest answers. Hey, it's like telling me I'll hit the tennis ball better if I don't think about it while I'm swinging. Not until I get into the zone myself." She laughed, mimicking my latest sports phrase.

"I can't argue with that part. You're still pretty stubborn as a matter of fact." I shook my head. "I'm just really out of the zone when it comes to this girl."

"Paul, I'm going to be there if our child and she want to meet someday. I'm not running from her. I can understand wanting to. I'm not pretending the reality is easy. But her existence, her presence even, is not going to make my beliefs any less real either."

"Stubborn."

"You bet." My head began to spin. I was trying to figure out what to say, if I did write. Finally, I figured what plagued me was that you, I, Lisa and our child didn't add up. Our sum was too big for its parts. But in my pragmatic world, all things do eventually total out. If they don't total at first, you add them again. That is one of the first things I learned.

We're not accidents, meant to be dispensable. Your child isn't. You're not. I believe that. Maybe it is that our souls will meld. Then maybe it's as Lisa will have it—the finite becomes infinite.

Work through this in your own way. There is little I can give you except to tell you what's happened. Store my moments in your memory. They should be yours too. Build on them and know that your child's hair has changed from red sprouts to near shoulder-length platinum blonde. That she finger-paints multicolored clouds we've hung on our kitchen cabinets, and that her smile lights up our hearts. That her eyes have gone from blue to hazel, that her pink and black ballet outfit is her favorite, that she laughs at her own jokes, and that the other night she asked if we needed the Honda to get to heaven. Know, too, that she responds to our affection with embraces that seem to make her twice her thirty-three pounds, and that her legs are double-jointed and we're constantly reminding her to keep her kneecaps out front. And know that she memorized "The Pledge of Allegiance," still loves *Goodnight Moon* at bedtime and sings along whenever the new James Taylor song comes on the radio. Know she'll be a brat when we won't put sherbet on her Cheerios, and that she saves her most dramatic fits for when Lisa picks out clothes she dislikes.

Know that she'll learn to love you, Lorraine. Her name is Christa May Taylor.

"A Picture of the Family" first appeared in *Northeast Corridor*, V1, N2.

John Azrak is the chairperson of a secondary school English department in New York. His work has appeared in the anthologies: *Bless Me, Father,* and *XY Files.* He has been a finalist in story contests sponsored by *Apalachee Quarterly* and *Northeast Corridor.* Additionally his stories have appeared in *West Branch, Another Chicago Magazine, The Artful Dodge, The Santa Barbara Review, The Santa Clara Review,* and *Fine Madness.*

From Silence to Silence

He wears the words,
suits himself in escutcheon,
protects, withdraws, denies:
my son toughens himself behind
modern fibres: emotional armor
is effective cover: violence masks pain;
there's safety in anger,
a knife severs
bites of nourishment,
it is designed to separate love from anguish—
stab breakfronts, kitchen cabinets,
striate furniture instead of flesh;
scissors clip night gowns, dresses, shoes and sheets.
Rage subdues what is intolerable.
Examination of this pain
only fuels the fabric,
buttresses resolve.

He eats the words,
digests them into pulp,
then shits them out, in fury:
sustenance is inadequate when prolonged
starvation has already caused
viscera to invert to consume itself.
Fault?
Some children suffer cancer, some abuse—
physical and sexual.
They rail against themselves
when they are older, if they survive.
How can this adoptive parent cushion
neglect inflicted in the crib;
brain chemicals, attachments, rapport
haywired against screams of
no kindness, no caress, no soothing sounds.

Now sound is an assault.
Lessons, explanations, reminders
turn to bile and revenge is paramount;
there's no guarantee that love and time
can penetrate such misery.
So I more and more hold back
laments and supplications,
trust his doctors—rely on medication—
assign consequences, punishment

for every damaged object, every lie,
to teach him to connect behavior
with outcome, success, jeopardy,
that his choices rule response.
But he is my baby, my deepest treasure,
all I want to do is hug away
those animalistic fears, and speak low,
speak, speak.

Claudette Bass

How He Will Remember Me

I will be the mean bitch, the witch
shouting rules like incantations
bat's wing, frog's toe, respect property,
my black garb will obscure
his tantrums, the screaming
hitting, pounding, smashing
of fists and feet
into bathtub porcelain, mirrors,
the skull against the bedroom wall
like a skillful game of chicken.

It will be my coarse voice—
an evil God upon the mountain—
lightning, thunder, commanding
thou shall not
that he tries desperately to eradicate
raging bile, vomit, diarrhea,
a brew bolder than Hitchcock's birds,
lashing, thrashing as I hold him to the roof:
thou shall not hurt thyself;
thou shall not obliterate thy mother.

He will recall my evil nature
the demagogue, monster, storm
which denied him flight,
an immovable, hated object
when memory serves up
those pre-medicated electric weeks
after Dad had gone to Texas,
long past the endless neglect of a
Korean orphanage where he lay
unfed, undiapered.

Will the calm show through?
our laughter, giggling, touching,
the fierceness which evaporated
into a mild, if stubborn, boy?
When I am dead
and watching if my soul permits
his growing adult strides,
will he recall the dedication
or abusive preservation
of his life?

Claudette Bass

31

"How He Will Remember Me" appeared in *Staple,* Derbyshire, England, 1995, and in *Vigil,* Somerset, England, 1996.

Claudette Bass was born in Detroit and raised in Bronx, New York, and North Brunswick, New Jersey. At fourteen she went to Miami, Florida, to live with aunts and attend high school, college and work in educational and commercial television. She moved to Los Angeles in 1978 and wrote screenplays and novels. Her poems and short stories have appeared in three hundred journals in the U.S., Canada, England, and Australia.

For My Husband's Mother

Those months I carried Sara
I'd think of your mother,
the woman who carried you
though she could not
keep you.
        This woman
we do not know, this girl
whose life was changed
in ways we'll never know,
who wanted or did not want
who loved or did not love
who chose or did not choose
but, willing or reluctant
carried you.

Easily, like the grass that sprouts the pasture green
after first fall rains; or in great pain,
volcanic, slow,
the creaking
cracking of the earth, she
birthed you.

We do not know her name
or what she thought as her fingers soaped her taut
belly in the bath,
as your kicks reached her
first uncertain, then
definite, firm rabbit thumps.

We do not know if she could
keep food down, if
her legs cramped,
if she grew dizzy in the grocery
had to drop her head between her knees
to keep from blacking out.

We do not know if she held you in her hospital bed,
if her breasts were bound to keep the milk from letting down
or if they drugged her and she woke
only to the new softness of her belly, like dough.

We do not know
what friends or family criticized her, if they
sent her out of town and brought her back
as though she'd been on holiday.

We know only
there was a woman who gave you
the food of her blood
the bed of her flesh,
who breathed for you.

We do not know
if anyone ever
thanked her.

Ellen Bass

Originally published in *Ms.* and included in Ellen Bass' volume *Our Stunning Harvest.* Used here with the author's permission.

Ellen Bass was co-editor with Florence Howe of the first edition of *No More Masks! An anthology of Twentieth-Century American Women Poets.* She has published several volumes of her poetry, including *I'm Not Your Laughing Daughter, Our Stunning Harvest,* and *For Earthly Survival,* which won the University of Cincinnati's Elliston Book Award. Her poems have been included in magazines, journals and anthologies.

The Adopted Daughter's Lucky Loop

Lucky she had the good sense
to give you up.

Lucky we had love
and love to spare.

We plucked you
from a steamy state

with inferior schools.
You smiled, almost

wisely, as if you knew.
Lucky your lazy eye

could be corrected.
What a relief

we looked like family.
In your case, consider yourself

a Jew—doubly chosen.

Remember those tentative steps?
How the TV turned the astronauts blue?

We bit our tongues and let you learn
at your own pace.

Lucky she had brains enough
not to begrudge you

a better life. It's best
we never met her—

what if we'd found flaws,
then saw them in you?

In our house we hoped
we'd never find you in her

unfortunate fix. With luck
we'd keep you

from feeling the loss
of a wonderful bundle like you.

Dina Ben-Lev

Letter to My Unmet Mother

If the embroidery of this dream wears down,
if my syntax unstitches, if I slouch, blankly

watching the window, the highest buds
whitely swaying. If spring's dumbfoundingly

bright through the screen, if I breathe in to my depths
but exhale hours I hoped to meet you.

If I breeze over the ellipses of my beginnings,
if twenty-some years of blurry

ideas about why you relinquished me
can't change my case sealed in steel

in upstate New York. If my file names a man
whose machismo swung his sight south

away from the women he wooed. Maybe
it mentions injurious jokes, a sky blue skirt

too high on your thighs. Maybe it notes
a savvy acceptance of loss

or the slopes of gray under your eyes.
Mary carried the Lord, but couldn't save him;

Moses cried in the bulrushes, yet parted the sea.
And me, I've counted our country's star-spangled lies,

and still felt lucky to live here, where hope stretches
such ludicrous lengths. A friend with AIDS shoots shark

cartilage into his veins. Another, not quite
free of Sara Lee, will have her stomach stapled. Absurd

and unsendable, this letter's a loop through a hole.
In all tenderness I'm trying to picture you well

in the somewhere that surrounds you.
I'm hoping you have the strength to stand up

if someone unsteady needs the seat.
I've seen doves nest so slovenly

all their eggs fell. If a hapless pair
drags their tails down your driveway, I trust

you'll throw crumbs. And when a neighbor
knocks to ask if you noticed the moon,

I hope you'll stop
whatever you're doing and join her

outside, saying, Certainly, it was a perfect platinum half.

Dina Ben-Lev

Broken Helix

The sexy talk show host nods and nods. Beside her
a bald man begs to meet the mother he's never known.
Slowly, in front of fourteen million, the curtain
rises with applause—surprise! Before a camera closes in,

I shut my eyes. Down in deepest Florida, in a hospital
winged with a sanatorium, you named me Cheryl.
Then signed me away. At 22, were you tired
of trailer parks, truck stops, drive-thru

windows of worry? Did an old, world-weary nurse
warn, Only one skill you'll be properly paid for.
Impressive, said a man with his hand on my resume . . .
But hell, you'll ruin marriages

with such heavenly hair. Walking out of that white room
and out of that black building, I thought of your leaving—
thirty years ago, those minutes it took
to exit, empty-handed but for one slim bag.

In the cool, antiseptic lobby, you might've stopped
at a fountain. Bending, maybe you moved your whole
face into the water. Were you glamorous in sunglasses,
pushing open the door to the heat? You'd never see

your daughter settled in Seattle, where sun's uncommon
and painful. Never know her new name. Did you
ride a bus alone through battering light, past the hundred
hotels of Miami? At 20, after phoning and phoning and failing

to find you, I fell off a chair in the Fontainebleau.
Pink drinks paid for by a lawyer who liked me best
on my knees. Did my father rub your feet
when you returned? Or did you dream

all night, alone, one light left on?
Blurry on gas, I spread for suction
and scalpel. A nurse held my head
At 24, with a Master's in Fantasy, I ached for escape

from the dirtiest, snowiest section of Syracuse.
A taxi took me home, where sleep came on a green
Goodwill couch—bought with the man of my dreams
who later burned poems in the bathtub,

shot fist-wide holes through my Nova.

And the next day, did you turn to the TV
for comfort? And now, half a lifetime later,
in the kitchen / living room / bedroom / only room,

watch the same talk show host? How she moved
a microphone to the mouth of the bald man's mother?
How she asked, OK tell me, would you do it again?

Dina Ben-Lev

Poems here are reprinted, with the author's permission, from her book *Broken Helix*, Mid-List
Press (Minneapolis) 1997. ISBN 0-922811-31-8

Dina Ben-Lev is the author of two award-winning
chapbooks, *Sober on a Small Plane* (1995) and *Note
for a Missing Friend* (1991). Her poems have
appeared in numerous literary magazines, and she is
the recipient of two Academy of American Poets
awards, the Elliston Poetry Prize, and a Poetry
Fellowship from the National Endowment for the
Arts. She has received degrees from Oberlin College,
Syracuse University, and the University of
Washington, and is currently pursuing a Ph.D. at the
University of Cincinnati. Her recent book of poems
Broken Helix is the winner of the Mid-List Press 1996 FIRST SERIES AWARD
FOR POETRY.

A Different Kind Of Birth
Rabbi Lenore Bohm

It is Mother's Day, and I am grateful for the opportunity to put these thoughts on paper. I intended to call this memoir "Alena's Story," but I realized that is something she will have to write herself, and I hope one day she does. Instead, this is my story about Alena, how she came to join our family, and how she helps me grow in ways I never anticipated—as a person, a mother, and a student of theology. For this I am profoundly grateful.

My husband and I truly felt blessed with the birth of three sons in '87, '89, and '92, but a longing remained persistent within me, and that longing bore the name "daughter." In no way did my sons, with their incredible beauty, innocence, energy and spirit, disappoint me. They were and are infinitely precious to me, but sometimes people feel a calling for something beyond what has been attained or has been given, and this call came to me in the form of a longing for a daughter.

That we pursued expanding our family with a daughter through the somewhat unconventional path of international adoption was both serendipitous and bashert (Yiddish for destined, foreseen). How it was bashert I will address at the close of my remarks. It was serendipitous in that we didn't know any people who had adopted internationally and deciding to adopt internationally was not the reasonable outcome to a well-thought-out assessment of options. In July 1992, I read a paragraph submitted by an attorney arranging for the adoption of Jewish children from the Ukraine in the *Reform Rabbis' Newsletter*. Did we rabbis know of any congregants who might like to consider this road to parenthood?

I read this when my son David was 5, Daniel 2½, and Ari a mere 4 months old. After the initial moment of intrigue with this possible avenue for fulfilling my desire for a daughter, my next thought went to my husband Paul: He is never going to go for this. I was wrong. Paul keenly and compassionately felt the depth of my longing and agreed to proceed with inquiries. Ultimately, our contact with an attorney proved fruitless, but I feel indebted to him for having provided the prologue to this story

Through the first attorney, we learned of all the paperwork we needed to complete: dozens of sheets, including FBI checks, police records, credit statements, personal references, three visits—the "home study"—from a licensed social worker, our marriage license, our and our children's birth certificates, assessments from their doctors, and on and on. Paul handled the paperwork and legalities with infinite patience and good humor. We proceeded with the collection of these bureaucratic items through the fall of 1992 and spoke to no one about our plans. Conception of the idea had taken place and initial growth had begun, but I wasn't, so to speak, ready to wear maternity clothes. There was nothing yet "to show."

In December, I was teaching an Adult Education class. I overheard a participant talking about the son she had adopted from Romania. She was now once again ready to contact her "stork" (the individual who makes the adoption arrangements and accompanies the baby/child to his/her new home) to plan a second adoption, this time, hopefully, of a daughter from Russia. I was elated to meet someone who had successfully accomplished what we were struggling with. We talked at length of our shared hopes and dreams.

My friend introduced us to Bal Jagat, an international adoption agency in Chatsworth, California, that services families like ours. Bal Jagat means "Children of the World." It was founded in 1983 by a most loving and unusual Indian woman named Hemlata Momoya. She has united close to 500 children with about 400 American families. The children come from Russia, India, Paraguay, Bolivia, China, Mexico, and Guatemala. They comprise a rainbow of colors, faces, voices, handicaps, talents, limitations and gifts. Hemlata describes her mission: "Our goal is to unite orphaned children from around the world with loving and stable families in America." She herself is an inspiration.

In March 1993, Bal Jagat suggested we contact a woman in the Washington, D.C. area, who has a personal, on-going relationship with two orphanages located near where she grew up in Angarsk, Siberia. For a fee, she escorts small groups of American would-be parents to these orphanages to arrange for sanctioned adoptions. The children need to be selected and approved in advance, but otherwise, the procedure is relatively straightforward.

We were told that children are always available, but not always the children expectant parents wanted. We were asked, "What exactly did we want?" Our reply was, "A healthy girl, about two or three years old." Many people ask why we didn't want an infant, someone whose earliest memories would be of/with us. The answer is two-fold. Since we already had three children, we were familiar with infancy and early toddlerhood. We didn't feel the need to experience that again, and we recognized that for many adopting parents this would be a priority, since they had no other children. Also, we felt that a child of this age would be least disruptive to the birth order of our "existing" children.

Within days, we received a picture of a sweet-faced, though rather sad and frail-looking, three-year-old child. We were told she was an economic orphan, relinquished by her mother/parents because they could not afford to care for her—an increasingly prevalent phenomenon in Russia since the fall of the Soviet Union. The child had received all appropriate inoculations, already had chicken pox, was out-going and bright. Soon she would be moved to an orphanage for school-age children, and then she was far less likely to be adopted. We decided to go for it.

It was now April and we were busy preparing for Seders and Passover. As we planned Paul's two-week trip to Siberia, the freedom theme for the season took on intensified meaning. We built and decorated a new bedroom for Alena, like typical expectant parents, with great excitement and slight trepidation, Paul and I readied the house. Meanwhile, Paul read up on Russia and Siberia and had lengthy conversations with our local Russian friends, who gave us excellent information on Russia in this post-Communist period.

Exactly how and when we began telling people about this addition to our family, I don't remember. I do recall sitting one night with David, six, on his bed and explaining that Daddy would be gone for a few weeks because he was meeting a little girl, who had no family, and he would return with her to join our

41

family. He asked, "Why our family?" I responded, "Because our hearts and our home have room for her." He looked very seriously at me, as he is still wont to do, and said, "We're doing the right thing, Mommy." His teacher told me he spoke about the pending events enthusiastically, and that he showed his classmates Angarsk, Alena's hometown, on the map. We practiced some basic Russian words, and several times in the days prior to Paul's departure, I remember mentally and physically holding our family close and thinking, "It will never be the same. Please, God, make this a good decision for us all."

Many people were astounded that we had been moving in this direction for several months, and that there was a young girl in an orphanage almost half-way around the world who would soon be part of our family and community. Many gasped at the news, but those gasps were small in comparison to our friends' reactions when they saw Alena for the first time. Her beauty, even in those first days and weeks, was so pronounced, her manner so expressive, her zest for living so apparent—few didn't fall in love at first sight. And that's pretty much how it's been since. But let me return to those two weeks in April when Paul took his incredible journey.

Fortunately for us at the time, the adoption laws required only one parent to accompany the child to her new home. I was relieved to stay in Encinitas where I could keep our sons' lives as normal as possible. Part of me was sorry not to experience the earliest moments of Alena's connection to us, and not to see, first-hand, her living situation. But I also appreciated giving Paul the privilege of midwifing this birth.

When our sons were born, of course Paul was present and even held them before they were laid in my arms, but with Alena I really felt Paul was the parent giving birth. I welcomed the opportunity for her to know him first and for him to meet her in unique fashion alone. This reminds me of the reaction of good friend who looked at me in disbelief and said, "Most women I know won't let their husbands pick out a piece of furniture, and you're letting him choose your daughter!" That Paul spent several days with Alena before I had even seen her is very meaningful to me, to him, and to her. For me, Paul will always be the birthing parent to our daughter. This is a role few fathers know and fewer know how to appreciate.

I would like to share a few entries from Paul's travel journal that give voice to his feelings and impressions as he prepared to meet his new child.

April 14, 1993: There are two things quite difficult for me to realize—one is that I am in Siberia and living in a place I thought was nothing but a giant snow bank; but more amazing, tomorrow I will see my new daughter for the first time! We will visit the orphanage soon and I'm not sure I am ready to walk in and have a little girl say, "Papa." I have certainly thought seriously about this, but somehow the enormity of it has not hit. It is now a matter of fact that I am taking this enormous step for our family for generations to come

April 15: Tax Day seems 10,000 miles away—and it is! I had a wonderful night's sleep and awoke to a glorious day in Siberia with sunny blue skies. It is a fitting day to see my new daughter. We had a 40-minute drive to the orphanage. It is well kept and bright. First we met the orphanage director, a doctor named

Vladimir. There were more introductions, and then some nurses came in with Alena. She was wearing a big yellow ribbon in her hair and immediately came running to me, calling, " Papa, Papa." Of course, I melted. She was very cute and personable. She sat on my lap and I felt the whole trip was now worth it. I gave her the first doll of her own and she had a big smile on her face. As everyone watched, we became immediate friends and all of a sudden, I realized its done! We have a daughter! Alena and I took a long walk outside and played on the swings. She seemed very happy, and we continued to play silly games and laughed.

April 16: An amazing thing happened today—we adopted Alena! We returned to the orphanage, and she once again ran into my arms yelling, "Papa, Papa." She was even more beautiful than I remembered. She is bright and cheerful and full of laughter. She has green eyes and a face that could melt a continent of snow. We left the orphanage to attend the ceremony, which formalized the paperwork guaranteeing the adoption, and then we celebrated with vodka toasts and dancing.

April 20: I awoke to snow, a terrible storm. This was to be Alena's last day at the orphanage. We finally made it, and she was ready at the door waiting. Some of the nurses were crying—they had known her since birth—but she seemed happy to go with me. A whole new world awaits.

On this end, as the days of waiting decreased, and Paul's and Alena's return was approaching, my anxiety level increased. What if this was the wrong decision? What if she just didn't fit in? What if the boys resented this imposition on them of a new being, a sister? What if I couldn't handle four kids? What if? What if? I tried to stay calm. I don't think I did.

On the Monday Paul and Alena were due to return, my closest friends had planned to accompany me to the airport and videotape the arrival was highly emotionally charged all day. My aunt and uncle would meet Paul and Alena in N.Y. when they arrived and wait for them during the customs ordeal. Then they would call me to relay their impressions. Can you imagine your relatives meeting your child before you? It was very strange.

The flight to LA was late, and consequently, the plane to San Diego was cancelled until morning. I couldn't wait until morning. Paul's brother and sister-in-law, who live in Orange County, were kind enough to retrieve the weary travelers from the LA airport and drive them to our front door. They had been in flight and in airports for over 26 hours and were exhausted. Although they were now father and daughter, they barely knew each other, and didn't speak the same language. Paul really was heroic in his handling of it all.

I had alerted my friends that the airport arrival wouldn't come to pass, and readjusted my thinking to greeting Alena and Paul in our front yard. Fortunately, it being 1 A.M., the boys were all asleep, and my dear friend Ellen was considerate enough to keep me distracted on the phone. Every so often I would shriek, "I think I hear something! But no, not yet."

The night was very cool and clear and I was thankful that I couldn't distinguish my internal shivering from the external cold. I purposely put on satiny, cream and rose-colored pajamas and a soft, terry robe on top because I wanted Alena's initial sensory experience of me to be inviting and peaceful. Her room was ready, fresh flowers had been planted in the garden to greet her. A warmer welcome could not have awaited her. I kept thinking, if the first time she was born was not under the best of circumstances, let this second birth be all that she could dream of.

Finally, the delivery car drove up and the door opened. I didn't know where to look first—at Paul's face or Alena's. I kept going back and forth—and only ten seconds had passed. Paul looked totally drained, but very happy and relieved. Alena looked thin, pale and frightened. Paul put her in my arms and we went inside. He said to me, "Here is your daughter." And with great tenderness, he said to Alena, "Here is your Mama."

She held on so tightly, I was surprised by the strength of her underdeveloped arms. I thought of the verse from the biblical Book of Ruth 1:14: "And she clung to her," because of the ferocity of the need expressed in that initial embrace. I don't know how long we sat there. It seemed like forever. Then I pulled back a little to really look at my new daughter and to wonder in amazement that all this came to be.

The ensuing days were filled with confusion, interrupted sleep, lots of crying from my sons, enormous tension and strain. I will not dwell on these moments. Suffice it to say, they were not unlike what I experienced each time a child of ours was born in the traditional sense of the word. However, here there were no raging hormones (or were there?) to attribute to the panic, and the panic was very real. In retrospect, I realize that in the weeks and months surrounding the births of our biological children, I did feel self-doubt, fear and exhaustion, but these emotions vied for center-stage with great love and trust in the being evolving before our eyes. This time, neither transcendent love nor total trust held sway. These were uncharted waters I was treading, and there was no one to guide me, no one I knew well who had swum here before.

In no way did I blame Alena for the difficulties of this initial period of adjustment. To the contrary, I was constantly amazed by her resilience, her eagerness to participate, to be accepted and to function as one of the family. From the first, she was full of curiosity and delight. Her intelligence was obvious, as she explored every room, every drawer and every corner of our home. She ate with great appetite, particularly relishing fruits. The large, juicy strawberries were her favorite. She was friendly to her brothers, affectionate to us, energetic and anxious to please. She had little sense of limits and boundaries but caught on quickly to what was expected.

To this day, Alena is known for her warmth and embracing personality, her ready laughter, her delight in new experiences. One of her teachers described her as "all heart." She plays with abandon; she adores animals; she is tender to her dolls and to younger children. She loves fireworks and scary rides, dress up and swimming. She sings and dances, loves to color, to pick flowers and to be chased and tickled by any willing tormentor. Many who get to know her without learning of her background are amazed that in two years she has integrated herself so completely. I often see people looking at her with wonder—a child whose destiny could have been so different.

People often ask about the treatment she received at the orphanage. From an emotional standpoint, it must have been excellent. I say this because Alena is so incredibly open and loving, so gentle to animals and babies. I can only assume that this is modeled on behavior she either witnessed and or experienced first-hand. Her trust level was high from the start. It is a great credit to those who cared for her during her first three years.

Paul told me, "I worried when we finally departed the orphanage that, in the moments when she realized she was actually leaving everyone and everything she knew, she might panic and run back to the arms of familiar people, to the sounds of a familiar language." I ached for both of them—for anticipating that crisis, the uncertainty, and the turmoil. Paul felt great relief when she eagerly took his hand to exit the orphanage premises, she smiled her magnificent smile, waved and never turned back. Her courage, willingness to belong, to give and to receive love so wholeheartedly have made her, in these two years, an integral, and dearly cherished part of our family.

Many thoughtful adoptive parents address at different times along their journeys the question of whether and when an adopted child really feels like yours and can it ever be the same kind of yours when the child has biologically emerged from your body. For us as adoptive parents, who also gave birth three times, the perspective is enhanced. Without hesitation, I can say that for about a year after Alena joined our family it did feel different. We did not treat her differently than we did our sons in terms of less nurture, care or affection, fewer toys, treats or privileges. If anything, perhaps, both Paul and I made extra efforts to express our love toward her and to bring into her world what she seemed most to need and desire.

The turning point came one night when I was putting Alena to sleep and noticed, as always, her porcelain beauty and the delicacy of her features. As I lay beside her, safe in mother-child intimacy, I noticed how our breathing was in harmony and how her breath seemed to enter my body, and then when I breathed out, it was as if I was breathing into her, as well. What came to mind for me was the verse from Genesis where it says, "And God blew into Adam's nostrils the breath of life." (Gen. 2:7)—and thus creation of human life commenced. I thought of our shared breath and breathing as a primordial life-force of creation passing from one body to another. I recalled a verse from the Indian poet Tagore, "Once we dreamt we were strangers. We wake to find we are dear to each other," and I thought of the birth and creation Alena and I made possible for each other— our creating a life for her filled with opportunity and family, she creating for us a life touched by a daughter, and a heightened sense of responsibility for all children everywhere. In a sense, by changing one world, we had changed the entire world. It was a great risk, a great responsibility, and a great privilege.

If the theology of bringing forth biological children finds its roots in the creation of human beings from substantive material, i.e. the dust of the earth, as Genesis also describes and our own genetic pool through which many of us get to experience the miracle of creation for ourselves, then the theology of bringing forth adopted children can find its pertinent metaphor in children being breathed into life as was Adam by God and as was Alena in our home that night.

Further, in Genesis 2:18 the words, "It is not good to be alone," usually used in conjunction with marriage, have come to mean to me—it is not good for a person, a child, to be alone in this world without family and a community to guide and nurture her. Although, to me mothering never felt like a biological call or function, it was always more spiritual. I don't think I recognized the fullest dimensions of mothering, until Alena came into our lives. For me, pregnancy, birth, lactation, and even those fleeting firsts—first smile, tooth, steps, words—were not nearly as compelling or as binding as the continuity of the relationship and understanding I was building with each of my children on a daily, weekly basis. And now that I have experienced two years of being Alena's mom, and have watched her grow and flourish and struggle, I can say assuredly that I feel no different toward her than I feel toward our sons. She evokes in me the same pride, tenderness, rage and frustration, and I am charmed and challenged by her in equal measure to our sons.

Through Alena, I am able to experience life differently. Where I am careful, she is carefree. Where I am spiritual, she is spirited. I am earth-bound; she flies high. My laughter is reserved; hers would fill a reservoir. I am manifestly a feminist; she is quintessentially feminine. Through her, as through each of my other children, I have come to inhabit worlds heretofore unfamiliar to me, and I rejoice in what I learn through them.

I try to honor what makes each of my children unique. I hope they will grow to appreciate the differences between them and me, and between themselves and all others whose paths they will cross. To the extent that living in a multicultural family will help prepare our children for a multicultural world, I believe Alena's adoption will be, for her brothers and for her, a valuable key to functioning well in society at large.

Alena arrived in San Diego on April 26, 1993. One month later we named her in a memorable ceremony at the Temple Family Service. We dressed her in red, white and blue, and our ever-generous friend made her a beautiful flower tiara for her hair and a bouquet to match. In August, we all drove to LA's University of Judaism to enact Alena's formal conversion through immersion in the mikvah, another very meaningful event for us all. Many asked if she knew what we were doing. Of course not! She was only three and a half then. We did tell her and our sons that we were taking part in a ceremony to seal Alena's Jewishness, just like the boys' brises had done. To Alena, I added, "And we get to go swimming in a small pool with lots of people watching and smiling." To her, it was another adventure to relish.

In January, about nine months after Alena arrived, we celebrated her fourth birthday and her first within our family. We made a big Russian party, catered by a Russian friend who is an excellent cook. We decorated tables with Russian trinkets, enjoyed festive music and a big cake.

Initially, I focused on the party and its details, but as the day approached, I found myself thinking less about the event and more about the woman who gave birth to Alena. I began to pray for her. I prayed that she was in good health and had enough money to meet her needs. I prayed that she was at peace with her

decision to deliver Alena to the care of an orphanage and that she was not tormented each year on the anniversary of the day she gave birth. I prayed and cried for her, and hoped that the winter winds—the same winds that carried Alena on the plane to us—would carry my prayers to her. I had come to view the sky as a birth canal. Through it, Alena was born into our world, and now I viewed it as a means of communication for bearing my prayers for contentment and resolution to a woman I am sorry I will never know, but who I imagine to be bright, fearless, and flamboyant, strong and passionate, perhaps a great dancer, a talented musician or some other kind of creative artist, certainly someone who celebrates life.

This unexpected thinking of Alena's first Mom taught me, in ways I had never fathomed before, the true meaning of motherhood, the deep, underlying connection between all who give birth and bring forth life, and the responsibility we have to recognize in each other shared stewardship of the young. In a wonderful book, *Also A Mother,* a Nicaraguan woman is cited as writing to her daughter, "A mother isn't just someone who gives birth and cares for her child. A mother feels the pain of all children of all peoples, as if they had been born from her womb." And, as I alluded to before, I again realized the secondary and relative place biology plays in the construction of the ideals of family and in the building of community bonds that matter. You see, along with everything else Alena has taught and given me, this revelatory experience of the true meaning of motherhood, has filled me with humility and insight and a new understanding of what it means to authentically propagate life.

I am pleased to tell you that this story doesn't have a happy ending. It has on-going beginnings, perpetual rebirths I and others will be privileged to experience at both predictable and unexpected moments. One of those unanticipated beginnings had its roots planted a few months after Alena came to be with us. We were taking a family vacation in Santa Barbara, and we met another family with two domestically adopted daughters of their own. I recall a pleasant conversation we had, but little else. A few months ago, I received a letter from the mom stating she was so moved by Alena's story that she has been working ever since to create a foundation to foster awareness of international adoption, and has set up a fund to grant interest-free loans to families who would like to adopt from Russia. She named her organization Domoi, Russian for, "Let's go home." She remembered Paul telling her those were among Alena's first words to him and the nurses at the orphanage translated. Domoi's brochure explains the general circumstances under which Alena joined our family, and her picture in the orphanage and at home with us graces the pages of this pamphlet. Ideally, her face and story will now inspire others to open their homes to wonderful children just like her.

Earlier I mentioned Liz, who hoped to adopt a daughter from Russia. Days after Paul's return with Alena, Liz's husband made a pilgrimage to the same orphanage that was Alena's first home. He returned with a new sister for their Romanian-born son. Miri was a baby. Though she and Alena were housed in the same institution, they had had no contact with each other. Even so, Liz and I agreed to encourage a friendship between the girls. At some point, this might mean a great deal to them both.

Finally, I stated early on in this presentation that in some ways it seems that our choice of international adoption was bashert, destined, foreseen. Both my parents were born and raised in Vienna and only left at ages twelve and seventeen under the horrible circumstances of the approaching Nazi onslaught. My parents' immigrations to America, their learning of English as a second language, their living between two cultures, all that they left behind, all that they gained from their new life in our incredible land of freedom—all these were relatively silent but deeply powerful themes in my growing up years. Unlike many who were victimized equally, more, or less, my parents chose to use their experience as raison d'être for reaching out to others, for embracing the stranger and building bridges to those from different backgrounds. Throughout my youth, people visited our home from dozens of countries where they spoke many different languages, ate unfamiliar foods and were culturally displaced for at least a short period of time. Although at the time I objected to their presence in our lives, I see in retrospect the sizeable impact it had on me. For me, foreign might mean different; it could never mean undesirable.

That my daughter was born elsewhere and owes her earliest allegiance to a different culture makes her more like my parents than I ever was! It feels like an identity coming full-circle. Several years ago, my sister and I contributed, in our parents' honor, a donation to the Ellis Island Immigration Museum. Their names are inscribed on a wall with the names of hundreds of other immigrants. In honor of and to mark the first anniversary of Alena's arrival, I sent a donation to this same museum. I doubt if their names literally rest side by side, but in my mind they do and always will.

This past April, we celebrated Alena's second anniversary with us by having an ice cream party to celebrate her many devoted friends. Someone thought it was her birthday we were celebrating, but she corrected them. She said, "We're having this party because I am adoption." She certainly represents the very best of adoption and of life itself.

May 14, 1995

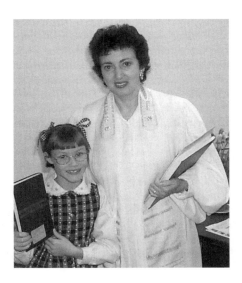

Rabbi Lenore Bohm was ordained from Hebrew Union College in 1982. She teaches and preaches Judaism from a feminist perspective. Having served congregations and worked with women's groups in San Diego County for fourteen years, in 1997, she and her family moved to South Australia for a two year sabbatical. In Adelaide, she works with the only Progressive Jewish congregation in the region, Beit Shalom. Rabbi Bohm has published guides for observance of Jewish holidays and Rosh Chodesh for Women of Reform Judaism. Her reflections on various Torah portions are included in *Beginning the Journey: A Women's Torah Commentary.*

Family History
Jody Lannen Brady

I sit at the dining table in my fiancé Stephen's childhood home. Out of the corner of my eye I see Stephen fidgeting beside me. He thinks it's time to leave, but I can't take my eyes off his father Max at the other end of the table. I watch Max's fingers. They are big and stiff, and Max rubs them almost constantly across his chin while he speaks.

Now he moves his hand and one of the fingers rubs his brow. His fingers never stop. They perpetually rub each other or something on his face, but he appears completely unaware of their presence. Stephen doesn't watch fathers the way I do. Once I asked him if Max was always like this and he looked at me as though he had no idea what I was talking about

Max is telling me something about his twin, a man I haven't met. I have trouble listening to Max's words as I watch his fingers rhythmically stroke the left side of his chin. "Watch out," Max says, and points at me, "they run in our family." He throws his head back in a laugh. I smile dumbly and nod, then I realize what Max is laughing about—twins. He is warning me twins run in the family. Stephen's entire family talks about children as though they are already a certainty, not some possibility down the road for Stephen and me.

"Sleepwalking. That runs in my family," Stephen's mother Rita puts in. "But don't tell me if you know all about that already."

We all laugh as we are expected to. I look at Stephen. His face is flushed. I see he doesn't like where the conversation has led, isn't certain of its effect on me for a number of reasons. Stephen stands and says, "We have to go." He puts his hand on my shoulder and I rise obediently. I don't know what runs in my family. I want to tell everyone at this table, but I would never be that impolite or honest.

When I am at my mother's house the next day, I am still thinking about our dinner conversation on families. My friend Susan has been after me to call my birth mother and ask her for a family medical history. Susan has a child with epilepsy and she is pregnant again. Her anxiety has turned her into an expert on every possible genetic defect that a parent can pass on to a child. She has made it her mission to prepare me for the childbearing she sees in my future. For Susan's peace of mind, I agreed weeks ago to see what I could find out. She gave me a form I had no intention of filling out. Last night after dinner with Stephen's parents, I find myself wanting to call, though I don't really know why.

My mother is getting ready to move out of the house she has lived in for over twenty-three years, almost as long as I've been alive. Granny lived here even longer. When Granny died last year, the moving process began. Today's job is packing up and delivering to the Salvation Army things we have decided we are willing to part with. Mom holds up a teapot, turning it in front of me to show off its shine. She's like a pushy sales person pitching her wares. "You'll be sorry about letting this go," she says. "Stainless has a good whistle."

"Then you keep it," I tell her.

She puts the kettle in a box. We put pots and potholders, a carving knife, and a set of mixing bowls in the same box. We move to the pile of clothes and I try to get started with what I want to say, but I can't find the words.

My mother won't be upset. She has always been willing to talk about my other mother, as she refers to Sharon. My mother has found ways to bring up the subject over the years. When I was a girl and I asked about a woman's swollen belly, my mother explained the birthing process and my story. When I was a teenager, she told me Sharon's story as a real-life example of unplanned pregnancy. "While her pregnancy has been a blessing to me," my mother told me, "it was a very painful experience for your other mother. She was a very angry, very unhappy girl." And even recently when I told her that an old friend miscarried her second baby, my mother nodded solicitously then asked me to tell my friend, that if she ever wanted to talk about adoption, to give her a call.

"What's on your mind?" Mom asks.

She startles me and I drop the shirt I am folding. If I ever have children, I will at least pretend that I can't read their minds.

"I'm thinking of calling Sharon."

My mother nods but doesn't say anything. She gathers up the edges of the plastic bag in front of her and leans on it to squeeze out the air. She pulls it up, sends it spinning around, and then whips a twist tie around the bag's neck. My mother is always neat, even when she's getting rid of things. She is waiting for me to tell her whatever I need to tell her.

"I want to know more about her family," I say. "Susan says I should know things before I think about having children."

As soon as the words are out of my mouth, I realize this is what I didn't want to say. It is something of an indictment. You wouldn't know about these things is what I'm afraid my words might sound like to my mother, who tried for years to conceive a child before she adopted me. I bend down and busy myself putting a stack of folded clothes into another bag.

"That's wise," is all my mother finally says. She picks up a shirt and begins to fold it. It is an awful, flowered print I loved in high school. Then she bends and lays the shirt carefully on a stack of other folded shirts. She reaches over and puts her hand on my shoulder.

"You'll make a wonderful mother someday," she says. I look at her. My mother's smile reassures me. "Why don't you go call her now."

"Later," I tell her. "Let's finish."

We go back to folding clothes. I feel better, so I hum along to the radio we have set to an *oldies* station. It's playing a song I vaguely know—a song that came out at the same time we wore some of these clothes.

The next Friday at the end of the workday, I wait for the last person to leave. I want to be alone when I call. I want the computer in front of me and file cabinets all around to remind me that the phone call is just business. Finally from the next cubicle Charles calls out as he leaves, "Don't stay too long."

In front of me sits the medical history form Susan gave me. Two columns run down the form, one for the mother's family history and one for the father's.

I don't know who my father is, but I'm hoping Sharon will tell me enough to fill out that half of this form.

"Expect nothing," my mother warned me the first time I called Sharon. I remind myself of that.

The few times I spoke with Sharon, there was always the same guarded tone in her voice. "What do you want from me?" the voice says, no matter what the words are saying. I know Sharon only by this voice. When I try to picture what Sharon might look like, I can only imagine a forty-year-old version of myself, but with a pinched, wary face.

Expect nothing, I remind myself, as I dial Sharon's number.

"We don't have any problems, if that's what you mean," Sharon tells me.

I go down the list anyway. "Cancer?"

"My mother's father died of cancer of the liver. Is that what you want?"

"Yes," I say and scribble down the information. There's not enough room on the line and I have to use the space in the father's column. I move on. "Heart disease?"

"No."

"Blood disorders?"

"No."

"Respiratory disease?"

"Like asthma?"

"Yes," and get my pen ready to write.

"His sister had asthma."

"Whose sister?" Sharon doesn't reply. As the silence on the phone line settles, I feel something like electricity shoot through me. I tingle. Sharon has just slipped. Though she has forbidden me to talk or ask about my birth father, Sharon has just done it herself.

Finally Sharon says, "You got anything else you need to know?" A pause and then, "Any more diseases?"

" I'd like to know about the asthma." I take a deep breath and then lie, "I've been having some chest pain and the doctor asked about any family history of respiratory disease. I told him I'd find out." No reply. "It really would help." Silence, then a deep sigh. I wait.

"She only had it bad a couple of times. The rest of the time she just used one of those little cans she would spray into her mouth. She could run races and everything."

I try to think quickly. How can I keep her talking without scaring her off? "No one else in the family had asthma?"

"No." It sounds like an accusation.

"The doctor will want to know how she is related to me."

"She was your father's sister. All right?" Her voice sounds angry now.

"All right. Thanks." I don't push. This is a start.

I have had three mothers. When my father died and my mother and I moved to live with my grandmother, I was a baby. Granny spent days with me, while my mother worked in a doctor's office. Two mothers hovered over me, and the third mother, this disembodied voice on the phone, birthed me. I don't remember the father I briefly had. I know him only by pictures and stories.

"Your father," my mother would say and point to a picture of a man in a checked hat with a big moustache. "Your father," she would say to me and then tell me about the man who ran a printing press and prided himself on never having ink under his fingernails. My mother knows nothing about my birth father, and Sharon won't speak. I rarely wondered about him as I was growing up. It was as if Sharon had done the whole thing on her own—sixteen-year-old girl who goes ahead and has her baby.

Now as I play with Susan's son and watch my other friends have babies, I think about having children and I wonder more about the whole father thing. I would like to know the kind of father my fathers—the one who conceived me and the one who adopted me—might have been. I find myself wondering what type of father Max was to Stephen growing up—the strict type, the talkative type, the pushover type—and what type of father Stephen will be, if we have children. Stephen says, "There aren't types of fathers," but he takes the concept of father for granted. He doesn't notice them the way I do, and he doesn't understand the exotic creatures they are to me. I learn about them in books. I shake hands with them when I meet them. I listen to them tell jokes about my friends. But I don't really know them, and I don't know what part of them becomes a part of their children.

I don't tell anyone about the phone call to Sharon, not even Stephen, though I've always confided in him before this. My mother knows, of course. But even when I am back at her house packing up the things I am taking—pictures and sentimental things I associate with Granny and growing up—she doesn't ask. I want to make light of the whole thing. I planned to volunteer the information that Sharon's family appears to be relatively clear of genetic time bombs, but I can't bring myself to share anything.

When my mother carries Granny's scrapbook out to the car for me, she says, "Bring Stephen over soon." I promise. As I drive away, I feel like a traitor. I have spent the entire week thinking about the phone call. I keep wondering what pieces of me are pieces of Sharon and what part of me comes from the man, or boy, who fathered me. I've always been genuinely laid-back about Sharon She's been out there. I've had a few awkward conversations with her, and her connection to my life has been tangential. Now I find myself wanting to know if my blue eyes come from her? Does my height come from him? I try to imagine what he might have been like, but Stephen's father is all that comes to mind. I picture Max's big hands holding me as an infant.

His sister had asthma. My mother has told me that Sharon wasn't certain who impregnated her, that she'd had a one-night stand, or something of the sort Now I know this can't be the case. Sharon knew who made her pregnant well enough to have known his sister, to have seen her use an inhaler, to have seen her running, and well enough to know the sister only had a couple of asthma attacks growing up. It makes everything different somehow.

At work I sit trying to think of ways to trick Sharon into revealing more. I face my computer screen, but I can't concentrate on the budget spreadsheet I'm supposed to be putting together. On Monday my boss will ask for this spreadsheet on her way into a meeting with the executive committee, but I can't muster up enough panic yet to make myself focus on the numbers. I keep thinking about driving to the town where Sharon lives. I think she grew up there. I could snoop around. I could check libraries for high school yearbooks and look for pictures of Sharon with boys. I could make a list of potential fathers.

The phone rings. It is Stephen. I tell him about the budget, boring him on purpose with details. "They'll never approve Katherine's training request but I have to put it in here anyway." I rattle on. Stephen knows something is wrong, but I have denied it every time he asks. He asked me last night if I'm having doubts about the wedding. I tried to reassure him. I told him the only thing I was having doubts about was my wedding dress, but he wasn't fooled.

"Can we do something tonight?"

"I don't know when I'll get out of here," I tell him.

"We still on for a ride tomorrow?"

"I'll have to call you." I hang up but keep my hand on the receiver. I feel rotten about what I'm doing to Stephen. From down the hall Peter chooses this moment to march in and tell me that he never received the revised budget schedule so he won't be coming in tomorrow, Saturday, to help. This is a lie but not a big one for Peter, who can come up with much more elaborate excuses not to do his work. He is a conniving coward, unwilling to face up to his problems—like me, I realize.

"Fine," I say to Peter. "I'm not coming in, either."

Peter looks nervous, as he backs away from my desk. He's afraid I might be serious, that I might leave us both hanging. And he's right to worry because I really have decided that I'm not coming in.

I'm going home to call Stephen and tell him when to come over in the morning, and before he comes tomorrow, I'm going to call Sharon.

I call her not too early but before Stephen will get here to go bike riding and before the stores open, because Sharon told me once that she works retail. I put my dog out back and I make sure the front door is locked so that Stephen will have to knock. I practice what I will say. Then I blurt it all out differently once I have Sharon on the line.

"I want to know who my father was."

"I never told him," Sharon answers me, not attempting to mask her anger. "Why should I tell you?"

"Please. I can't stop thinking about this since we talked last time." I hear a car outside and I listen for it to pass. It is too early for Stephen to be here.

"You want to call him too?" Sharon asks me. "You want to ask him all your questions?"

"I just want to know. I want to put this behind me. I won't call him, if you don't want me to."

"I don't care what you do," Sharon says. The bitterness in her voice sears me. "He wouldn't believe you, anyway. He'd tell you I was lying."

My dog Norman is barking now. He wants to be let in. "Can't you just tell me something about him?" I plead.

"You trying to get back at me?"

" No. I just need to know. Please."

"What do you need us for? Don't you have a nice life there?"

"I've never had a father." I never intended to say this, but I find myself explaining to Sharon: "Long ago my father died. He's someone I think I should love for my mother's sake. My mother can't understand he doesn't exist for me, anymore than the characters in books we read over and over together when I was young. He's just one of the kindly and reassuring characters but not real." I tell Sharon about Stephen and getting married and about my fear of having children. I've never called it fear before. When I finally stop talking, the silence is so long I'm afraid Sharon has walked away from the phone. "Sharon?"

"He's not going to want to be your father, honey."

Sharon's voice is transformed. It is soothing, almost southern in its soft slowness. I can't account for the change. I want to keep this new voice talking. "I just want to know about him."

"It'll just be more of the same thing."

"That's okay. I'll know his story. I won't have to sit here making one up and thinking about him all the time."

A sigh comes from Sharon's end of the phone. "He was cheating on me. Going out with another girl. Sleeping with her."

"Oh," I say, because I can't think of what else to say.

"So I thought if I did it. If I slept with him too, then he wouldn't cheat on me."

"I'm sorry."

"Why are you sorry? I'm not telling you this to make you feel guilty, honey I disappeared and he didn't care. He never tried to find me."

"But that's not your fault. I'm just sorry you had to go though that alone."

"I wasn't alone. I had you, and I knew I was doing the right thing. That's something I've always felt good about, no matter what else has happened."

"You felt good about me?"

"I still do. About having you and about giving you to good parents I didn't know about Mr. Morrison dying. I'm real sorry to hear about your father."

I try to keep my voice calm I try to think of all I meant to ask and to say to this woman, but it's difficult to think at all. It's difficult to believe that I am speaking with the same Sharon who was so reluctant to speak with me the few times before when I called.

"You've never sounded like you felt good about me. You've always sounded like you didn't want to talk to me."

"I don't," Sharon says, her voice hard again.

This doesn't make me feel good. Norman starts barking louder. I stretch the phone cord far enough to open the door and let him in. He frantically licks my legs I cradle the receiver and rub my hands down his back. He twists his head to lick my hands. Still I don't say anything to Sharon.

"You open up old wounds," she finally says. "You bring me back to the worst time of my life."

I can't think of anything to say.

"I gave you life and I gave you parents. And that's all I have to give you. You understand?"

I try to think of an objection, but I realize I don't have one. "I think I understand."

"No, that's wrong." The soft voice is back. "I guess I have something else."

"Yes?" I wait for Sharon to go on.

"Give me your address I saved some things from when I went with your father. I never knew why, but I couldn't throw them out. Guess I was saving them for you."

"Thanks."

"You be careful if you call him," Sharon tells me. "Someone told me he has a family now Don't expect anything."

It was the sort of advice my mother gives me all the time. "Don't expect Sharon to want to see you. Don't expect Stephen's parents to like you. Don't expect having children to be easy."

"Okay," I say to Sharon. "I won't expect anything." This is the answer you are supposed to give a mother.

I sit at my mother's dining room table. We are hosting a farewell dinner. Farewell to the house, that is. Max sits at the head of the table, rubbing those big fingers against each other as he tells us a story about a little boy Stephen asking for a raise in his allowance. Rita sits next to him shaking her head but enjoying the story every bit as much as my mother and me. Stephen jumps up and offers to find another bottle of wine. He will bide his time until this story has ended and it is time for my mother to tell on me again. Stephen comes back with the wine.

"A toast," Max proposes. We raise our glasses and Stephen walks around the table to fill them.

"What will we toast?" mother asks.

"To children," Max says.

We clink our glasses and echo his toast. No doubt it means something different to each of us, but we all mean well with our toast—a family around the table, telling stories and trying our best to love one another perfectly in this imperfect world.

"Family History" was previously published in *Confrontations*.

56

Jody Lannen Brady won the 1998 F. Scott Fitzgerald Short Story Contest. Her story, "Family History," was originally published in *Confrontations*. Two of her stories appear in recent anthologies, *At Our Core: Women Writing about Power,* Papier Mache Press; and *A More Perfect Union: Poems and Stories about the Modern Wedding,* St. Martin's Press. She lives in Annandale, Virginia, with her husband, Bill, and two children, Matt and Kelly.

Open Mind, Open Heart

I.

In Changsha, China, in dark orphanage rooms, hundreds
of abandoned baby girls wait. Legend has it that Lao Tsu,
riding off to the desert to die, sick at heart at the ways of men,

was persuaded to write down his teaching for posterity.
*The Tao, which can be told, is not the eternal Tao. The name
that can be named is not the eternal name.* At the Office of the

Secretary of State of Massachusetts, they affix the proper seals
to our documents. They used to throw them in the river or
bury them alive. *The nameless is the beginning of heaven and earth.*

My husband's birth certificate is lost in the gray cubicles
of New York state. Lao wrote the *Tao te ching,*
The Way of Virtue, in the sixth century B.C.,

essence of Taoism. Now they leave them near the orphanage,
pretend nothing happened, try again for their one chance
at a boy. *The named is the mother of ten thousand things.*

How long it takes to collect the required papers! *It is important
to cast off selfishness and temper desire.* I'm learning
about patience. *He who is attached to things will suffer much.*

II.

Lao Tsu, ancient master of divination and sacred books,
in Hunan province where my future daughter waits,
is said to have met the young Confucius, telling him to

beware of his pride and his ambition. *Being open-hearted,
you will act royally. Being royal, you will attain the divine.*
Confucius, hurt, took the message to heart, and found

he was changing. He looked at Lao Tsu and saw
a dragon rising to the sky, riding on the winds and clouds.
Being divine, you will be at one with the Tao.

He vowed to be worthy of the great master, though he
knew his way was the way of the every day.
Though the body dies, the Tao will never pass away.

III.

Breathe in, breathe out. How many approvals left to go?
In the universe great acts are made up of small deeds.
In Changsha, she waits in a sea of baby girls,

all needing a name. It's not over at six months, or six years,
it's never over She may have a place in her that is desolate,
a land I can never reach. I dream that

I am standing on top of a cliff looking down on ocean
under a full moon. In front of me there is a staircase
of stone leading down to churning waves of water.

The stairs are narrow and steep, with no railing, and
I am afraid of heights. I want to go down barefoot
on cold stone, a shimmering below where the tide

hits the land, and above a light bathing me in something
both animal and ethereal. I know I will go. But for a moment
I stop and listen. *Darkness within darkness. The gate to all mystery.*

Karen Braucher

©1997 by Karen Braucher, *Heaven's Net,* Bacchae Press, 1997. First published in the journal *Nimrod* as a finalist for the Pablo Neruda Poetry Award.

Travel Instructions for China

Travel lightly. The itinerary can change at any time without
notice. Don't express anger or frustration; they will not
understand. The size of your baby is unknown. Do not
trust the birth date given. The notarials ask, "How much
money do you make? Why can't you have babies? Why do you
want a Chinese baby?" Do not insult their culture. Do not mention
all these babies are abandoned because they are female. No
immunizations are required to travel to China. The Chinese
will be very helpful if you smile. Then you will go to the
orphanage and meet the baby, but you can't take her
with you back to the hotel. You will be required to throw
several banquets for various officials. Bring a nasal aspirator,
Vaseline jelly, hydrocortizone cream, sixty diapers, a pocket knife,
clothes of correct size, a baby thermometer, a flashlight, jugs for water,
formula, Q tips, bottles, nipples, pacifiers, bibs, bottle brushes, bonnets,
and Pepto Bismol. Travel lightly. Paperwork will then go to the
Ministry of Justice in Beijing. You are a woman so you should know
what to do with these nursery items. The size and weight of your baby
are unknown. Travelers on usual tourist routes are not at risk
of malaria. The baby you are assigned may be different from the one
you finally get. Americans should be cautious about carrying
into China documents, literature, and letters which might be
regarded as objectionable. Schistosomiasis has been reported.
Avoid swimming or wading in fresh water such as lakes,
rivers, or ponds. The hardest part will be the tour of the
orphanage. New York to Tokyo is fourteen hours non-stop, and
from there you must go to Beijing and then Changsha, which is not
on the usual tourist routes. Before you leave China, you must fly
with your baby to the U.S. Consulate in Guangzhou to obtain a
U.S. visa for her. She will not be tested for hepatitis B, now raging
through the Orient. Then you will fly from Hong Kong.
Bring baby wipes, cotton balls, cuticle scissors, Tinactin solution,
Caldesene ointment. You are a woman so you should know.
Your baby is liable to suffer from understimulation. She will be in
culture shock. Your life will be permanently changed. In China,
everything is difficult but nothing is impossible. Bring coffee.
Bring comfort foods. You are a woman. Travel lightly.

Karen Braucher

©1997 by Karen Braucher, *Heaven's Net*, Bacchae Press, 1997.
First published in the journal *Iowa Woman*.

Brand

I'm in Changsha Children's Center Number 1 holding only
the baby assigned to me. Although it's bright outside, in here
it's dim, heavy with heat and infants flat on their backs on bamboo.
For some reason, all the helpful Chinese women caretakers
are gone. There are at least forty babies sprawled in the half-light,
and most of them are crying. Perhaps one is hungry, another
thirsty, one burning in a soaked diaper, and I am here
holding only one of them. I look across the room and see another
ashen-faced American, a man, holding only his baby.

Our eyes lock like two refugees, two prisoners, and we shake
our heads slowly and do not speak. The miniature bodies around us
continue to cry, roll and writhe, crane their necks trying to get someone's
attention. No one picks them up. No one is going to pick them up
for minutes, hours, and we know you can forget all that crap
about helping others and all that fluff about loving one another,
because we are looking at the unwanted, the cast-offs, no matter how
you try to paint it in some other light. The moment passes. We look at
each other again, veterans, and he says, "We've got to get
our babies out of here." And I think, yes, that's the way it is, you can't
save them all. Courage and ruthlessness rise like the south China heat.

Karen Braucher

©1997 by Karen Braucher, *Heaven's Net,* Bacchae Press, 1997.
First published in the journal *Iowa Woman*.

On Tiananmen Square, 1992

Swarms roam the square, which can hold a million
A huge color portrait of the late Chairman
hangs from the Gate of Heavenly Peace
in front of the Forbidden City where emperors
lived with hundreds of concubines. Nearby,
the Great Hall of the People stands, where,
according to our guidebook, the "dictatorship
of the proletariat" is conducted. But here
in front of the Museum of the People's Revolution,
there's a gigantic green inflatable beer bottle,
so out of place we laugh at the hint that markets
are opening. So much gray concrete, scrubbed
clean of blood. Who cares now about Mao's
permanent revolution? Who cares now
for the wisdom of Confucius or Lao Tzu?

Perhaps there is some new way for this country
to rise up. I wish I could speak to these mothers
with their only daughters, dressed in layers of frills.
I approach them sitting on the sunny square. They
rise politely smiling, willing to pose for a foreigner.
They speak no English and I, no Beijing dialect.
I want to say my daughter is Chinese; these photos
are for her. Pictures she may study years from now
when she considers why her birth mother
might have let her go, why that mother might
still dream of her from a compound
near the rice paddies, imagine her, happy.

Karen Braucher

©1997 by Karen Braucher, *Heaven's Net,* Bacchae Press, 1997.
First published in the journal *Baybury Review.*

First Chinese New Year

Bundled like the richest Manchurian girl,
you were held up by your father to see
the dragon dancing through red firecracker
paper and snow in Boston's Chinatown.
High on Peking duck, whole crispy fish,
shivering, dodging sparks, I went click, click,
a silly woman really, silly with happiness
and wanting to save fragments for you,

wanting to remember our breath rose
in the frigid air like we were the dragons,
not the men in grimacing masks jazzing
the street with neon, grabbing money
hung from the restaurant foyers.
Bathed in the finest ginseng soap,
wrapped in red silk, you laughed
through the banquet's sweets and sours,
Lapsang Souchong tea, while boys outside
didn't lose fingers setting off kabooms.

Born in the Year of the Monkey,
all fire and rascal, you will receive
so many official scraps, hotel receipts,
snapshots, Chinese paper cut-outs,
flurries of crisp confetti. But this day
could go to gray haze—I forgot
to put film in the camera—like your
first nine months and nine days.

Were you found in Hunan heat,
cavernous train station, drab department store,
were you torn from your first mother's arms,
or did she hide, cradling you, trying
to leave her baby somewhere auspicious—
there's no detail, no hue. Betty Li Bai,
the faded orphanage clothes you wore
when you first were handed to me
are wrapped in tissue. Blue Chinese pantaloons
with a drawstring, a shirt with a cartoon cat,
I'd take them with me if the house were on fire,
bottom drawer, left-hand side, of your dresser.

Karen Braucher

©1997 by Karen Braucher, *Heaven's Net,* Bacchae Press, 1997
First published in the journal *Iowa Woman.*

Karen Braucher grew up in Massachusetts and now lives in Portland, Oregon. She has worked as a high-tech manager, consultant, business writer, and teacher. She holds an M.F.A. in Writing from Vermont College. *Heaven's Net* won the Bacchae Press 1997 national chapbook competition. Ms. Braucher also has won the Worcester Poetry Prize, the Grolier Poetry Prize, and was a finalist for the Pablo Neruda Poetry Prize. Her poems have appeared in literary journals including *Nimrod, The Spoon River Poetry Review, Iowa Woman, The Worcester Review, and Puerto del Sol* as well as in anthologies. She was awarded a 1996–7 Oregon Literary Fellowship in poetry.

Meeting Eve
Nicole J. Burton

At the foot of the winding staircase leading to Selfridges' coffee shop, I gazed up to see if anyone was looking for me. At twenty-seven, I was embarking on the most perilous leg of my long voyage to meet my birth mother for the first time.

I met my birth father in Nottingham the week before. Now I was in London, poised in the doorway of discovery, facing the possibility she might not show. At the top of the stairs, I looked again. Perhaps she'd cancelled at the last minute after I'd already left the house. Maybe she had to pick up her husband early. Then, there she was, sitting at a table for two.

She didn't see me at first. She was pretending not to look around amid the bustle of morning tea. She had wild, grayblond hair and wore a snappy black jacket and jeans. She was younger than I expected, younger than my adoptive mother, still youthful and defiant I could tell from across the room.

She saw me.

I smiled and walked over to the table. "Eve?"

"Yes."

I sat down. We chatted about getting there, the temperature, and traffic. Then she said, "You look exactly like him."

"Yes, I do." What a joy to know it was true. My olive skin and intense eyes had been his from the start.

"You don't look a bit like me," she said, looking me over. I couldn't tell yet if that was accurate. She was not exactly pretty. Still, you couldn't help but notice the generous nose, large gray eyes, and angular cheekbones framed by a riot of hair. She was petite and shapely and looked as if she worked to keep her hips in line. This was how I might look in middle age.

"How did you meet Philip?"

"My adoptive mother knew who he was. I don't know how. She's from Nottingham too. I think a family friend was involved in the adoption. Anyway, she told me his name two years ago, I mean his last name. I always knew you named me after him, 'Pippa' short for 'Phillipa.' My mother took me to his curtain store on Upper Parliament Street, and later, I called and met him at the factory in the Lace Market."

I recalled walking down the long corridor, announcing myself to the receptionist, who rang his office. When I saw him, at first I couldn't speak

Eve acted uninterested, yet she obviously felt something—resentment, heartbreak, or just plain old pain.

"What did he say about the circumstances of your birth?"

"He told me you'd gone together then broken up. He went out with a friend of yours or you with friend of his, and a few months later you wrote saying you were pregnant and he was the father. He said it was awkward because by then he was engaged to someone else." A nice Jewish girl he could take home to Mama, I thought, privately.

65

"It wasn't quite like that," she said, and folded her hands without elaborating. Please tell me, I thought.

"The best I can explain it," she said, paused then continued, "is to say it was the fifties, puritanical, I never felt like I fit in. There was a very good book by David Lodge called *How Far Can You Go?* I remember reading it and thinking, yes that's just how it was.

"I wasn't promiscuous but I was romantic, sensual, always falling in love. I was much happier in the sixties and then on, I can tell you. Philip was from a conservative Jewish family. His mother would have died rather than have him marry me. His family paid my bills, but I never heard from him, ever. When you were born, I remember looking at you. You didn't look a bit like me. I remember thinking, there lies a perfect stranger."

I kept my face immobile, but she'd cut a circle of flesh from my heart. She dragged on her cigarette and looked away. Across the table and the miles of years, this was obviously how she'd felt. What an odd woman! I wanted her to feel at ease, give us a chance to know each other, prove I wasn't a stranger but her daughter.

"Shall we get coffee?" I asked.

We went through the self-service line, each pouring a cup of coffee. At the table, she lit another cigarette then offered me the pack.

"No, thanks. I quit last year. I was a hopeless fiend."

She smiled. "Good discipline, then. I've never had much discipline. You're almost twenty-eight now?" she asked, as if she didn't know.

I nodded.

"And will you be back home for your birthday this year?"

"Yes. I'm going to Spain and Germany, but I'll be back in the States by the end of June."

"I always think of you on your birthday, July 25th."

"I think of you, too. I always knew no matter what you were doing the other days of the year, on my birthday, you must be thinking of me."

She stared for a moment. "I only told one friend, a dear person who never breathed a word. But I have another friend whose daughter's birthday is the same as yours. I always gave her presents. Once she asked me, 'Eve, how is it you always remember my birthday?'"

I pictured her giving presents to another child. It stung.

"Last year I was in Italy on your birthday. I made a pilgrimage to the frescoes of Fra Angelico."

I perked up. "I lived in Italy from age 13 to 15. My high school there took a field trip to see the frescoes of Fra Angelico."

"How strange. And I've been to United States many times. My husband Thomas owns a textile company. We often go to New York and Washington, and to the mills in North Carolina."

"My favorite beach is in North Carolina, the Outer Banks. Do you know it?"

"Yes! We were there, oh, two years ago in September, I believe."

I thought back. "I was there too after Labor Day and stayed about two weeks.

Perhaps we passed on the beach." Our paths had come close to crossing. How uncanny, I thought.

"And what kind of work do you do?" Eve asked.

"I'm a playwright. I have a small theater company I write for and help manage."

"Do you act also?"

"Sometimes, when drafted. Actually, I like acting. But it takes time from writing. I'd rather do that."

"You could do well in the movies with your looks. You'd stand right out even from the back row."

She'd complimented me. I was surprised. "I'm going back to college to finish my degree in literature."

"I love American literature. Not so much the colonial writers, but, oh, Emerson, Whitman, James, Wharton. I couldn't live without them! I have another daughter who writes. And one who paints. The other one, I don't know yet. I think she enjoys business, like her father."

"Weren't you an art student? Somehow, my mother knew and told me, though I was afraid it just a nice thing to say."

"I went to London Art College. I didn't finish my program, but I've painted ever since. I don't know how good I am, probably not very."

She lacked self-confidence. Here she was also negating her work. I made a mental note to be on the lookout for this trait. It was so self-destructive. Might be genetic. I wanted to know more about her, about the shape of her life. But I didn't want to scare her with questions. I probed, gingerly.

"Did you ever work, you know, a job?"

"No, not really. I had you and . . . well, it wasn't a very happy patch in my life. A few years later, I was engaged. We were on the verge of getting married, and he left me for someone else. I was pregnant again He knew and his leaving was quite a shock. But I said to myself, 'Eve, you can't go around leaving babies all over the place,' so I kept her. That was my daughter Angela.

"When I met Thomas, he fell in love with both of us. After we married, he adopted her. We had two more daughters, Marianne and Jules—Juliet. Angela's the one who writes; Jules is the painter."

For a moment, I saw myself with my three sisters, all madly writing and painting, and there in our midst, our mad matriarch swirling oils on a dark canvas. I smiled. I came for these connections. Ciphers for the blood that coursed through me.

She broke my quiet thinking by adding, "I never told anyone except my friend, not even my parents about you. It was different back then. I was married, with the girls. What was I supposed to do? Sit down at dinner one night and say, Thomas, girls, I have something important to tell you."

I thought, yes, that's what you should have done. What you should do now. But instead I said, "I understand." I said what would soothe her. "I don't expect anything from you. I have my family. I have a boyfriend and a life in America. I don't expect you to disrupt yours for me."

She brushed off my words. Looked relieved. "Perhaps I shall write to you occasionally. I could send you the name and address of my friend and you could send letters to her house."

My restraint had paid off. "I'd like that. By the way, what time was I born?"

"Oh God, why do you want to know that?"

"I want to have my horoscope done."

"You don't believe in that nonsense, do you? How appalling! It was the morning, around eleven. I don't remember exactly."

"How old were you?"

"I was twenty-three."

"So now you are . . . ?"

"Age has never been important to me," she said, with forced casualness. "I just had my fifty-first birthday Monday."

I jotted down her birthday on the back of an envelope in my purse

"May I take your picture?

She shook her head. "I look terrible in photographs, absolutely dreadful."

I liked the way she looked. She must have seen rejection cross my face. Her tone softened when she spoke, "One of my daughters has taken a few pictures that aren't quite as hideous as usual. I'll send you one of those." She looked at her watch. "I must be going. Will you walk out with me?"

We rose and walked downstairs into the crowded mass of people. She touched my shoulder. "Well, you look as if you had a nice middle-class upbringing." Her hand smoothed my tailored jacket.

"Oh, yes."

She must have been relieved I didn't grow up cold, hungry, and poor—every birth mother's nightmare. Relieved, too, I didn't want anything. At least, I wasn't going to create a humiliating scene involving her family. Then she added, "I should think something in brown wool would look very nice on you, keep you snug in those fierce American winters."

Her desire to clothe me warmed my heart. My adoptive mother was long-gone by the time I enjoyed clothes shopping. While we were in Italy, she and my father separated. When we returned to the States, she stayed there.

Eve and I walked to the Underground.

"I'll write you," she said and hugged me briefly. "I'll never leave you again, you know that, don't you?"

I looked into her eyes and nodded.

Then she was gone.

I walked down Oxford Street, looking in shop windows. Up to Marble Arch, around the Serpentine Lake, over to Hyde Park Corner. I looked for a Lyons Corner House, but they were gone, victims of McDonald's and Pizza Hut. I walked along Park Lane, back down Oxford Street, and into the Golden Egg for an omelet.

I felt lonely, so I went back to Selfridges and sat at our table and wrote postcards. This was our reunion place; I had to be here. I thought about the brown, wool jacket she mentioned, and about her gray eyes that alternately mocked me and begged forgiveness. I thought about her at the airport, collecting her husband returning from China. I thought about my sisters, their jackets, and their big warm house in Hampstead.

After sitting there for some time, I went downstairs and I looked at shoes. I was leaving the next day. You deserve something sprightly, I told myself. I did it. I met my mother and my father.

I looked down the rack of shoes. "You've reached your destination," whispered a pair of red and black sandals. I hesitated a moment, then forked over a small fortune, slipped on the snazzy red tiger-striped sandals, and sashayed out of Selfridges, into the blur of London streets, as a reunited adoptee.

Excerpt from *The Secret Daughter, Memoir of an Adoption Search,* ©1998 Nicole J. Burton.

Nicole Burton is a Washington, D.C. area playwright, author of *Last Call at the Marble Bar; Starman, Wish Me Luck; The Memory Club of America,* and other plays. Her award-winning dramas and comedies have been produced up and down the East Coast in theaters and venues as diverse as federal prisons, homeless shelters, and the U.S. Capitol. Her screenplays and treatments include *Mickey Berlin Loves Women* and *Southwest Remembered,* a film about urban renewal in Washington, D.C. that won the CINE Golden Eagle Award for Best Documentary in 1991. She has a B.A. in English from the University of the District of Columbia and is an Internet analyst at a federal agency. She lives in Riverdale Park, Maryland, with her husband, Jim Landry, and their son, Miles. *The Secret Daughter* is her first book.

Noah

Seven years of a boy
who got older and taller
a boy I love completely
a boy who began his life
in Chile,
then came to us
through difficult miracles
through problems
turned to a deep and full
solution: this boy,
now a Chilean Jewish Armenian
New Yorker,
our only child
a Noah whose seas
are our floods
whose paintings
our walls.
He believes
in ducks,
in fire and dinosaurs,
in Spaceballs and toys
and donut holes,
in ships
and dogs
and iguanas
named Iggy and Ziggy,
in friends and swimming
and cookie dough ice cream
in miniature golf
and Berenstein bears,
in cupcakes and ghosts,
in Caribbean suns
and guests for dinner,
in the idea that miracles
like the three of us
can sometimes happen.

Esther Cohen

Noah
Esther Cohen

". . . to think larger than one, to think larger than two or three or four
this is me
this is my partner
these are my children
if we say, these are my people, who do we mean?
how to declare our bond
how to keep each of us warm?"
—Melanie Kaye-Kantrowitz

Now he is eight, my funny son Noah. He draws but does not like art classes where everyone makes the same thing. He likes to draw when and what he wants. He often draws objects he sees—lobster boats and bicycles, televisions and dinosaurs in the museum. His other frequent subject is aliens. He usually shows them arriving. These aliens are creatures who suddenly appear from other worlds. They are in planes, or big, round, egg-shaped, silvery star ships with small doors. His aliens descend down long, straight ramps right to earth. In their strange way, they are smiling. I often wonder if he is drawing Peter and me, when we arrived to meet him in Chile one June eight years ago.

On the night he was born, the night I did not give birth to Noah, I had dinner with a French heart surgeon named Joseph. Joseph is a friend of a friend. An urbane man, witty and talkative, Joseph visits New York once a year. We ate in a warm, red and white restaurant. We were talking about music when Noah was born. After dinner, we went for a drink. I got home around eleven. Peter was writing numbers on the back of an old envelope. He seemed very nervous. I heard him say, "Esther's home. I think she would be better at this."

That is our delivery story. A woman I didn't know very well told us about a baby boy. I was not exhausted. Neither was Peter. The call was unexpected. We'd been told that adoption takes forever, and the baby was born two months after we'd decided to adopt. But it was not a simple process.

We saved the envelope where Peter wrote down the baby's length and his weight. We had twelve hours to decide—were we and this baby boy born in a village in Chile destined to become forever intertwined? Birth parents don't think about that very much. But I do know this—I wanted a child more than anything I've ever wanted before or since. I didn't care at all about the details of the child's life, sex or color, height or weight. I didn't want to live a life without a child. I don't know exactly why, although it seems as simple as wanting to live in a room full of light.

We said yes to the 6 pound 10 ounce baby boy. We knew almost nothing about him except that we would name him Noah. A few months later, we received his picture, an out of focus Polaroid of a baby facing away from the camera and wearing something blue. Somehow the picture made it seem as though we couldn't see him, and he couldn't see us either.

71

We adopted Noah in the midst of two large-looming myths—that technology can solve infertility problems and that biological children are somehow better. Even the news media refer to biological children as *natural,* implying that others are not. Especially in these last few years, author after author writes articles and books telling painful stories of all the tests and suffering and pain they've endured to be a mother. These authors sound as if all the many homeless children around the world won't do, as if they want to parent a perfect child, and as if that perfect child can only be born from them.

Both myths deeply effect a large segment of society—people who want to be parents, but only if they can have this perfect child. Several hundred thousand people a year participate in fertility treatments. The number astounds even RESOLVE, a national organization dedicated to helping people cope with infertility in the same way that AA members, for instance, cope with alcohol.

When we began the process of adoption, neither of us had thought very much about families. We did not have friends who adopted, so at first we called strangers in the way that you might if you were visiting a far away country they knew. They often told us dramatic and difficult stories of how and where they met their children—their own stories of delivery. They met their children in country trailers, near Paraguayan waterfalls, in Brazilian villages, orphanages in Bombay, or on dirt roads in El Salvador. Sometimes, it was more simple—a hospital room in Buffalo, a lawyer's office in Texas. The stories often had a dazed and mysterious quality to them, not unlike childbirth, or summer. None prepared us for the loud knock at our door in a huge hotel in Chile. An hour after we'd arrived there, a smiling, nervous woman named Dorys handed us a baby and he became ours. In this strange greenish room with a luminescent painting of a sharp-nosed flying fish, we three became a family.

Two adults drinking Cokes a minute before only half suspected the truth of what would happen, the coincidence of events, our random choice of Chile, our number in the adoption line, the modern day lottery our families have become. There were no breathing classes to prepare us, no outward signs of a pending momentous event, or no difference between the sexes in how we got ready. Becoming Noah's mother was instant. But even now, I am still a little surprised by people's reaction to adoption and what they say. "Maybe someday you'll have a real child," or "I've heard of couples who adopted, and then they had one of their own." It is hard to imagine how one child could be less real than any other, particularly to a parent.

People talk about families as though they never had one themselves. Maybe the Hollywood myth looms large—that families are all harmony, station wagons and apple pies. In fact, we live in a time when families are changing dramatically, no longer limited by old definitions, by genes or sex preference, by race or religion. Today, everyone can have a child, be part of a family. In my kindergarten class in a small Connecticut town, family meant only one thing. In Noah's class in a New York public grammar school, there are nearly as many kinds of families as there are children.

We three are connected through love, through choice and dailiness, through all those mysterious forces that brought us together. Not by blood, or similar eyes. We are a family.

Esther Cohen is the curator of *Bread and Roses,* a labor union arts program. She teaches writing in several places, including Parsons School of Design. She runs Workers Write, a writing workshop with readings and publications by union members. She is the author of the novel *No Charge for Looking* and is presently seeking a publisher for a second novel.

Balbriggan
Janis Cooke Newman

Balbriggan is not a tourist destination. Forty-five minutes from Dublin, it is possibly the only town in Ireland that does not have a quaint pub or a house with a thatched roof. Instead of Aran sweaters and key chains made of old Guinness advertisements, its shops sell pork chops and discontinued shoe styles. It has a beach, but the only thing that appears to go near it is the train up from Dublin.

We were the only people to get off that train at Balbriggan station. My father and his second wife, Ellie. My husband, Ken, and our two-year-old son, Alex. Me. American tourists with new sneakers and money belts that made our sweaters bulge out in odd places. We had come to Balbriggan in search of family. At least those of us with Irish blood had. Ellie was German by way of Kentucky, Ken was a Jew whose ancestors had come from a small town near the Polish border, and Alex was a little Russian boy who'd spent the first fifteen months of his life in a Moscow orphanage.

My father looked over the concrete wall of the train station and took a deep breath of Balbriggan's foggy air, as if it might awaken some forgotten genetic memory. His mostly black hair was squashed down into the shape of the Irish tweed cap he'd bought almost as soon as he'd gotten off the plane. The same cap that was now on Alex's blond head, floating around his ears. Ellie was singing to Alex a Country and Western song about a lonesome train, while Ken tried to open the stroller without damaging the print, slide, and video cameras he had slung around his neck like the bandoleers of a Mexican bandit. I, too, tried to wake a sleeping genetic memory with a deep breath of Balbriggan's damp air. It smelled largely of car exhaust.

George Cooke, my father, spoke to the stationmaster. "We're from the United States," he told him, as if he thought the man might find the news surprising.

"Tony McCormick," the stationmaster said, reaching up to shake my father's hand. He was a small man with white hair and a blue uniform.

"My family came from this town," my father said, "name of Harford."

"And would you be knowing old Freddy Harford then?" stationmaster McCormick asked. "He'd be living just up the road next to the hairdresser's."

"Freddy, huh?" my father said. "We should invite him to the pub."

"You'll not be wanting to do that," the stationmaster told him. "Freddy's a pioneer."

"A pioneer?" my father asked.

"Have you not heard of the pioneers? They never take a drink."

"Freddy doesn't drink?" My father sounded as if the stationmaster had just told him that our new-found relation had been born with three legs. "Are you sure he's a Harford?"

"Oh, is it Harford you're saying? I thought it was Harper. Old Freddy Harper's the one lives next to the hairdresser's. I guess he wouldn't be a relation of yours then, would he?"

We decided to ask stationmaster McCormick for directions out to the old cemetery, where we'd been told we would find a family grave, and leave it at that.

Like all Irish directions, McCormick's were as dense, as beautiful, as baffling as a page of *Ulysses*. "What you'll be wanting is the road that bends and leads off the main road, past the video store where the wall is painted a yellow-gold, like sun shining, and sends you down past the old factory where there's been no work for a good long time now, to the butcher shop on the corner where the Benson and Hedges advert's been painted over the old kiln bricks."

We set off walking, Ken pushing the video camera in the stroller, Ellie looking in the windows of Balbriggan's stationery shops and newsstands for an Irish sweater. Up ahead, my father had taken Alex's hand, and it made me think of the things we'd done together when I was a child. How my father would lie in my bed at night and tell me stories until he fell asleep; how he'd put on his plaid bathing trunks and join me in the bathtub; how one time we'd stayed up all night filming pictures, with an eight millimeter camera, for my history project about World War I battlefields.

The old cemetery was perched on a green hill off the main road to Dublin. An ancient church stood at the top, and the white headstones of the graves marched up in neat rows like a small army. My father and I walked through wet grass looking for a headstone with an inscription that matched the one his mother had recited from memory before she'd died. It was her grandparents' grave. My father found it almost immediately. It had a rectangular stone with a large Celtic cross on top and the family history carved into it. Listed among those who had died in America was Marianne, my father's grandmother.

My father ran his fingers over the carved letters on the headstone. "In a few more years," he said, "you won't be able to read it at all."

I found drawing paper and a green crayon in Alex's diaper bag. Putting the paper over the rough stone, I rubbed with the crayon. The words *Erected in Loving Memory* appeared. As I rubbed, the words came letter by letter, the way they do on a Ouija board. I felt as if I was receiving a message from the grave.

When I reached the last line, it started to rain and I gave the crayoned rubbing to my father, who rolled it up and tucked it under his jacket, as if it were a rare and valuable parchment. Then we crossed the road to a modern pub that had a sign advertising conference rooms.

The pub was paneled and carpeted and had two color TVs tuned to the same soccer match. We sat in a corner booth and ate oxtail soup, while Alex walked around behind us and made animal sounds into the backs of our necks.

"If it's living relations you're looking for," the bartender, a tall man with red hair and a pink face, said, "you should be talking to Sean McNally, the undertaker. He knows everybody."

We took a taxi to McNally's Drapery Shop, an old fashioned clothing store with racks of men's sports coats with plastic covers over the shoulders. The man behind the counter wore a shirt that still had creases where it had been folded in its package. He told us, 'You'll be finding Sean at home. Just go back up the road away from Dublin, past the Church of Our Savior, and look for the tallest of three tall houses all in a row."

My father and I wanted to go off in search of the undertaker, but the last train back to Dublin was leaving in fifteen minutes, so we headed back to the station.

"Did you have any luck?" Stationmaster McCormick asked when we returned.

"Not really," my father told him.

"This might be of some help to you then." He was holding a small white piece of paper. "T'is the phone number of Monica Harford. She reckons her husband Patrick might be a relation."

Two days later, the five of us returned to Balbriggan in a rented car to have lunch with Monica Harford at the Mile Stone Pub.

The Mile Stone smelled like old cigarette smoke and gravy. There were dead flies caught between the screen and the window behind our table, and above the bar a small color television set was tuned to the sheep dog trials.

Monica arrived in a flurry of face powder and conversation. "I'm expecting a fax from the Fingal Heritage Group," she said. "I've a friend over there looking up Harfords in their database. They'll send it round about three-thirty." She pronounced it 'tree-turty.'

"Would you like a drink, Monica?" my father asked.

"Vodka and white lemonade," she said.

"Just white lemonade?" my father repeated, not having heard the rest.

"Now what good would that do me?" Monica told him. Her hair was standing straight up on one side of her head, as if that was the side she slept on. Between bites of the Turkey and Ham special, Monica told us about the Harfords who were still in Balbriggan.

"Of course there's my Patrick, and Patrick's three brothers," she said. "And Christy Harford the bomb maker, sure and he's dead now."

"The bomb maker?" my father said.

"Have you not heard of Christy Harford?" she asked. "Made up bombs for the IRA, he did. Made them right in his basement." A large drop of brown gravy fell onto the front of Monica's pink blouse. "The Gardai arrested him ten years ago. A pub owner in town paid his bail, and sure and if Christy didn't disappear right after."

"How did he die?" my father asked.

"One night about five years after, men in Balaclava's brought his body back to his house. He'd died of natural causes," she said. "There's still bombs today they call a Harford after Christy."

The fax from the heritage society arrived, a document that traced the Harfords back to my great-great-grandmother's baptism in 1847. My father pored over it.

"It's grand what you Americans do," Monica said, "tracing your ancestry. It's important to know who you belong to." She smoothed the curled pages of the fax flat on the table. "Not like some. A schoolteacher and his wife here adopted a baby girl from Romania. Now that child will never know who her real family is, will she?"

I looked over at Alex, who was sitting at the bar with Ken and Ellie watching a horse race on the small television. He was wearing a little Irish tweed cap my father had spent the morning searching Dublin's shops for.

My Irish father, his wife that wasn't my mother, my Jewish husband, my Russian son. The day before, we'd stood and listened to a soft-voiced Irish actor recite from Beckett, and I could sense them standing around me. It had made me feel the way you do when you discover that someone who loves you has been watching you sleep. I folded my copy of the Harford database and put it away. I could feel no real connection to the Richard Harford who was married in 1870, or the Christy Harford, who manufactured bombs in his basement. Real family was not found in Heritage databases or carved on headstones. It was found in the man heading to the bar to get Monica another vodka and white lemonade, the woman explaining to Alex what that thing on the jockey's head was, the little boy dropping a plastic hippopotamus into a glass of Guinness.

When lunch was over, we stood in front of the Mile Stone and Ken took pictures of us with Monica. Then we walked back to the rented car, Alex and my father up ahead in their matching Irish tweed caps, moving past Balbriggan's used furniture stores and ladies' dress shops.

"Balbriggan" was printed in the *San Francisco Chronicle, the Philadelphia Inquirer,* and will be included in *Travelers' Tales, Best of Family Travel.*

Janis Cooke-Newman lives in northern California with her husband, Ken, and their son, Alex. Ms. Cooke-Newman's work has appeared in *Country Living, Sesame Street Parents Magazine, Backpacker, Salon* on-line magazine, the *Philadelphia Inquirer, San Francisco Chronicle, Denver Post,* and the *Chicago Sun-Times.* One of her stories is included in *Travelers' Tales,* "The Farther You Go, The Closer You Get: The Best of Family Travel." Her memoir about her son's adoption from a Moscow orphanage, *The Russian Word for Snow,* is being published by St. Martin's Press.

Mother

You gave me life, then left,
taking little bits of me with you—
the wound remains gaping and raw.
I'm the only brown-eyed girl
in this family, my freckles
stand out too much in the family photos.

When I was young,
I'd pretend you were a spy
or a dancer.
A little later, I'd imagine you
a painter, a musician,
barefoot and blue-jeaned,
auburn hair in a messy bun—

a sharp contrast to my
adoptive mother,
with her frosted bob,
clicking efficiently around the kitchen
in her navy blue pumps.
I'd imagine you looking for me,
at the grocery store,
on the highway, the movie theater,
searching every little girl for a trace
of your eyes, your lips,
my father's nose.
And always I'd imagine
you coming back for me.

When I turned eighteen,
Catholic Charities told me
you'd named me Michelle,
that you were Irish and Canadian,
twenty, Catholic, and unmarried.
My heart broke for you
for what you went through
to give me life.
I cry for both of us on Mother's Day.

If I meet you,
if I ever get the courage to look,
I'll tell you that I never forgot you,
of the sacrifice you made,

even though all I have
to remember you by
is me.

Amy Cronin

Amy Cronin is a freelance writer residing in Johnson,
Vermont. Her feature articles and fiction appeared in
The Rock and *Basement Medicine*. Her poetry was
published in the anthology *Dreams of Yesterday*.
Currently she is working on her first book of poetry
and pursuing two Bachelor degrees, one in Journalism
and the other in Political Science.

Adoption Piss Off

You can tell it in their rounded voices,
where the accent nearly falls, then lifts:
You have an adopted daughter, haven't you?
And you have a birthed son, right? I nearly reply.

Even grandparents stumble. Asked,
How many grandchildren do you have?
reply, *Nine,* proudly, catch
themselves, *TEN, with the little adopted one!*

Let us introduce you to our adopted grandbaby . . .
and here's our lovely birthcontrol-failure nephew,
our sperm implanted-on-time, in-place grandniece
Now, does everybody know everybody?

The scent of blood is what we believe in.
Gnaw on the split umbilical cord:
this deformity amongst us.

Mary Cummings

In Six Parts: Tarot Words

For my daughter Ada, born in China

I wanted to give her what she'd need to look—
stored in drawers and mind things to know
to make the hungers and blanks go away.
How could she not have them, the questions
of face, and race, of the bodies that contain her
first truths, first father, first mother?

Before me, there was another mother
of my child. And did she try not to look
at her swelling body or know herself as container,
ripe and sacred, not to seek or know
what would come? Did she ask questions
of her mate, her family, to find a way

to hold, and not send, this so precious girl away?
Will my child—like me—love, honor and hate this mother?
There's rightness, and balance, but always—questions.
The moment seeing her baby's sex, wet and declared, in that look,
what story appeared on her face? did she give sound to her *NO*
or did practicality and acceptance contain her?

There may have been a blanket with the plastic container
she set the baby in: her final smoothing and touching. She went away
from the father, the others—paid bus fare, hoping she'd know
the best place to leave the baby where a new mother.
could grasp this pulsing umbilical cord and look
at last upon her daughter, without questions,

in recognition. Still, at the station there were questions:
how the baby came to be there, and how to contain her
cries, if she did. Or perhaps she slept. People must look
at what's alarming; first they'd have turned away,
then stared at this bundle left from the flight of a mother
All around, a hovering flutter of fear, an unspoken *NO*.

I wanted her to be born to me. For my body to know
her from the smallest, first cell, without the questions
of would she ever come, how long to wait to be mother
to her. My womb was an empty, listening container,
but found the seed, somehow, incomprehensibly far away
and bloomed at her manner, her look.

We are daughter and mother: but there is more to know.
How to knit together the *away* with the *here,* to look
at the questions, speak them reverently, to hold, to contain her.

Mary Cummings

Wild Cards

Do they deal them like face cards in a deck?
Baby pictures in adoption workers' hands:
seven laid out on the table
by these professional gamblers.

Official documents link them up
in a two-step march:
baby   baby   baby   baby   baby   baby   baby
family family family family family family family

There is no sleight of hand here, but
the agency workers stare at this configuration.
Their presumptuous task embarrasses them.

Someone becomes playful, sees a truth.
Says, "This baby seems to go with them."
Can't explain, but there's
a look, a shape, a grimace in that baby
that reminds them of something in those parents.

An arm reaches diagonally across the table top.
"This round little one
fits over here, don't you think?"

Pictures shuffled, files shifted and the deck
becomes Tarot. These dealers must connect fates.
They grope for texture, seek skin and scent
beneath these papers to whisper "yes."

And if this seems oddly random,
consider molecular comedies in sperm
million upon million tumbling and jockeying
to seize one gliding orb.

Ardently seeking one child to become particular,
are such parents more like sperm or egg?—
Waiting moonlike and full as any egg
for that most fundamental fusion.

Mary Cummings

Joined

A connection is made.
Across continents, across universes.
A psychic incision and stitching together.
The one does not know its match:
the particulars of the other.
Only the abstract fulfillment
of mutual need.

A womb that can't bear its own children.
A womb that can't bear children of its own.
Circumstances conspire.
Practicalities of my body.
Practicalities of her life.
It's like that race where you tie legs together
to make three and hop as best you can.

Between us strapped a cocoon, a preciousness.
Sweetness distilled into shape.
Called into being by one,
brought into being by the other.

Just when the laying down of pattern, of bone
and thrust commenced, neither of us knew. The unheard
music of biology at life's start began by chance,
by error, in regret or tragedy.
Still, there is flowering.

But does this cocoon, this becoming-child
sense a chamber which can not greet, a lap
which may not hold her? And does she receive
in arms not yet emerged from the darkness—
a signal showing the way towards nurturance,
the distant, awaiting embrace?

Mary Cummings

"In Six Parts: Tarot Words" appeared in *Families with Children from China-Midwest.* "Blessings" appeared in *Newsletter.* "Wild Cards" appeared in *Artword Quarterly.* Reprinted here with author's permission.

Mary Cummings has recent and forthcoming poems in *100 Words, Grasslands Review, Studio One, Ekphrasis, Loonfeather, The Aurora, Hodge Podge* and *ArtWord Quarterly.* She is Education Director at The Loft, a literary center in Minneapolis. Her daughter, Ada Lorane, was born in China in 1994.

Meeting My Sister

1

After work, we meet at the Dojo
on St. Marks. We pick up corresponding
halves of pita, select different
herbal teas. She tells me
the details of her day: trying
to close an issue long overdue,
the magazine trying to find
its shape amid all the chaos.
Later, she'll return to her
apartment, fill out the necessary
forms. She'll revise the family
landscape, set aside two places
as her own.

2

My favorite photograph: me waiting with open
arms to hold my brand-new sister the first
time. Then, just visible above the largeness
of her drum, she marches in the elementary
band, plays softball at the Concord at
thirteen. And girls. I was away at school
and didn't understand.
      Jamie   Rebecca   Hillary

3

For her I save the infant jeans,
the xylophones and bibs. After
endless debates and Donahues: "How
Single Parents Cope," "Should Gays
Adopt?" my sister accepts
with certainty that she does need
something more than visiting my
kids. This child would come from
Mexico or Washington Heights.
We could ride up on the *A* train
and come back down with her son
or daughter sleeping on her lap.
Her tiny studio would stretch
like a woman who gives up her child.

4
In tonight's dream, she breaks
the news again. Our parents
draw the blinds, observing darkness
for seven days. We hold each other's
hand and continue our difficult walk.

Sally Lipton Derringer

Reprinted here with author's permission. "Meeting My Sister" was included in *The Grolier Poetry Prize Anthology, 1997,* published by Ellen LaForge Memorial Poetry Foundation, Inc.

Sally Lipton Derringer is an instructor of Poetry and Fiction Writing at the Rockland Center for the Arts in W. Nyack, New York. She also teaches English at the State University of New York at Rockland Community College. She has an M.A. in Creative Writing from Antioch University. Her poetry manuscript was a finalist for the 1996 New Issues Press Poetry Prize from Western Michigan University, and she was a runner-up for the 1997 Grolier Poetry Prize. She received Honorable Mention in the 1998 Pablo Neruda Prize for Poetry and was a semi-finalist for the Paumanok Award. Her work has appeared in many journals including: *The Quarterly, Nimrod: Awards Issue 20, Denver Quarterly, New York Quarterly,* and *Passages North*. She has also been published in the St. Martin's Press anthology, *A More Perfect Union: Poems and Stories About the Modern Wedding*.

How It Is to Look Like Someone

In my twentieth spring, I first met my father,
saw him through his diner's window,
that big curly-haired Greek
counting his money,
cigar clamped in his teeth,
smoke rising, coiling around him.
March rain carried odors of onions and starch,
his heavy-lidded eyes looked like mine,
his hands like mine, the Mediterranean nose,
the tilt of his head, his scowl.

Ten years later on a bus in Athens
I look at people in their seats
all scowling, the old woman
who coaxes me into my primitive Greek,
the exclamatory wave of her hand
to show me she's impressed,
the same hand beating out
the sign of the cross on her heavy bosom
each time we pass a church,
and her husband with his bags
of artichokes, his bright beads,
he could be my uncle, he has hair
like my father, she could be
my *yia yia,* she smiles like I do.

And I am back in Michigan that March,
standing in warm night rain,
watching through a glittering window
a dark man who sired me.
I look like him. I look like them.
I look like a person.
I look like a nation.
We scowl,
we pound our chests,
we lower heavy eyelids
all the same.

Lonnie Hull DuPont

He Sees

He offers me coffee,
tells me I am mistaken,
says he is not my father,
that I do not look like him.
When finally he asks,
Who is your mother?
I say her name, it's all I know.
I watch his heavy face sink,
watch him try to pull it back.
He sees what I see.
He has the look of a man
who has just opened a window
but not to the sun.

Lonnie Hull DuPont

In Real Life

I dreamed I lived in a high-rise project in Detroit
and you drove by in a black Cadillac.
In real life, you were dying.
Johnny promised to deliver a letter to you.
Remember me? it read. I am your daughter.
I hear you are ill. Call me. And other things.

I dreamed you talked to me, smoked your cigar.
In real life you died, silent. I stayed away.
I look so much like you, people talked.
Johnny promised to take me to the cemetery.
We drove there through patches of April snow.
He couldn't find the grave.

Lonnie Hull DuPont

Poems reprinted with author's permission from *Child of the Left Hand,* San Francisco: eyelet press, 1996.

Lonnie Hull DuPont lives in Michigan, where she is a freelance editor and an author of biographies for young readers. The poems included here are from her chapbook *Child of the Left Hand,* a collection of poems focusing on finding her biological roots. She writes that while searching for her mother, she found her father.

Mother of the Bride

I. Prelude

Strangers say curiously, "Do you
have any children of your own?"
I have five children.
I am the mother of the bride.
That is my daughter coming down
the aisle on her father's arm.
She is delighted with herself;
she knows who she is. She knows
she'll not be given away.
Smiling at her guests in welcome,
she nods and whispers hello.

Panicked by curiosity,
strangers say over and over
"Where are your real children?"
The strangers are there in my dreams,
they turn and twist in my nightmares,
they are obsessed with wombs.

II. Sestina

The family gathers, and this becomes a holy place.
Two sisters and one brother fidget, side by side:
the bride knows none of them are any longer children.
She doesn't often wonder, but today she wonders
about the odds against this woman, her mother,
standing at the end of this long chapel aisle.

The bride is calm: music will help her down the aisle.
Her father, ill at ease in this still place,
smiling, has told everyone, "I paid the bills. The mother
of the bride planned this affair." Side by side
the father and the bride wait patiently in wonder.
One day when she was twelve, when they were children,

she, most sullen among blond and blue-eyed children,
said, "I'm tired of being different. I'll
tell you, I wish strangers would not wonder
why we are all these different colors." The place
went quiet. Face still, hand limp beside
her daughter's smaller hand, eyes cool as frost, mother
instincts braced for truth, she answered, "Your mother
is most different of us all." Children

know: and now, having faced strangers side by side
for years, being different doesn't matter. "I'll
go down the aisle to meet Sentoso, and though my place
is now with him, I'll not be given away. I wonder,

though, why strangers like to ask? Can they really wonder
what right this woman has to be my mother?
Do they think she doesn't know her place?
How can they say, "Do you have any children
of your own?" Today, and in this aisle,
there'll be no nightmares. On either side

sit friends and family, pressing side by side
to watch a woman overwhelmed with wonder
who knows her daughter coming down the aisle
will not be given away, who knows she is the mother
of the bride, who knows she'll always have five children,
and also knows no one could take her place.

The members of the wedding are in place, safe inside
their dreams for one another. The children watch in wonder
as, smiling at her mother, the bride walks down the aisle.

III. Postlude

We have an answer for the strangers;
we can be gentle with them in our dreams.
We every one know who we are:
our mother is the mother of the bride.
We are a plaited circle that cannot unbraid,
figures on an Escher staircase, themes
in point and counterpoint. We are
like sudden turns in a modern fugue,
a curiously comforting Mobius strip.

Our mother wasn't there at the beginning.
She was there before, and she has told us,
"I walked alongside God before
He ever imagined Eden. I stroked His hand,
saying, Lord, you may have Paradise,
but these are my children,
give them to me. And God trembled."
That's what she says, and smiles.
We watch our sister coming down the aisle
on our father's arm.
Our mother is the mother of the bride.

Diane Engle

92

Diane Engle is an attorney, musician, and poet by profession. She has published articles on adoption and education in newspapers and magazines, and was included in the anthology, *The Adoption Reader*. She and her husband are the parents of five children, all adopted and now grown, and the grandparents of five. Partial list of credits: *The Formalist; Calopooya Collage; Elf Magazine; Pearl; ENvoi* (U.K.); *Queen's Quarterly* (Canada); Sparrow; *Karamu; Anthology: The Muse Strikes Back.*

Report to the Natural Mother
Christopher Fahy

It's already his birthday again, and the fantasies start. It's hard to believe how the time has gone and the fantasies persist. I meant to write this long ago but kept putting it off. It always seemed foolish, still does, but my urge is stronger than ever this year, so here goes.

Strange weather, unusually warm for December. I wore a light wool sport-coat and it made me sweat. We waited in a battered room with child-size tables and chairs, sad toys. Our obligation suddenly huge, we tried our best to joke. Somewhere a door slammed shut. Smiling, the social worker said, "I think I hear a baby." We were sick and ecstatic. She got up and left us and soon she was back, and that's how he entered our lives.

He screamed for over half an hour, as we cradled him in our arms and paced the floor, and then he fell silent, face puzzled, for the photo session. On the ride, he slept. When we stopped for a light or traffic, still not believing, we turned to look at him there in his car bed. At home we laid him asleep in the crib with musical mobile and Furry Bear, and we felt like thieves.

We watched his sleeping chest move up and down. The room seemed huge; his crib was a ship adrift on a wide dark sea. I thought of chance, wars, famine and abandonment, and saw him alone in the world except for us, two strangers. In spite of my joy, I wept.

That night as I fed him a bottle, he watched my eyes—his pupils widening, sizing me up. Not even six weeks old and he sensed I was someone new. A sudden rush of love demolished me. Seven years of love and pain and tears hadn't worked and now, because of you, I had my son. I marveled at your courage and your loss.

For days I could hardly sleep. His every movement woke me to thoughts of you. Twenty-one and your firstborn gone to us, to strangers who'd failed. Five and a half weeks out of your womb and given to us with your blessing. You looked on his face and eyes and tiny hands and held him close, then gave him away with your love.

I kept wondering where you were at the start, when he was a world unwanted, feared, a nagging worry in your rapture. In a car? A rented room? How did you feel that day, and who was your lover? Lover—is that the right word? How long had you known him and what were your plans? When panic spread, what made you decide in life's favor? Were you thinking of people like us when you went for your checkups, felt his kick?

He slept well, ate well, thrived. He was ours and we ceased to believe in you. His laugh was ours, his tears were ours, his name, the smell of his diapers—all were ours. You became shadow, fiction. His infant song at the top of the stairs when we put him in for his nap was never yours but ours, all ours, and filled our hearts with sun.

Snapshots:

Ten Months: Crawling over the lawn in his funny white hat, the wide, blue universe framing him.

Two: Throwing handfuls of grass at my face and laughing, running until I catch him. "Don't tickle me, Dad!"

Almost three: I carry him into a field of goldenrod buzzing with bees. He puts his hands over my ears and I laugh, "Hey, what are you doing?"

"I'll cover you, Dad, so you won't get stung."

Same age: His mother has a stomachache. He hugs her gently, says, "Oh Mom, do you have a pain?" then sings to make her well. Midsummer, and the song is Jingle Bells.

The chickenpox was nothing, but that croup at three and a half! Those nights when I lay awake with his fever and labored breathing, scared to death. And that chronic winter cough. It stopped right away when we moved from the city. His health has been fine since then, but which one of you gave him those teeth? So many, so huge! Two hospital trips to take care of that, with Seconal and Halothane both times. You weren't there to hold him, pale and vomiting, to see the gauze fill up with blood, to see how brave he was.

Well, that was years ago. Now his braces are gone and his smile is simply fantastic. Such a handsome kid. When people say he looks like us, we're flattered. Actually, he looks more like his brother, who is also adopted. An amazing trick of flesh. Or is it? How much does flesh count?

He's smart. At eighteen months he made funny monster faces. At two he invented the *lions and tigers* game. He started to read at four. He's been on the honor roll all through school, and he's a whiz at math. Did they tell us you majored in math? I think they did. Also, very unlike me, he's good at sports. He won the *Most Valuable Player* trophy in Little League. I never even made the team. Flesh counts.

Two curious things:

We almost gave him the name you gave him.

My wife and I are left-handed and so is he.

A while ago, his aunt said to his mother, "When you were pregnant," then laughed abruptly and blushed. "I forgot. I completely forgot."

It's an easy mistake. It's so hard to accept he is not of our bodies, as hard to accept as our deaths. We keep telling ourselves the truth. It comes to us as he stares out the window, lost in whose pattern of thoughts? Whose eyes does he see through. Whose dreams does he dream? What do his veins and sinews dictate? Where is his magic's source?

We told him the truth from the very beginning, of course, the truth about flesh. There are books about it for children like him. They call you the *natural mother, birth mother or biological parent*. When he was five, I read him the story about the people who wanted a baby and couldn't make one and what their solution was. I read the book matter-of-factly. After I finished, he smiled and closed the cover then looked at my eyes and said, "Dad, don't be sad."

Child of your flesh and blood, and I am his father. It says so on papers filed in the proper places, paid for and sealed and covered with dust by now. But law is the smallest part of it. Babies imitate the words of others with their lips before they learn to speak, before they even learn to understand. We are all he knows of parents, we are the print on your film.

When he was six and faced with something new for lunch at a friend's house, he said, "My other mother gave me that when I was a baby, and it tasted bad." That was the first time he'd mentioned you. The story made us laugh. But then out of nowhere he said, "I guess she didn't like me." We talked about it, and he listened calmly in that way of his—a way that isn't ours—and seemed all right. But for years he tossed and ground his teeth from dreams of somebody stealing him in his sleep. We talked, we kept a night light on, we couldn't stop the dreams.

In fourth grade he had an assignment: My Story (fill in the blanks). "When I was born the day was (blank) and people were (blank)." He frowned at the paper and said, "I'm adopted. I can't do this." The last line of the story: "Someday I will (blank)." He filled in *die*.

One night he was watching the news on TV about an abortion protest. Tears flooded his eyes. "What's the matter?" I asked.

"I hate abortion," he said.

I asked him, "Why?"

"It could have been me."

Snapshots:

At seven: An expert on planets and dinosaurs. He makes a biplane out of wood and paints it a rainbow of colors. A paper train that he worked on for days surrounds his wall. A friend is careless with a stick and cuts him under the nose. The scar's still there.

At eight: He is pushing a toy sailboat in the Luxembourg Gardens. Blond hair, red boat.

At nine: Dusk is falling on the lake. No fish, then a sudden swirl, a huge eel. The astonished look on his face as he reels it in.

Ten: Twenty-three points in pee-wee basketball. The way he steals the pass and drives the lane.

Thirteen: Working nine hours straight on his project on evolution and taking first place at the eighth grade science fair.

Especially on this day and after all this time, we think of you. Green eyes? Blond hair? A birthmark on your thigh? Did you marry him after all? Marry somebody else? Have you since given birth again, a joyous birth? Have you heard infant songs at the top of your stairs?

You're divorced, perhaps? Remarried? Perhaps you've died? Or maybe you weren't able to bear more children? Cruel trick of fate. I think of you lying awake in the dead of night, as I've lain awake. As I've lain there wondering how I can say things right, so that no one gets hurt.

It's beginning to hit him now. He told his first girlfriend that he is adopted. He said to me, "It's something I never thought about much before. When I thought about it, I didn't like it."

"What didn't you like?" I asked

"I didn't like it that somebody gave me away."

We talked again. I told him as much as I could, but you have the missing parts. You have the albums he wonders about, the snapshots of you as a girl In pigtails? On a swing? With your brother and sister? Your dog? These fantasies are absurd, but can't be helped. I told him the world was different then, your circumstances were impossible. He understood you cared enough to give him life. I said, "You can call me by my name if you'd like that better."

"No," he said, "you're Dad."

This birthday it's clothing, books and a basketball. His hair is no longer blond but brown. Has the time passed as quickly for you as it has for us? Soon he'll be gone to the world and his own life, carrying what we gave, our flaws and fears as well as our strengths. Gone with your eyes and hair or your lover's eyes and hair, that softness in his smile, that mole on his cheek, our love and your love too; we're sure of that.

Maybe he thinks about you on his birthday. He's never said and we've never asked. But you're thinking of him as you always have and always will on this day. All the questions come back—and the pain.

Too much of imaginings, of fantasy. This letter is the smallest part of it all. I know it's been brief, but I hope you can picture him now—now that his childhood's gone. We can't do anything about your pain, but want you to know he's fine. Our son is fine. We can't imagine our lives without him, and send you our thanks.

Christopher Fahy is the author of six novels, among them *Eternal Bliss* and *The Fly Must Die.* His poetry collection, *The End Beginning,* was published by Red Earth Press. He won the Maine Arts Commission Fiction Competition for his book of stories, *One Day in the Short Happy Life of Anna Banana.* He and his wife, Davene, have two sons, Greg and Ben. The son, Greg, featured in this piece received his Ph.D. in May, 1998, and now teaches philosophy at Boston University and Brandeis. How time flies! Ben is an archeologist and lobsterman.

Child of My Soul

brown bruised used
abused
white affected selected
protected
God's hands swept us
up
set us
down
in a river of tears
we crafted a
boat
sailed to the sea
searched for heaven

storms marched across
our bow
great winds capsized us
together we righted
our boat
set sail again and
again
encountered sea monsters
with tongues of
fire
jonah's whale
moby dick

i have had a
child
born of my
womb
i have had a
child
born of my
heart
but you are the
child
born of my
soul
with whom i have
slain dragons
crossed oceans
reached heaven

anne fitzgerald

Anne Fitzgerald lives in Pennsylvania. She is the mother of three. Her oldest daughter, age 25, is Apache Indian and first came to her as a foster child. Anne also has a 22 year-old daughter and a son, now 15, the subject of the poem. When he was 16 months, a maid she employed left him on her doorstep. He was subjected to unimaginable abuse from a deeply disturbed and chemically dependent mother and now suffers from severe learning disorders. She writes, ". . . he truly is the child of my soul." Anne Fitzgerald is an R.N. working ER for 26 years. She writes poetry, paints, is active in community theater, and is the National Champion 45–49 in 1 meter and 3 meter spring board diving. She says that she is also computer illiterate and a lousy housekeeper!

First Name

Before she wrapped the blanket,
tucked its ends, handed you
to the agency lady,
what did she call you?

And when, years later,
you tracked her down,
on a tree-lined street
with other daughters
entitled to her arms,
was there a name
that anchored you
to blood and salt?

When you were mine,
I gave you the best I had,
my father's gentle name,
withheld from two sons
for you, my daughter,
a link to my blood
I wish flowed in your veins.

I understand: I do.
How that first missing name
is an empty place,
unknown letters,
a gap easy to fall into
and find deep.

Who is there
to reach down, whose hand
will you accept? I hope
her arm is willing
and long enough.

CB Follett

Lost and Found

My daughter has found her birth mother.
Soft rocks the cradle.

Hard scrabble, this search,
this last search, begun in her gut
somewhere around eight.

Loss colored all her stables.
Rejection rode the winning horse,
balked at the fences, and threw her
in the mud. Again and Again.

One day, she got an answer. Hired
a detective, who took her clues
to the head of the line, and so
she sent a letter. Got one back,
and some pictures. Now at last,
she looks like someone,
is somebody's daughter.

And I wish her
the joy of it, as she rises
out of the mysterious density of loss,
and I fall toward it.

CB Follett

Soft Letters

The word *adopted* with its soft letters,
the *p* nudged against the *t*.
Adopted should be a word of nested boxes
instead of the barbed wire
you've erected between us.

It is on your birthday I miss
our never having interwoven.
You inside me
curled against your coming out
our blood mingled so that what I ate
you ate, what I breathed in, might have
breathed to you there in the sac,
the warm sea of your beginning,

but we were never yoked and that
for you has made all the difference.

CB Follett

Implied Space

Adopted implies space I never felt
but you made ocean-wide.
By twenty-five, you piled
so many jag-edged boulders between us
my knees cannot overcome them.

My skin has loosened
where you rattle beneath it
like gravel
I can neither expel the grit of you
nor coat it into pearls.
Your star fingers, your organs,
transplanted themselves in my life;
never your heart.

Increments of rejection in whose gears
the sweet confection of you
slowly sheds your young-girl
skin, shaken into dust
around the house, draining yourself
of me who only wanted
to build a landing field to return to
when you needed refueling,
the flexion of your wings, wings
that should be tensile for soaring
over new landscape, wings
you strut instead for escape;
flying ever away.

CB Follett

Drawing Blood

Stalled by the daytime moon
gibbous pale above Tallac,
above the lake, I am struck
by its roundness. Staring
seems to draw it looming near.
In it I see my daughter,
her early faces
when she still loved me.
She turns her head to the right,
looks into middle distance,
the distance of the space between us, playful, ready to smile.
I have not seen that dimple
where it lies drowned in truculence.

She yowls at me across the miles,
green eyes aslant and her fur matted;
I cannot lick it soft,
I am not her mother
but she's my daughter,
this face in the moon,
blooded from a different source.

She seeks someone else for blond hair
who loves sunrise, and words.
She needs it not to be me.
Moon with my daughter's face
yet not my daughter,
but another's; full of heat
because of it, hating me
who would make of her a daughter.

I want to scratch behind her monotone,
draw blood that will seep
below her mask.
I need something, something to be there.

CB Follett

104

"First Name," "Lost and Found," "Soft Letters," "Drawing Blood," "Implied Space," were published in *Visible Bones,* by CB Follett, Plain View Press, 1998. "First Name" was originally published in *convulvulus,* Fall 1993 "Soft Letters" first appeared in *Sweet Annie Press: The Eclectic Woman,* Winter 1997. "Lost and Found" first appeared in *Encodings,* 1991.

CB Follett was born in Connecticut, went through high school there, and graduated from Smith College. As an only child, she wanted lots of children. When that didn't happen, she and her husband adopted three—two boys and a girl. All of them are now in their 30s, and one has three children. She loves being a grandmother. She is also an artist, working in acrylic mixed media in her studio, where all the goodies are available. She met her husband in college. When they married, they moved to his home base California. They lived for many years in San Francisco and raised their family. Later they moved to Sausalito, where there is less fog and great views. Her poems have been published by *Calvx, Green Fuse, Perejzrine, The Cumberland Review, Rain City Review, Ambit (England), The MacGuffin, Birmingham Poetry Review, New Letters Review, Psychological Perspectives, Without Halos, The Iowa Woman, Heaven Bone, Americas Review, The Taos Review.* Her work has also been printed in several anthologies. Several poems have been awarded contest prizes, including Third in the Billee Murray Denny, Honorable Mention in New Letters and finalist in the Eve of St. Agnes. Two poems were nominated for a Pushcart. She was runner up for the Robert H. Winner Memorial Award, the George Bogin Award and finalist in the Alice Fay Di Castagnola Award, all from Poetry Society of American.

Stupid
Sarah Freligh

I got pregnant in college. This was before the Pill, before abortion was legal or middle class, when getting pregnant was the worst thing that could happen to a girl, much worse than dying because you had to live with the consequences.

At first I didn't want to believe that my body had turned on me, had gone and done this thing to me that I didn't want it to do, so I tried to pretend my pregnancy away. Then it was too late to do something. That's what my friends kept telling me, you have to do something, although at the time there wasn't much I could have done. I didn't have a thousand dollars to fly to Sweden and didn't know where to get a thousand dollars. Even if I had, I knew I couldn't go through with it. I couldn't trust the airplane to get me there without crashing, or the taxi to take me to the clinic without a collision, or the doctor not to sever an artery which would cause me to bleed to death. I was afraid to die, but every morning when I leaned over the toilet to throw up, I wished I were dead.

Marriage was not an option. I was only 18, and my condition was no love thing—nothing but a drunken roll in the hay with a frat boy named Alex or Alec, I was never sure. He had orange hair and pale, see-through skin, but he danced like a black guy, all shoulders and subtle hips. That did it for me. I got drunk enough to pick him up and forgot to tell him that it wasn't a good time of the month.

At first, I tried to starve it out. I ate an apple for breakfast and yogurt for lunch and a green salad with vinegar, no oil, for dinner. I did that for a month. Then one day I went to breakfast in the cafeteria, and without thinking, I ate a plate of bacon and eggs and went back for seconds. I didn't eat an apple or yogurt again for years.

I wore girdles and jeans a size larger than normal and got through the first five months without anyone suspecting. Then one day my stomach rebelled and stuck out big and hard as an unripe cantaloupe, and it was no use pretending anymore, I had to do something soon, now.

I went home and told my parents. My mother cried and my father didn't talk to me for a week. When he did, he wanted to know who the father was so he could kill him. They were all emotions for a few weeks, like they were pregnant, not me. When they settled down and became their rational selves again, they decided the best thing for me would be the Blessing Home. The Blessing Home had been a dark little joke at my high school. "She was blessed," we'd say about girls who dropped out of school one year and were back the next. Hoody girls who screwed their heads off, or mousy, unlikely girls who did it once and got caught. Stupid girls. Now here I was, a blessed joke.

The Salvation Army ran the Blessing Home as sort of a boot camp for girls like me. We were required to attend Morning Prayer services and sermons in the evening where Major Bernadette swayed and shouted at us about chastity and the healing power of repentance. "Your body should be a vessel for the Lord, not no receptacle for some young man with lust in his groin." My parents hoped that heavy doses of piety would cure me, but all it did was make me tired. I yawned my way through the Lord's Prayer and mouthed the words to hymns, anticipating the moment when I could take off my shoes, unfasten my bra and sink like a stone into bed. Once there I would close my eyes, hold the swell of my stomach and pretend some man was touching me. What a waste, I thought. Here was my body, ripe as a garden in August with no one there to enjoy it.

Time was huge, heavy and slow as an elephant. At night I marked each day off the calendar I kept, counting down to the red X of my due date. Between meals and prayer services, I lay on my bed, watching the second hand on the clock radio move from one minute to the next. I thought about things. I thought about what my life would be like after it was over, labor and the rest of it. I thought of my life as a treadmill, moving along without me while I took this brief detour. How after this was over I'd jump back on and start going forward again.

But my body kept bringing me back to the present. My stomach ballooned, splitting the elastic panel of my maternity pants with a farting sound during Morning Prayer service. My breasts filled with lead. I imagined I could hear my pelvis widening, my skin stretching and tearing. "Construction Under Way!" a sign might say, my teenage body disappearing under the edifice of bulky middle age. I even walked like I was old: back bowed, duck-footed, led by my stomach.

Finally, finally, when I couldn't stand another second of being pregnant, I went into labor. Time shifted, sped up, blurring experience—the cold metal of the examining table on my bare butt, the pain that made me sing high and loud, the baby on my stomach like a hot, wet pile of pasta.

The next day I leaned on the arm of a nurse and looked through a thick glass window at the baby asleep in his bassinet. "Your boy is just beautiful," the nurse said, but she was wrong. The baby looked exactly like President Eisenhower. And he was never mine, just something I might have been borrowing for a while.

That afternoon I packed my suitcase and dressed in real clothes. I wore a pad that bunched between my legs and leaked metal-smelling blood all over my underpants. In the car outside the Blessing Home, my mother rested her forehead on the steering wheel and without looking at me said, "I think it's best if we try to put this behind us, hmmm?"

"Okay," I said. I did. I tried.

Sarah Freligh's short stories have appeared in many literary journals, including *Iowa Woman, Cimarron Review, Third Coast* and *Painted Bride Quarterly*. Two stories from her short story collection, *The Absence of Gravity*, earned honorable mention in the Mississippi Review's Special Workshop Edition. She is currently completing her second short story collection, *The Madonna of the Highways*.

Reunion, or the Hole in Time
Paula Naomi Friedman

Number 3—on the door was the large number 3. The woman opened it; I stepped inside.

I said, "You're my kid." He had risen. There were tears in his eyes. My arms had opened; we were holding each other. Shutting the door, the woman said, "Take whatever time you like, we close at five."

He had thick curls now; my hands were stroking them. It was his tears on my shoulders and cheeks.

"I didn't know we'd . . ."

"What? Be 'stylistically identical'?"

Abruptly we laughed, for two hours we talked and sometimes we laughed, we hugged each other and touched each other's hands and cried. Soon it would be eight hours, sixteen hours, sixty, each tolling and chiming the lost years and new world.

Later I would return to it—his wide-open eyes upon me as we hugged goodbye, the clarity of his profile, feel of his skinny shoulders, warmth of his known long hands—all these fragments calling, burrowing into memory, fastening in so deep the usual content—what was said, the images—seemed lost before the stillness and peace.

The regular world had taken over again—my job, my young teenager—clamoring for attention. But later that first evening, when I could lie down and recollect, only bits remained—and the *sense* of him in heart and womb.

Days alone, I would return to the agency, the long walk with the woman down the corridor, her, "Have no expectations," and the people in the lunchroom glancing up, the number 3, the opened door, the lightness of those curls, his chin upon my shoulder and my hands upon his hair.

I showed him pictures. We gave each other pictures. I wrote his telephone number underneath his name. I gave him what I once had made and saved across the years. As if there is a bridge across the years.

The leftover chicken had been sautéed for lunch and I would be driving my teenager to Kids' Connection ("We welcome youth with problems") in an hour. The phone rang; I was beside it, kneeling on the floor.

He said it was he; I said, "Thank God." He said he too had had to work. I said, "I know"; these voices were deepened, not our own.

After stopping by Kids' Connection, it was not much longer. Cresting the hill, I saw the park, the fence, some people by the slides and on the grass. Nearer the bridge, he was moving toward me, holding something over his shoulder. Really he, really here. My eyes "found it easier" not to focus; I stretched out my arms.

Our voices had no words. For the next eight hours we would hold each other and cry—on a bench, on a golden lawn. Any doubts, any puzzles, would be left behind. There were two birds on a branch; later I would buy a book to discover they were Steller's Jays. There was the creek below, the light that changed, the sunset—and the fragments, glistening by light so bright, by light that chimed (that seemed to chime—it is the tears and widened pupils create this effect, we know).

This is the tenderness of paradise, the souls re-met, the source; this is beyond all other love, is only love.

We were each totally vulnerable.

Beneath the trees and on a curb—another afternoon we clung beneath a staircase in the rain. Later he would give me one portrait so caring it hurt to see. We would query with the voices' slow return. One afternoon he leaned upon my shoulder and I would have kissed the child to sleep. *Where are the years; our arms encircle a peace.*

In between came days to wait, the biding time, the hours of weeping as if reaching in the first days after birth, tenderness turned by waiting to mourning or fear. Learning to remember this person, rediscovering how to move through the pallid furnishings of a changed world—my damaged teenage son, the ordinary jobs and limits—how to make pass safely the days that came between.

I had given this kid up in adoption. This baby, now grown up, had found me.

"My life has been happy so far," he would assure me.

One day he said, "I asked how many found each other there;" I worked the figures in my head—so few. "It's over now," he soothed.

"That expression," he added, "comes close—it was like having a hole, a void, inside."

I could hold him; in the rain beneath the now-old stairs, still wordless in that earlier-than-language, that voice barely mine, surprised by its struggle, had cried, "It wasn't that I didn't love you." Conscious he already knew this.

He could hold me. *We really are here.*

There is no knowledge or ritual for this, no understanding of how little in tales or books is true, how wrong the theories of only loss and fear—

When he had phoned the agency, they had located my picture and letter in the file. Those parents had also signed a waiver; by state law of recent years, the rest was not physically hard. Then there was his wait and for me the corridor, the number on the door.

"No, you were right, I wasn't two weeks old." He'd asked that Mom and Dad. "I'd been in foster care two months."

I said, "I have no picture of your father; photos came of ego, of the system we struggled against—Vietnam, the war. I had none of you, until I went back and they gave me this—you, one month old; after ten years, their policies had changed. That day, she left the file out on the desk; I never touched it. I thought that will be up to him. I have no right."

Turning from his worktable, he said it had become frightening to think of the randomness, the other possible lives. I exclaimed, "But you're the way I'd have you be! It wasn't right, those years you didn't know who . . ."

They say these early hours will pass, like—yet so very unlike—mother and newborn, lovers, myth of the return; they say these hours will pass, their joy and utter vulnerability, with the first harrows of the hole in time. They say one must let go these moments and it is hard to let go, one must let grow the new world. They say too much; I mustn't again lose this child to others' fears.

In the quiet of your living room, we can sometimes even gossip and laugh. But then you see me watching you and again say, "What?" I shake my head and smile or weep.

You said that adolescent story I had written was exactly what you had felt.

There are already shared remembrances, humor. But what in words this time is for you, what fears or images of other selves, what relocations of your world, I cannot know. Your tears are drying; I would hear you and protect.

It is not right we had not met, not right we must fight for time to meet. It is not right our love, our bonding, seems too intense, as if romance, to those who cannot feel the ruptured time—not right time not have been.

Mornings in the office, the sobbing returns. It is as if (I told you, in that changed voice, "I would die for you") my body cries like a hungry baby calling the vanished mother, cries as you too have cried, in tenderness, not separate—not phoning, not wanting to have to trade for your presence your respect.

I thought there would be time, time to listen and understand. We have laughed so much, but sometimes your voice is crisp and humor fades. I would tell you to take care, maternally stroke your hair.

We have said, "I know" and " I am glad."

The sun-motes fill the room; leaf shadows dance on your walls. The poem was:

> Shiver and shake yourself dear tree,
> and silver and gold rain down to me

in the illustrated *Seven Swans* of my own youth. Childhood is so huge. I would cloak you with glimmer and jewels, would have sung you lullabies.

When you answer, "No, come over," I can deny I've heard the change. But it is real; I must let separate, let grow, although I know this child, more swift to descend the mountain, would gladly stretch out a hand and is my child and not rejecting me; but rather I feel bereft, as when I wakened yearning for my baby after you were gone—this broken love a mourning in the hole in time.

In what depth you must have then mourned me.

There are those who are not found.

"You inherited my nervous system." "Hey, I know." I remember telling you of one demonstration, and your eyes as you heard; I feel like the little fir tree remembering the attic. I love you so much. Sometimes the tears have been to reach, sometimes from sorrow; sometimes I did not dare express the happiness.

But for the tears and joy, the tenderness in the fragmented light of those early hours, care for the vulnerability of these chiming weeks, and afternoons and hours still—blessed those hours, blessed this wood—for the lost return in paradise, the simple love of here, there are no words; there is this deepened, softened, different voice. Blessed be the love.

The years took us far, and in the middle of January, the new war was on, and people dying from our bombs as on our streets, the first big march would happen the next day and then there was the letter ("Some years ago you wrote this agency.") in the mailbox.

Very soon the war was over. Then the corridor, the room, the number on the door.

Your picture shows you holding a beautiful cat; you've a shy young adolescent smile; the cat is startled by the light but obviously calmed in your arms.

Now you are a man.

You came from my womb in the very early morning, flying out into the doctor's arms. Three times in the hospital I held you; you had already those long fingers and fine features, and your eyes, then dark blue, saw me, *but I cannot be his mother, children need two parents, how could I raise a child like this?* Those very arguments I would resolve mistakenly, years later, for that other son, because finally I could not do it twice. Once I held you, rocking in a silent room on the courtyard of the agency, only a little while and then the time was over and—*for* you, but over the abyss of chance—I signed the papers. I signed the papers; I signed the papers.

You said, "I remember once when my grandfather . . ." You said, "My Mom used to . . ."

If I start to cry, if you start to cry, your hand, my hand, not very different, is immediately there; in the glance of an eye, "I know."

You looked away, leaving "these" (seeking a soft word) "first spaces"—the early unity, the *adoration*—where I remain. Has my slowness to let go been cause, or is this natural return to the pendulum of time? You feared to hurt me by acknowledging your distance sooner; I'd sensed it, child, yet your compassion moves my soul.

Your life has been happy, I know. I am so glad you found me, so thankful you exist, that you are you.

You reached out, said, "I don't want to lose you."

The love tears my heart.

Reunion—Second Year

This is the second autumn
since the spring
you found me

The yellow leaves the sky
are neither more nor less
bright than usual again

This is the second year
I know you are here,
and not in the
nowhere
I put you

"for his sake"
your sake

not ever expected

here,
This is the second year.

Paula Friedman

Note from the Invisible Mother

to you
that cradled babe came
through inviolate space,
    the empty places
of jigsaw his bounds
plain like fog, white paper
unpopulated as the empty floor
he'd later spread big puzzles on,
    wondrous at the figures phantomed in the grain.

Yet the invisible mother
was here all along. You
knew her
in his eyes

    Knew
no gush
of waters, terror, cramps
turned your womb
to thrashing thrust of Earth, Gaia,
        bringing forth
this savior, bearing
this bearer
of you who've borne your cross
across your nights, his life

until our eyes
watered twined tears.

You were/are his Mommy,
I his first universe.

Paula Friedman

Before you leave/Image of this child against the sky

Your bones like frail glass,
profile delicately
different from each angle
tumbling
in three overhanging
            ledges—
                        brow, nose, chin—
your little wedge-shaped face
by sharp bones defined
eyebrows and eyes so mirroring mine
(but your lashes from nowhere reach
where no one's ever known a lash to be)

Beside you on this trestle table I observe
your wrists' thin whiteness silhouette
before the darkening pines
previewing sunset light,
your fingers longer than the setting world,
as fragile as my own.

Bare arms' hairs framed
in this lens lift,
each isolate; cove crosses sky,
light fills, here, curves
gracefully in
to your child's neck—skinny as we were,
once. Pleased,

you lean, for a moment again,
but the evening chills, history
looms, gulls perch, eye
us. I am half your origins.

I would be careful
as you, in your sensitivity,
your fine concern.

Paula Friedman

After the year after / reunion

1.

after we speak
speaking of the ordinary
as if

You tell me
the tender weeks bonding,
the distanced months,
time, had
not not been but
are not now

Child
approaching the topic "reunion,"
tensions in your voice then mine
just alike
rise, until you say, "Don't get defensive,"
gently, as I think, no, you were,
Neither can stand
the hurt in the other's taut nerves

2.

over a year
since reunion

the crying sorrow-joy in my throat
at work, unable to listen
to anybody   today
to look at the lights
again
I am opened, raw
would give you time
to take your time,
or whatever you need,
only the ancient womb-knowledge ours

3.

New mother and child
Love resonant in laughter
Identity of tears

Paula Friedman

"Reunion—Second Year" was published in *Chain of Life,* Fall, 1994. It is republished here with the author's permission.

Paula Naomi Friedman is a birthmother, reunited since 1991 with her first son, and also the single mother of a second son. An author, editor, and publicist in Richmond, California, she has published short stories and poems in *Work: A Literary Journey, Vietnam Generation, Buffalo Bones, Chain of Life, Quantum Tao, Neovictorian, Jewish Women's Literary Annual* (forthcoming), as well as in other publications and anthologies. She has received a New Millenium Award and Pushcart Prize nominations. Initiator/facilitator of the Greater Bay Area Adoption Writers' Workshop, and a participant in the "Writing It out: Authors' Panel," American Adoption Congress's 1998 Southwest Regional Conference, she has written on adoption issues for the Jewish and mainstream press. She directs the nationwide Rosenberg Award for Poems on the Jewish Experience, in 1993 publishing *Songs for Our Voices,* Berkeley: Magnes Museum, a selection of winning entries. Founder and editor of the Open Cell literary review and an editor of the women's poetry anthology *Gathered from the Center,* she has edited books for university and other presses.

To an Unborn Child Somewhere South of Ponmonjon

While eating kimshee for the first time today
    I thought of you
When my wife and I stoke passion in our barren union
    we think of you
The two of us are so anxious to carry you across
    the threshold of our lives
To place you in the empty room
    at the center of our hearts
We've gone without for so long now
    that our own souls seem stillborn
Even as our bodies move inexorably
    toward His time

Sometimes I lie in bed and I am thousands of miles away
Who are the man and woman — the boy and girl?
    we must thank
    for creating life for us?

Are your parents rural?
A son and daughter of Keunhwa Hyang, the Land of the Rose of Sharon?
Could they be students?
A boy and girl come together in a short, sweet spring?
Or blue-collar workers?
A man and woman caught in the collapse of the choebals,
your country's great industrial conglomerates?

Know this:
My wife and I are growing with you
    as you nestle into the womb's nourishing wall
When you kick
    we shall kick
When you turn
    we shall turn

And when you, our child, are prepared
    to soar
We will be here to receive you

Mark Funk

 Mark Funk is a 44-year-old public affairs consultant and former newspaper reporter living with his wife, Pam McGaffin, and infant son, Casey Jin Kyoo Funk, in Seattle. His child was born on February 28, 1998, in southeastern Korea, probably near the city of Pusan.

One Frame of the Adoption Flow

Bill's hand holds one edge
of the image, mine the other.
We lean toward white shades
illuminating
from a dark swollen core.

A curve runs along my hand,
my arm, flows across chests,
down his arm, his hand.
The curve joins at the paper's center—
light between two "X's."
Our child to parent, perhaps.

As we hold this chance in our hands,
we hold her, a woman's body
wrapped around a child. Waves
of rushing grays flow through her,
feed the child who knows her voice
and she, his touch.

Across the top, her name misspelled
with an extra "r." Age, 17 years.
I keep the picture
in my top drawer.

Emalee Gruss Gillis

Mother Rhythms

ba-doom swoosh
ba-doom swoosh
Around me.
ba-doom swoosh
ba-doom swoosh

Long tunnel.
Blinding light.
They place me
on her chest.
I hear it, softer.
ba-doom swoosh
ba-doom swoosh

When different rhythms
beat beneath me,
I feel my heart stopping,
I cry, they place me
on her chest.
ba-doom swoosh
ba-doom swoosh

I cry and I cry—
I cannot hear her,
feel her, smell her,
all I hear is
ba-din hhuhh
ba-din hhuhh.

My heart is stopping,
all I hear is
ba-din hhuhh
ba-din hhuhh.

ba-din hhuhh
ba-din hhuhh
This beat
beats with me, too.
Stays with me now.
ba-din hhuhh
ba-din hhuhh

When I'm surrounded
by unfamiliar rhythms, I cry.
They place me on her chest.
ba-din hhuhh
ba-din hhuhh

Emalee Gruss Gillis

Molecular Motherhood

from my doctor: "post-partum symptoms are common
among adoptive moms of newborns."

Bill's thumb strokes the unopened hand of a child,
seven days old. Sleeping between us,
the child stirs when we turn, listens
to the sounds of our breath.

Infant lungs reach for air and push it back again. His energy electifies mine,
molecules awaken deep within, connect to the son I hold. His breath
brushes my neck, quick, but steady like I've grown a second pulse.
Enzymes ignite like fireworks, shoot through me as I hold him closer.
Molecular motherhood. Days run together as hormones stream
to swell tender breasts, release strands, then clumps of hair in celebration
as if my body had birthed him.

Our chair rocks and he sleeps as another slow dawn lights. I want to hold
this moment, feel the love that pours through me,
overflows the circle where longing for a child once grew. My love for him
gathers in pools, flooding, forming waterfalls that sing.
I kiss him on his rolling chin. His eyes the color of sea water open.
"I love you," I tell him. As he falls back asleep, I whisper,
"My body believes I birthed you."

Emalee Gruss Gillis

Adoption is a Noun

Adoption is a noun.
The word names
a process. A way
something happens.

"My son joined
our family
through adoption."

Son first, then
talk about how
he joined our family,
if you must.

Please.
Not an adjective—
"adopted son."
"He is adopted."
Adopted does not
describe him. It describes
what happened
in a court room.

Really. Just the words
"my son" will generally do.
How often do we name
the process through which you
joined your family?

Emalee Gruss Gillis

Adopted

As if the others aren't.

As if a child is a simple mix of two,
not a combination of thousands of years
birthed one through the other.

As if a mother can find her exact shade
in the thread that drifts from her daughter's spool.

Child in my arms,
you take me for your mother
and I take you for my son
as we listen to repeated rhythms
held close.

Colors blur,
as we spin,
discover the dance
of family.

Emalee Gruss Gillis

Emalee Gruss Gillis began writing poetry next to a kerosene lamp while living in Africa. Villagers went to sleep at six, while she stayed up till midnight. Six hours alone each night for two years without a newspaper, magazine, or TV and limited batteries for a tape player made the need to write suddenly become obvious. Her work is included in two anthologies by the New Market Press. Emalee holds a masters degree from Pennsylvania State University. She and her husband built their family through adoption and currently live in Olympia, Washington.

Michael's Search
Lila Guzman

Michael Gibson glanced at the speedometer and jerked his foot off the accelerator. "Eighty! Man!" He looked in the rear-view mirror, expecting to see flashing blue lights, and blew out a huge sigh of relief. Not a police car in sight. A ticket is the last thing you need, he told himself as he set the cruise control at sixty-five miles per hour. Keep your mind on the road. But no matter how hard he tried, he couldn't.

Today, one way or the other, he would meet his real father for the first time and learn the truth.

Michael hated himself for deceiving his dad, who thought he was going direct to Georgetown University to start his sophomore year. Maybe he should have talked to him first. And say what? "Dad, who's my real dad?" Michael shook the thought from his head. How could he ask that question and risk hurting his father?

As Michael raced headlong down the freeway toward the Texas sun—half-in, half-out of the horizon, he slipped a tape in the cassette player to break the monotony of the solitary drive from Houston to Austin.

A country song twanged from the speakers. Michael punched the eject button and shook his head in disgust. "Dad, Dad, Dad. I've got to do something about your taste in music." Eyes on the road, he riffled through the shoe box filled with tapes his father gave him the day before when Michael drove him to the airport.

"It's a long drive to D.C.," Dad said. "At great personal sacrifice, I've decided to loan you my favorite tapes. And I did say loan."

Michael smiled at the memory until he recalled why he had headed for Austin instead of D.C. The tapes were a loan. Was the name Gibson a loan too? Or was he a Parkinson?

Doubts began to gather two months ago, soon after his nineteenth birthday, with a telephone conversation he accidentally overheard.

Michael had returned home early from the construction site where he worked summers. He was about to call out "Mom! I'm home and I'm hungry," when her voice, low, angry, vicious, caught his attention. It sounded like she was talking to someone in the den. Michael headed toward her voice, but stopped in the doorway when he saw she was alone.

Mom paced to the window, the portable phone to her ear. "I've never asked you for child support for Michael," she snapped. "Not once! This is the least you can do."

Michael stepped back into the hallway and leaned his forehead against the paneling. At the sound of an ashtray smashing against the wall, he flinched. Mom was at it again. He stood still for a long time, listening to his mother's conversation punctuated by long pauses and profanity worse than any he heard at the construction site.

Now, in spite of himself, his mother's words played over and over in his head. Michael gripped the steering wheel. He had ordered a copy of his birth certificate from the Bureau of Vital Statistics and discovered the space for *father's name* was blank. Then, he checked his parents' wedding certificate. It hadn't been a great surprise to learn his parents married three years after his birth.

To erase unpleasant memories washing over him, he stuck another tape in the cassette player. Out spilled the tinny notes of a ragtime piano. He loved Scott Joplin. Dad knew that.

Michael settled deeper into the car's vinyl upholstery. Dad had bought him a light blue Oldsmobile with low mileage. Michael laughed. Of course it had low mileage. No one in his right mind would want to do major cruising in it.

"Any son of mine who earns a full scholarship to Georgetown deserves a set of wheels," Dad said when he brought the car home as Michael's high school graduation gift.

An expressway sign came into view. Austin. Next five exits. Michael sobered. He ejected the ragtime tape that didn't match his suddenly somber mood. He was here. What now?

Michael pulled into a convenience store along the access road. He slipped a coin in a pay phone and dialed the Parkinson number. It rang and rang. When the answering machine came on, Michael hung up.

He bought a Pepsi and a strip of beef jerky, leaned against the car hood and popped the can top. He took a sip and scanned the horizon. Evening turned the sky inky blue.

Michael checked the time. Seven o'clock. He drove to a motel and rented a room for the night. He showered, then flopped onto the bed, belly down, with the phone in hand. He called home to let everyone know he was OK. Cradling the receiver between his shoulder and ear, he dialed the Parkinson number again. This time a voice honeyed by years in Dixie answered.

"May I speak to Mr. Parkinson?" Michael's hands shook, but he managed to keep a tremor out of his voice.

"He can't come to the phone right now. May I take a message?"

Michael hesitated. In the background he heard a child ask for a glass of milk. "No," Michael said. "This is just a courtesy call. I'll try back later."

Michael rolled over and stared at the ceiling. Mr. Parkinson had a wife and a child. A new tidbit of information. To judge by the voice, the kid was in elementary school. Michael pulled a three-month-old telephone bill from his wallet and studied the numbers again. Heck! His mother had made a lot of calls that month. Michael had called each one, but most were dead ends, except the one to a lawyer referral service in Austin made after Mom talked to Mr. Parkinson. She must have talked to a lawyer about back child support.

Michael researched the issue of child support in the University of Houston law library. Eighteen was the cut off age, but his mother could file for it until he turned twenty.

Michael wondered what Mr. Parkinson did for a living. Eighteen years worth of money was a chunk of change. But Michael didn't care about money. He just wanted the truth about his birth.

His mother never mentioned the call to Parkinson or the lawyer referral service, and Michael didn't ask. He'd seen his mother explode in anger plenty of times. The least thing could provoke her. Dirty footprints on her kitchen floor. A lunch box left at school. Dad had saved him from Mom's wrath many times by herding him out the door and into the van for a quick trip to McDonald's before she went really ballistic.

At nine-thirty Michael dialed the Parkinson number again.

"He can't come to the phone right now," the soft southern voice said. "May I take a message?"

Where could Mr. Parkinson be at nine-thirty on a Tuesday night? "Is there a better time to reach him?" Michael asked.

There was a slight hesitation on the other end. "I'm sorry. I really couldn't say."

Michael hung up the phone and blew out an exasperated breath. He stripped down to his shorts, climbed into bed, drew the covers tight, and planned his next move. He had to be in D.C. within the week. That only gave him two days in Austin to meet his father and get his questions answered.

He wanted to know why his father hadn't married his mother. Why he was a deadbeat dad. Why he'd left his responsibilities as a father to another man.

Maybe he should have talked this out with Dad after all. He always gave it to him straight. None of the crap adults usually doled out. But the Oil Company had sent Dad to Saudi Arabia to solve some crisis. Dad was good at that. He'd be back in Houston around Christmastime.

Before he fell asleep, Michael left a five o'clock wake-up call. He had to be in front of the Parkinson house before Mr. Parkinson went to work. Michael was marginally aware that what he planned was considered stalking. Last night the phone calls had been a bust. He would follow Parkinson to work, get his work number from the telephone operator, talk to him, then head for D.C. around noon.

By five-thirty Michael was out the motel door and revving up the car. He grabbed a quick breakfast at the McDonald's drive-through, then drove to a Wag-A-Bag where he asked for directions to the subdivision where Parkinson lived. By six o'clock, Michael found the house located at the end of a long cul-de-sac. Two story. Brick. About two thousand square feet. A nice house in suburbia. A lot like Michael's home in Houston, only smaller. He parked in front of a one-story stone house halfway down the block, slumped in his seat, and devoured a now cold Egg McMuffin.

A streetlight cast a cone of light on the black top about twenty-five feet ahead of Michael. He drummed his fingers on the steering wheel and waited. The sky lightened. The street light blinked off. Michael's rear-view mirror reflected the morning sun rising over the rooftops in the subdivision. A garage door went up to his left. A square-faced man lugged a garbage can toward the curb. He looked straight at Michael's car, frowned, but went back inside.

Great! Michael said to himself. Parkinson would live on a street with an active neighborhood watch program. Michael expected a police car to pull up behind him at any time, but several minutes passed and nothing happened so he relaxed. It wasn't a crime to sit in a car.

The front door of the Parkinson house eased open at seven-thirty. Two children with lunch boxes and backpacks waved good-bye to a woman watching them head for school. She wore a long, pink robe, but the shadows of the doorway hid her face. Michael strained to see the children. He studied their faces to see if they looked like him.

A boy about ten years old and a much smaller girl, maybe a kindergartner, strolled by. These two could be his half-brother and sister. Michael's throat constricted. How often he had wished he weren't an only child. He watched them until they turned the corner and were lost from view.

His eyes on the house again, he waited. The minutes crept by. Didn't Parkinson have to go to work? It would be Michael's bum luck for Parkinson to have decided to stay home today. Or could he be sick? Eight o'clock came. The garage door rose. A mini-van backed out. Michael tensed. He put his hand on the key in the ignition, ready to start his car. The mini-van drove past. A woman sat behind the wheel. In the passenger seat a teenage girl, maybe fifteen-years-old, brushed her hair. She looked like an older version of the little girl he had seen thirty minutes earlier. Another sibling! Michael thought. That brings the count to three.

Eight o'clock became nine. Then ten. Where the heck was the man of the house? Time was running out. Dang it. I've come all this way and it looks like I've hit a blank wall. A little later the woman returned. Michael watched her pull into the garage, unload several blue plastic bags, then lower the garage door. Still no sign of Parkinson.

What now? Walk up to the door and knock? Pretend he was a Jehovah's Witness? A door-to-door salesman? Or should he just flat-out announce, "My name is Michael Gibson. I'd like to talk to my father." Michael decided to phone him again.

At a gas station, Michael dialed. The soft southern voice he spoke to the night before answered. He took a deep breath and squeezed his eyes tight. "May I speak to Mr. Parkinson?"

"He's not here."

"Is this Mrs. Parkinson?"

"Yes."

Michael swallowed hard. "Mrs. Parkinson, my name is Michael Gibson."

The woman said nothing. A sudden coldness hung in the air. Finally, she asked, "What do you want?"

His breathing quickened. "Do you know who I am?"

"Yes," she said softly. "My husband told me about you."

Michael gripped the receiver so tightly his knuckles turned white. He braced himself. Any minute now she would slam the phone down in anger. When he heard nothing but dead air, he said, "I really need to speak to your husband. Could you please give me his work number?"

Another long pause.

"It won't do you any good. He's in a pre-trial hearing all day."

"When do you think he'll be back?"

"Michael . . ." She was clearly weighing how much to tell him. "The hearing is in New Orleans. He won't be back until Tuesday."

Michael's shoulders slumped.

"Michael, are you still there?"

"Yes."

"I don't mean to be rude, but I'm hanging up now."

"No. Please. Wait. Don't hang up." When there was no click on the other end, he asked, "Are you still there?"

"Yes. I'm here. If this is about money?"

"I don't want any money," Michael blurted. "That's not why I'm calling."

"That's good," the voice on the other end said, "because we don't have any. That's what my husband told your mother."

Michael frowned. "Mr. Parkinson refused to pay child support for me?"

"Your mother didn't ask for child support. She flat-out asked for money. Your mother and my husband dated, but that was over twenty years ago. Out of the blue your mother called and told my husband the light company and the phone company had threatened to cut off service. At first, Tom thought she wanted legal advice. She only wanted money."

"How much?"

"About a thousand. When my husband told her money was tight right now, she reminded him that he hadn't paid child support for you. My husband informed her he couldn't possibly be your father. She became verbally abusive and he hung up on her. She never called back."

"But that doesn't prove Mr. Parkinson isn't my father. Just because . . ." Michael stopped short. He recalled the conversation he'd overheard. It matched what Mrs. Parkinson said. He had heard only one side of the conversation, but he knew Mom had asked him for money. Why? Dad made a six-figure salary at an oil company. Michael's heart sank. Unless she was gambling again . . .

"Are you still there?" Mrs. Parkinson asked.

"I'm still here," Michael somehow managed.

"Good. I didn't hear you breathe."

There was a hint of good humor in her voice. It was embarrassing to talk to her, but she sounded so kind-hearted. He liked her. Why couldn't his mother be as nice?

"Look, Mrs. Parkinson, I apologize for bothering you."

"You have nothing to apologize for. If I were in your shoes, I'd wonder too. My husband isn't your father."

"My mother says he is." The statement was out before Michael realized how rude it sounded. "I'm sorry. Don't hang up."

"I'm not that easily offended. I've been married to Tom for twenty years. In that length of time, I've gotten to know him pretty well. He's willing to take a DNA test to lay this to rest. He told your mother that but she didn't take him up on his offer."

The sudden silence buzzed in Michael's ears. His words had dried up because he suddenly knew why his mother hadn't agreed to that. Mr. Parkinson wasn't his father. And at that instant, he realized why his mother had made so many phone calls. Michael self-consciously touched the telephone bill tucked in his shirt pocket. She had hit on all potential fathers for money. She had no idea who his father was.

Michael twisted the telephone cord around his wrist. Oh, God. No. How will I ever find my real father now?

"I have some errands to run," Mrs. Parkinson said. "If you'll meet me at St. William's Church in a half hour, I'll prove to you that my husband can't possibly be your father." She gave him directions, then said good-bye.

Michael arrived early and paced up and down beside his car.

Right on time, Mrs. Parkinson pulled into the empty parking lot. She smiled, climbed down from the van and thrust out her hand. "Michael, I presume?"

He gave her hand a firm shake. "Mrs. Parkinson. Hello."

She turned back to the van and retrieved two documents that she handed him. One was a passport. The other military records with Mr. Parkinson's Foreign Service in Germany clearly marked. A thirty-six month tour of duty from 1976 to 1979.

Michael glanced up and forced a smile. "He was in Germany the whole time?"

"Except for a trip to the States in December of '78." She pointed to the stamps on the passports. "That's when we visited Texas to show off Patrick. He's our eldest. He was born in Germany in September of '78. For you to have been born in April of that year, your mother had to have gotten pregnant the year before in July. You can see from the dates stamped on the passport my husband was in Germany from June 1976 until the end of 1978."

Disappointment jabbed at him. He still didn't know who his father was.

"Well, Michael, I have things to do before the kids get home from school. This has been an . . . interesting experience." With that, she took back the papers she'd shown him, climbed into her van, and started the engine. Before she drove off, she rolled down her window, "Good luck in your search."

For several minutes he leaned against the car hood, folded his arms across his chest, and contemplated the blacktop underfoot. What did he do now? He climbed into the car and drove off. At the first stoplight, he put a tape in the player. Flamenco music blasted from the speakers. Michael ejected the tape and muttered, "Dad, Dad, Dad."

A smile grew in the corners of Michael's mouth. The search was over. He knew exactly where his father was. Michael drove to a gas station and headed to the nearest pay phone. He took out the calling card Dad had given him and dialed Saudi Arabia. A male voice answered the phone. "This is Michael Gibson. Is my father in?"

"He's in the field. Is this an emergency?"

"No. Would you tell him Michael called?"

"Sure. Any message?"

"Yeah. I'm on my way to D.C. Just wanted to let him know the car is doing just fine."

"OK."

"And tell him I think he has lousy taste in music."

"What? I didn't get that."

"Never mind. Just say I'm looking forward to seeing him Christmas."

"Got it," the man said.

"Thanks." Michael hung up.

Dad was in desperate need of some good music. "Asleep at the Wheel." "Dixie Chicks." "Velvet Hammer." Yeah. Those would be the perfect Christmas gift. And a CD player too. Michael couldn't wait till Christmas.

Lila Guzman has published short stories and essays in *The Roswell Literary Review, Pif Magazine, The Arizona Literary Magazine, Lines in the Sand, The Raintown Review Anthology,* and *San Diego Writers' Monthly.* Her young adult novel, *Lorenzo's Lambs,* has been accepted for publication by Arte Publico. She won an honorable mention in fiction from the National League of American Pen Women in 1996. She is a board member of the Austin Writers League and teaches an on-line short story course. She lives in Round Rock, Texas, with her husband and three children.

It's A Boy
George Harrar

"Laurie and Jeff announce the delivery of a healthy, bouncing boy! Andrew Donald is 107 pounds, 59 inches. First words, 'What's to eat?' Time in labor, zero. First day home he slept through the night. Mother and son are doing as well as can be expected . . ."

Late Sunday morning, the time of the weekend when she always worried about her life, Laurie McShane sat on the back deck of her home listening. The summer buzz of the locusts flooded her ears. It was an odd kind of sound, so loud that it filled your head, if you concentrated on it. But if you didn't listen closely, the buzzing seemed to melt into all of the other sounds of the air—the crows cawing to each other high up in the trees, the faint music coming from her radio in the kitchen, a distant lawn mower.

Inside the ranch house, in what used to be the guestroom, slept a twelve-year-old boy, their newly arrived son. She couldn't quite explain how it had happened—from infertile baby-boomers, the kind all of the magazines wrote about nowadays, to adoptive parents of an adolescent in just three months. They had been intent on finding a baby. They even filled out an application and paid the non-refundable $200 deposit to an agency guaranteeing a placement within a year. But then Jeff spotted a newspaper article about an adoption party at a local roller blading rink. "Children Need Homes," the headline said. They imagined toddlers, perhaps five or six-year-olds. He said, "It can't hurt to go see.' Leaning on the railing that evening, they watched dozens of boys and girls racing around the rink, nametags pinned to their chests. They pointed out to each other the cutest of the little ones wobbling along on shaky blades. They imagined teaching them to read, to swim, to obey, to trust.

There was no single moment when they agreed to give up the idea of adopting a baby. But she knew what it meant when he noticed that there were more children at the party than prospective parents. He was the sympathizer in the family, she the worrier. She worried about what a child might have learned growing up in an environment of neglect and probably abuse. She wondered if they could bond with a boy or girl whom they hadn't raised from infancy. She could have gone on and on with such fears and doubts. She might even have persuaded him that children come out of foster care were too hardened, too damaged, too difficult for a couple like them. But she knew what she would really be saying—they weren't good enough. How could she think she deserved a perfect child, she asked herself, when she certainly wouldn't be a perfect mother?

They watched at the railing for an hour or so. When they turned to go a boy skidded to a stop in front of them carrying a large photo album under his arm. "You looking for a boy?" he asked but didn't wait for an answer. He opened the book and pointed at his picture, a grinning kid on a mountain bike. "That's me. I know I'm kind of older, but I can't help it. I still need a family."

She didn't know what to say. Was this how an adoption party worked—the children attached themselves, like a stray dog, to adults?

"That's a great looking bike you got there," Jeff said. 'What do you have on it?"

As the boy told about tire width and gearshifts, Laurie could see in her husband's eyes his instinct to save the world, and all things in it. Old people, homeless people, injured animals, lost animals—he always seemed to find some living, breathing thing that needed him.

And that is why, she said to herself now as she gazed out into the rising mist of the yard, this boy Andrew had moved into their lives. The getting-to-know-you period of ballgames, movies, video games and museums had come to an end. Now the labor would begin.

The limbs of the giant willow tree reached gracefully to the ground, like a ballet dancer stretching. Laurie closed her eyes and imagined herself like this tree, able to reach up and down and out to the side all at the same time. When she opened her eyes, there was Jeff in his old torn jogging shorts, bent slightly forward to take in oxygen more easily. "Andy still sleeping?" he asked as he pulled himself up the stairs by the railing. He wiped the sweat off his forehead with the tail of his T-shirt.

"Still sleeping," Laurie said. And she wondered, would every encounter now begin with a question about Andy?

"I'm going for a shower," he said and kissed her on the forehead as he passed by.

She followed him inside. "I was thinking of making some calls,' she said. "It's time we told people what we're doing." It was not a chore she looked forward to. In a world where most people had babies, or adopted them, how do you explain that you're suddenly the parents of a baggy-pants twelve-year-old?

"Why don't we just send announcements?"

"I don't think it would come out right on paper. People will have questions."

"Then call everyone," he said. "Tell them it's a boy."

She began with the easiest call she could imagine—Grandma Lilly. Laurie gave her speech, and in a minute, the ninety-seven-year-old was taking down the particulars to enter Andy into the family Bible. Laurie moved on to the rest of her family, then a few neighbors and friends. By the tenth call, she had pared Andy's story for quick telling: He was born to teenage parents; neglected by mother and father; taken by the state and passed through five foster homes. Mother's exact whereabouts were unknown; father was committed to prison—about the only thing he seemed committed to. She soon realized she was relating Andy's life as a series of troubles. As her closest friend said, 'This boy sounds like a big challenge. How did you pick him?" Actually, Laurie explained, Andy had picked them at the roller blading rink. And he had a lot of good points, which she began adding to her description. He was a healthy, good-looking boy, inquisitive, full of energy, interested in everything around him. This last part was important to her and Jeff, because they were ready to offer Andy the world.

As the bells of the Methodist Church a few blocks away struck twelve times, the boy took off on Jeff's old bike with notice to be gone no more than an hour. When he left, Laurie felt relieved, as if some invading army had suddenly retreated from their home. But as they sat on the living room sofa and let their heads fall back together on the pillows, a tapping on the window surprised them. When they turned to look out, there was Andy looking in at them. He made a crazy face and waved for them to watch. He pedaled off to get up speed, circled the crabapple tree, and when he came into view again, he jerked up the front of the bike and sailed past on one wheel.

Jeff clapped as Andy looked over his shoulder to make sure they were watching. "I can't imagine a girl doing that," Laurie said as Andy headed around the house and out of sight. "Why are boys such showoffs?"

Jeff pulled her warm face close to his. "I guess he's practicing to be a man."

Two hours later, they waited for him at the door, considering the possibilities. Was he lost, in an accident, or just plain heedless of their instructions to be home in an hour? As Jeff got his car keys to go on a search, Andy came sailing down the street on his bike, his hands folded on his chest. "Are you going to yell at him for being late?" Laurie whispered as the boy jumped off his bike and came running across the grass.

"Why me?" Jeff said. "You yell at him, if you want to."

Andy burst into the house already talking. "Close your eyes," he ordered Laurie. When she did, he cracked open a plastic bubble and slipped a ring on her little finger.

She held up her hand, and her irritation at his lateness melted away. "It's beautiful," she said, "and expensive, I bet."

Andy looked confused. "You know it's from a bubble gum machine, right?"

"Really? I like it anyway."

"It's a friendship ring," he said, "but we can't be friends, 'cause you're supposed to be my, you know—mother."

"Mothers can't be friends?"

"I don't think so," Andy said seriously. "At least it ain't ever happened in any of the other homes I've been in."

Laurie winced at his grammar. "Not 'ain't,'" she said. "You mean, 'hasn't ever happened.'"

"What I mean," Andy said, "is that's why we can't ever be friends."

Throughout the afternoon, they heard strange sounds in the house. Jeff shrugged and kept at whatever he was doing, but Laurie went running. She found him playing war in the basement with her china animals. She caught him in the garage mixing liquid cleaners to make fuel for his toy rocket. She saw him in the kitchen drinking a bottle of Tobasco sauce. When she sent him outside to play, he came back in minutes for water or a snack. Each time he forgot to wipe his feet and tracked dirt on the carpet. She wanted him at least to say "I'm sorry" or "I'll try not to"—anything that would indicate he was listening to her. But he merely shrugged and went on his way.

Sometimes he disappeared for half-hour stretches of time, then ran back to the living room with something he had found in the garage or basement. He brought the object out from behind his back as if it were strange and special—a toy car of Jeff's, a wooden pirate's gun, a baseball signed by Joe DiMaggio. About each one he said, "I'll bet this is worth something." His last find was an old photo album of Laurie's family, the pictures stuck in slits on thick black pages. Andy carefully pulled each one out and turned it over, as if interested in the names on the back.

"That's my Aunt Liza," Laurie said, "on her annual summer trip to Lake Louise in . . ."

"Damn," Andy said as he pulled the last picture out of the last page in the album, then corrected himself, "I mean, darn."

"What's the matter?"

"I figured maybe somebody hid money behind the pictures. It'd be a perfect hiding place, don't you think?"

"Perfect," Laurie said, but Andy didn't hear the sarcasm in her voice. The old photographs lay haphazardly on the table. Her family was not, she realized, of any interest to Andy. He jumped to his feet and headed for the basement. "Whoa," Laurie said, "you have to put the pictures back."

"Later," he said and reached the cellar door before she could stop him.

She remounted the photographs in their slots and put the album in the top shelf of her closet where Andy couldn't get his hands on it again. She still felt annoyed that his greedy search for money had required a half-hour of her time to repair. She considered ordering him up from the basement to remake the album, but his disregard for her relatives bothered her. She didn't want him touching her family.

By dinnertime, she felt worn out in a way she never had before. She looked forward to going to a movie as Jeff had promised. At least there Andy would have to be quiet. But he had other ideas. "Why can't we just rent a video? Movies are expensive 'cause I'm twelve, which is an adult, except I still look eleven, so you could get me in cheaper, if you want me to lie."

"We wouldn't want you to do that," Jeff laughed. "You don't mind renting, do you, Laurie?"

"Of course not," she said, figuring that's what a mother was supposed to say.

A half-hour later Andy came running up the stairs clutching the videotape. "Some stupid animal movie," he told Laurie when she asked. He pushed her arm away from the VCR and hit the buttons until *Animal Farm* came on. From that moment on, he talked. Everything he saw on the screen reminded him of something. "I've seen *Old Yeller* about ten times," he said, "and I still cry when they shoot him. So I'm warning you, I'll be crying if any animal gets it."

"I cry at movies all the time," Laurie said to make him feel more comfortable.

He looked at her briefly. "So what?"

She didn't know how to answer. Her life, she realized, didn't matter to a twelve-year-old boy.

When the animals and humans battle for the farm, Andy punched the air and kicked as if in the fight himself. He took control of the remote and replayed Boxer's charge and the birds pecking at the men's heads. Later, when Snowball, the good pig, is chased away by Napoleon's hounds, Andy covered his eyes. "Did they catch him yet? Are they eating him?"

"No, they've disappeared into the woods," Laurie said, "so maybe Snowball gets away."

"Pigs can't outrun dogs," Andy declared as he looked again, "even in cartoons."

After his victory, Napoleon announces the new motto of the farm: "Four Legs Yes, Two Legs No." "Yes," Andy said. "Animals rule!" Every few seconds he repeated the phrase—"Four Legs Yes, Two Legs No."

After about the twentieth repetition and the third warning to keep quiet, Laurie gave him an ultimatum: "Say that phrase one more time, and we're turning off the movie."

"Say what?" he asked innocently, obscuring more of the dialogue.

"Just shut up!" she yelled.

Her words hung out in the air like a puff of smoke that takes a few moments to dissolve. Jeff looked at her, wondering why she was so angry. She wondered the same thing. What exactly had this boy done, other than a dozen little defiances? He'd only been there for one full day, and already she had lost her patience. How was she going to last?

"You shouldn't say 'shut up,'" Andy said. "You should say 'please be quiet.'"

She tried to ignore his insolence. But no one ever spoke to her like this, so why should she accept it from a twelve-year-old? She rose from the sofa to . . . to do what? Turn off the TV? Yank him from the room just for talking during a movie?

"Wait," Andy said, waving his hands, "look." On the screen, Boxer, now an old horse, was being carted away in a truck that said *Glue Factory*. Andy wiped the tears from his eyes and stood up. "This is a dumb movie," he said and headed down the hall, past the bathroom where Laurie had laid out a new toothbrush, and into his room.

"Well, that was a relaxing night at the movies," Laurie said as she sank into the sofa next to Jeff. "I feel like I've run a marathon with him on my back."

"He does suck the energy right out of you. But all kids do that, right? I mean, think of anybody we know with children, they're always tired."

Laurie nodded at his point, but she still felt a difference here. Most mothers understood their child's moods, at least to some degree. Most knew where the limits were drawn from years of trial and error. Most mothers, Laurie realized, started out with love for their child, not sympathy.

"You want to head to bed and read?" Jeff asked.

"I want to watch the end of this movie in peace and quiet," she said, taking the remote and rewinding the tape a little.

They rearranged the pillows so that they could lie out on the sofa side by side. He gave her a kiss on the cheek. She let her hand fall on his leg. Suddenly

Andy appeared in the hallway with a leap and stretch to the ceiling. "I can't sleep," he said, "'cause I keep thinking of Boxer."

"I told you before—no running in the house," she said, "and no jumping."

"You have to read to me," he said as if he hadn't heard her. He held up *Gulliver's Travels*. "It's got Littleputtans in it, and . . ."

"That's Lilliputians," Laurie corrected him.

"Whatever—come on."

Why was he asking *her*, she wondered, and not Jeff? Was he trying to push her beyond her limits?

"Now!" he insisted. She was just about to yell at him for being rude, but Jeff laughed. Obviously he didn't take Andy's tone seriously, so why was she? She got to her feet and reached the hall in time to see him jump one more time and touch the ceiling with his dirty hands. She didn't have the energy this time to yell at him.

As she read, Andy reached into his trash bag of belongings and pulled out a stuffed bear, white as a marshmallow. "This is Ted," he said, interrupting her. "He's my main bear. My last foster mom only let me have two bears out. She kept the rest in a closet. I don't think animals should be kept in a closet, even if they are stuffed, do you?"

"No," Laurie said, "I think they need to breathe, like people."

"You think I'm weird, right, 'cause I'm twelve and I still sleep with Teddy bears?"

She shook her head. "I took a stuffed rabbit to college with me."

"Yeah, but girls always do dumb things. Boys aren't supposed to sleep with stuffed animals at my age."

"That's for you to decide," she said. "Now it's time for lights out." He stared at her for a moment, and she wondered, is he expecting a goodnight kiss." She leaned toward him, but he dove under the covers. When she kissed the top of his head, he made a gagging sound, as if throwing up.

On the first day of school, Laurie tried to get Andy up on her own. She tickled him and threatened him and pulled on his arm. Finally, he struggled out of bed and into his clothes, gulped down some orange juice along with his Ritalin and headed for the door. The bus would arrive in five minutes. Should she try to hurry some cereal into him or insist he brush his teeth? Tomorrow, she vowed. Today she would just open the door and send him on his way.

She saw that a hard rain had begun to fall, and she instinctively grabbed Andy's jacket from the closet.

"I don't need that," he said.

"You'll be soaked."

"I don't care."

"I care," Laurie said, and that would have to do for both of them. Wasn't it her job to decide what was good for her son? How would it look if he turned up soaked at school? Besides, she had declared her position and couldn't back down now.

Andy pushed out the screen door, but she was on his heels. As she threw the jacket over his shoulders, he whirled with his elbow high and struck her nose. It was the first punch of her life, and it felt worse than he could have imagined.

She couldn't believe her own questions: Was she stronger than Andy? That's what she asked, as casually as she could, when Jeff came out for breakfast.

"Well, you're bigger than he is, at least for now. So I'd say you're stronger. But he's probably taken a lot of knocks from playing sports and fooling around, and I bet you never have."

Laurie turned away from him as if she needed to get something from the refrigerator and rubbed her nose. He was right, of course. She had never even thought about getting in a fight before that day. For the first time, she wanted to strike back, make someone feel the anger that he had aroused in her. That made her even more furious, that this boy could turn her into a raving parent wanting to slap away his cockiness. Maybe I'm just no good at this, she thought. I'm not a mother who knows how to accept disrespect as part of the territory.

"Why are you asking?" Jeff said.

She held the reason inside her. If he knew, it might be the end of the adoption plan, and she wasn't ready for that, at least not yet.

That morning, Laurie called Andy's social worker and got right to the point: Had he ever hit a woman before?

Alison didn't seem surprised by the question. "There's nothing in the records about that," she said. "But it's not unusual for boys to strike out sometimes. And they always target the adoptive mom, because their own mother failed them. I wouldn't worry too much at this point. Andy's bound to test you, to see if you get rid of him like his other families."

The simplicity of Alison's response infuriated Laurie. Just testing? Why was every bad behavior explained away as testing? Why couldn't Andy's defiance and rudeness be just bad behavior? Why did there have to be some deeper reason? Perhaps Andy was acting up not for fear of being rejected, but because he truly didn't like her and never would accept her as a mother. Who was going to sort through the possible reasons and find the right one? Laurie realized at that moment that Alison would be no help. She was on her own to work things out, just as if she had left the hospital with a newborn baby.

When Andy got off the bus that afternoon, Laurie watched from the front door. She had made sure to be home to face him on her own, with no Jeff to back her up. "So, you're sending me back, right" he said even before he came in.

The question shocked her. "Why do you say that?"

"'Cause I hit you by mistake this morning and you think I meant it, which I didn't, but that doesn't matter, 'cause you don't really want me here. Jeff does, but you don't."

She felt near crying. How would it be to think every time you did something wrong that your parents might kick you out? She hated to admit it, but perhaps Alison was right—Andy was testing her.

"You're not going anywhere," she said with a firmness that surprised her. "As a matter of fact, you're grounded for hitting me—whether you meant it or not."

Andy stared at her, wide-eyed. Laurie didn't know what to expect. Would he swing at her again? Yell and stomp around? Run out of the house? Maybe she had been wrong to do this without Jeff there.

"You mean like grounded in *my* room?" Andy asked.

Laurie could hear the pleasure this idea brought to him—that he actually had a room to be grounded to, and a mother who would keep him in—not throw him out. "That's exactly what I mean," she said.

"Cool," Andy said and took off down the hall. He jumped up to touch the ceiling as he went, but at the last moment, as Laurie was about to yell at him, he pulled his hand down and turned around and flashed a quick smile. "Fooled you!"

George Harrar lives in Wayland, Massachusetts, with his wife and adopted son. Harrar's fiction credits include *Story* magazine (Carson McCullers Prize for Short Stories Contest), *The New Press Literary Review, Side Show Anthology, Quarter After Eight* (Ohio University Review) and *Eclectic Literary Forum*. His recent novel will be published by Permanent Press in 1999. One of his short stories will be in the next edition of *The Best American Short Stories*.

Marking Him

Does my little son miss the smell
of his first mother? I wonder
as the mew of his mouth
opens toward a plastic bottle
which is not her breast.

In her good-bye letter to him
sealed in his album
with a birth certificate which now
lists my name as Mother,

his first mother writes
she nursed him briefly
after he emerged into
the second room of his
world.

I think of milk volcanic
and insistent, answering
the newborn's gigantic hunger,
a primal agreement between
generosity and greed.

Sometimes
I press my nose
to the glass of that place
where a mother and my child
belong to each other;
I cannot imagine coming
between them.

Sudden new mother,
I bury my nose deep into
his skull cap of ringlets,
his starry cheesiness,
want to lick him all over
with a cow's terry-cloth tongue,
to taste him, or maybe
to mark him as mine now

so if the other mother returns,
she will repeat the doe rabbit's
refusal of the kit I handled;
she will whiff the baby
smeared with my smell and
she won't take back my child.

Margaret Hasse

Basket, Water, Adoption

A baby is placed
in a well-woven basket.
It moves with the current
carrying its little fruit
from one woman
to another
who plucks
the bundle from the stream,
whose arms are ready
to tend,
whose body
has remained empty
of what
she is in need of carrying.

I stand at the river
that brought my son,
think
of the woman upstream.
How she could—
in the middle of hardship
and loss—trust
a basket, water,
that a person
would find her child,
lift him up, raise him
for many years, the
descendant of two mothers,
each who labored,
each who was faithful
to the river.

Margaret Hasse

Adoption Subject to Public Comment

in the style of "Sure You Can Ask Me a Personal Question"
by Diane Burns

Beautiful boys, where did you get them?

What country are they from?

Are they brothers?
No, I mean, are they really brothers?

Is the baby Italian?

Are you the children's grandmother?

Makes you *Pro-life,* doesn't it?

I just can't get used to white women
with brown babies.

Bless you for helping our people,
giving a home to
these little black kids.

How do you get to do this? I thought
we passed laws
to protect kids from being raised
in a different culture.

What do you know about
their real parents?

How could they?—I just can't imagine
giving up my child.

Are you parents of Baby M
I read about in the newspaper?

My neighbor/ sister/ cousin adopted a baby
from India/ Paraguay/ Georgia
with all these
hidden
medical
problems.

I hear that adopted kids rebel
as teenagers.

How will you feel when they search
for birth parents?

When they grow up, they won't
like you
because you're white.

My mother's sister adopted me
but they kept it a secret.

I was sent away to
California to have a
baby when I was seventeen
and I never even
saw her face.

When I bragged
to other kids
I was adopted,
they jeered, "Are not."
I asserted, "Am too."

When a social worker
placed the bundle in my arms,
his blanket
bright red,
I felt   like a firefighter

who carries a baby
        from a smoke-filled house,

discovering my life
        was saved
        by the child.

Margaret Hasse

Margaret Hasse has published two books of poems, *In a Sheep's Eye, Darling,* Milkweed Editions, and *Stars Above, Stars Below*, New Rivers Press. She holds a B.A. in literature from Stanford University, and an M.A. from The University of Minnesota, and is the recipient of several writing fellowships and awards including one in poetry from The National Endowment for the Arts. Margaret has a consulting business for the arts and other non-profit groups. She lives in St. Paul, Minnesota, with her husband and two sons. Her current manuscript in-progress is titled *Kin*.

Twice-Sacrificed
a song for my birthmother

He was darkness on top of her,
forced blood on white thighs as
jack-o'-lanterns grinned, flashing
their single-flamed teeth. Her secret

forced, blood on white thighs. As
she washes clean, her simple dreams
their single-flamed teeth—her secret
lives—rain down in autumn's leaves.

She washes clean of simple dreams.
Nine months, one—dark memory roots
lives. Raining down in autumn leaves:
blood red wings, gold prayers on wind.

Nine months, one dark memory. Roots
deep in her heart, and beneath it—a tiny
blood-red wing, a golden prayer. In wind
she sings these lullabies of longing, rising

deep from her heart. And beneath it a tiny
garden, enclosed and growing, of herself
she sings. These lullabies of longing rise.
Under blankets of winter-star skies, the

garden enclosed and growing. Herself
a ripening seed, awake and sleeping
under blankets of winter. Star-skies
conjure night's ghost body children.

A ripening seed. Awake and sleeping
summer's unnamed moon swells heavy,
conjuring night, ghosts. Body, child—
a single breath between. This haunted

summer, unnamed moon's swollen, heavy
descent, pushing. Hard bone against flesh
in single breaths, between these haunted
white thighs, blood, pink body, scream's

descent. Pushing hard, bone against flesh
twice-sacrificed offerings of innocence:
white thighs, blood, pink body, screams.
He was darkness on top of her.

Suzanne H. Heyd

145

Susan Heyd writes and teaches writing in Danbury, Connecticut. In addition to her own poetry and fiction, Suzanne is a writer for the terminally ill. She was adopted at birth and has recently made contact with her birthmother.

There

for Susannah

The same tall doors,
the church, the street light.
There, I suppose, are the same moon, stars.

The calendar
says March, nearly spring.
The air's still winter. Just as it was

that night. Oh, it
was best. I took good
care of her, doubled the blanket, left

a note with her
birthday—something to
know, without name or place. Now I can

recall her twice—
on the birthing day
(how easy!), then on that high stone step,

eight years ago,
tomorrow. Does she
hate me? Would she even know me,

now? The least hint?
The river's high, cold.
I won't let anyone take notice,

tomorrow. She
has a fine distant
somewhere to live in. What I have

left is certain:
the touch of her hand,
the sound she made as she took my breast.

As I left her
there wasn't a cry.
I could still see her from so far off,

that small, warm, misting breath.

John Hildebidle

147

A Long Distance Chat

to Susannah, still in Korea

With a watch
and a decent map
I could calculate back
from my time to yours,

and guess whether now
you're awake or not,
testing perhaps your few words;

or asleep, dreaming
in a foreign language.
But I'd rather
imagine you here

well-fed and sung to,
within arm's reach,
"home" at last

(as we like to say).
How we crave
your disorder
to re-center our lives,

summon our patience,
annoy away
our crust of habit—

"Come here, come home
for the first time,
for good," I could shout,
as if to summon you

across oceans,
across winds and continents,
and mountainous waiting—

come here, come home
to let us begin
this test of the heart,
of its gift of tongues.

John Hildebidle

Opposites: I

for my daughter Susannah

FAR is the country where someone
must now bewail your absence;
NEAR's the place where I'll keep you,
a world that holds no laments.

OUIET's the sound of your sleeping,
of the snore of your life, close by,
turned into sunrise muttering.
LOUD's the noise of my glee.

COLD is what makes the windowpanes
a scribble of lines and stars;
WARM's the grip of your fingers,
your weight propped on my arm.

EASY's the way we swoop and whirl,
waltzing this morning—to Telemann!—
all round the boisterous kitchen.
HARD is putting you down.

John Hildebidle

Opposites: II

for my son Nicholas

We thought, having been the all and only for so long,
you should know what it is to be one of an *and;*
was there, after all, really a Costello without Abbott,
a Jonathan without David? Maybe: but sadly diminished.

So (we did think about this) we decided to find dark to your light,
she to your he, short to your tall. We imagined quiet to your voluble
but we seem to have slightly miscalculated: oh well, in music
counterpoint's no better than antiphon. But on one count

we drew the line: having watched for those years of your sole
possession of us something rather closer to perfect than we'd believed
(sometimes) we did not feel it was advisable to go for flawed:
so on that score we found someone more directly after your fashion:

neither pole nor counterpart, but not only echo or shadow, either.

John Hildebidle

Riding, Holding Hands
for my daughter Susannah

Her idea, of a certainty. We'd come for the battleship,
    but she'd seen the carousel, demanded a turn,
        picked out a black horse, and pointed to one
    (grey and red-reined) just beside. Up and down,
up and down, faster than I'd imagined. Did she have
    a good seat? She put out a hand, called me,
        claiming ownership.

Just as well:
    no one even would have taken us for chums,
        she so Asian and (everyone says it) gorgeous;
        me bulging, ungainly, vaguely Teutonic.
        Now we're linked, and if no one was looking,
    I could cry, for the sheer joy of it.

I look over at her—bouncing, delighted,
    laughing. What a trail of abandonments,
        losses, what a crooked, improbable path
        brought us each here. Maybe it's evidence
    that things (complex, unavailing so often)
    roll (sometimes. This once.) toward
a good and necessary end. Who do I thank?

John Hildebidle

"Opposites I," and "Opposites II," previously appeared in *One Sleep, One Waking,* Enright House/Wyndham Hall Books. "There" previously appeared in *Defining Absence,* Salmon Books, 1999, and *Something Understood,* Every Other Thursday Press.

John Hildebidle has enjoyed a peripatetic, happy childhood, a life-long devotion to baseball and football, more Harvard degrees than any sane person can survive, jobs teaching at colleges and in public secondary schools, twenty years of marriage, two children (one birth-child now a freshman in college; one, adopted, flowering into elegant young womanhood, to her father's amazement and, yes, anxiety). His publishing credits include two books of poetry, one more in process, due in early 1999, one of fiction, and two scholarly works that helped earn tenure at MIT. John is a professor of literature with particular interests in contemporary Irish and American writing and the history of Anglo-American poetry.

Heartbeats Do Not Come From the Heart

Each of us lives in separate bodies
born into a unique universe—spheres of reality
containing only ourselves and all our possibilities.

> *When grandfather was dying*
> *we asked him to send us*
> *a child from heaven*

Yet during our lives each universe, each sphere, intersects,
interacts, with every other
creating new reality around each interaction.

> *since we are infertile.*
> *He said he would*
> *and we knew that he would*

We are, on earth, aware only of the points of contact
between our reality and others we encounter.
Only at these points do our perceptions, our expectations,
our dreams agree.

> *and that he could.*
> *Our adopted son*
> *is now two and asleep in his crib*

Yet these interactions extend beyond our imagining,
into the afterlife, connecting all levels of consciousness,
making our definitions of consciousness obsolete,

> *with the soul of his great grandfather*
> *beating*
> *in his heart.*

making our definitions of souls obsolete,
making our definitions of family, and of god, and of love
seem trivial in the face of what is possible from heaven.

Bradley Earle Hoge

A Safe Warm Place to Winter

We have adopted our child because we are infertile
and cannot have our own, but . . .

>Adopting a child is like bringing your dreams into reality
>like painting a landscape and planting it in your backyard,
>like finding the rarest jewel while digging to plant a tree,
>or finding your way to sunset without a map.

I look back on my life and ask, would I be better
off having made different decisions . . .

>It is like seeding a cloud with the thought of rain,
>like tasting the salt of the ocean with your toes in the sand.
>like running up a mountain to drink from a stream,
>then somersaulting down and landing on your feet.

where to go to college, different jobs in different
cities, staying together, persevering . . .

>Like taking communion in a Catholic church,
>like the slow impossibility of a great blue heron
>taking flight low over a tranquil halcyon marsh.
>Like a bittern raising its head to hide in tall chord grass.

But any decision I could have made differently
would not have led to the miracle that is . . .

>Adopting a child is like choosing a church in a new city,
>like your first day of college, as your parents drive away;
>like geese flying together from Canada to Texas
>to find a safe warm place to winter.

our adopted son.

Bradley Earle Hoge

Bradley Earle Hoge is a full-time, at-home dad of
two small sons. He is also a part-time research
scientist in global change at Rice University. His
poetry appeared in *the fractal, The Texas Poetry
Calendar, Kudzu, Kimera, Arrowsmith, Beyond
Doggerel, Musing,* and *Sophomore Jinx.* A
collection of his poetry is included in the anthology
Everywhere Is Someplace Else, Plain View Press,
August 98. He is the publisher and editor of
Quantum Tao and *Frontiers,* Blue Heron Press.

The Cake

That cake you brought to me at school,
chocolate with 7-minute frosting
and coconut,
my favorite,
I believed it as
Hansel and Gretel
believed the gingerbread.

Starved and desperate, they needed
the sweetness of that house,
the candy hearts, sweetmeats,
gingerbread better than the staff of life,
dark, spicy, full of promise.
Eager little fingers stuffed
fluff and nothing into searching mouths.

So, too, I took in
the animal pancakes on cold mornings,
the clothes, summers in Maine,
needing them to be for me,
pretending to myself.

Childless and evil with that hunger
you took me from my mother,
an adopted child,
more unwanted than H & G

Your sisters couldn't control the rage in you.
but Mattic took me to her heart,
saved me.
To pay us back
you let me watch her die.

The cake impressed the roomies.
I let you bask in the admiration
of girls with less extravagant,
more loving mothers,
girls who didn't realize
you'd eat them
if you could.
While you gloated and seduced,
I ate the cake
willing to be deluded one last time.

Cher Holt-Fortin

The Cake was written in an attempt to remember one good thing about my adoptive mother, an abusive narcissist, after I found my birth mother and felt free enough to look honestly at the lifelong unhappiness of my relationship to my adopted mother. The effort only succeeded in capturing the essence of our relationship.

155

Homecoming

Huge arid exotic, India lumbered into my small world
the summer, I was six;
a carny selling rides
on a broken-down circus elephant
looked like a maharaja to me.
I begged for days and Dad gave in
on Friday, while my disapproving mother
served barbecue amid the spicy, grease-flavored air
of the Pigstand next door.

Riding that elephant,
so far above the world I knew,
all of India was mine.
The sweet bronze bells on her harness
rang only for me
and I dreamt of silk and jasmine,
despite the itchy blanket beneath my legs,
the elephant smell, the nearby traffic—
a poor man's gift to his only daughter.

Years later, in an airport
a woman hands me a baby girl,
wrapped in an old quilt,
three days coming across the water,
India to Atlanta.
black eyes, elegant fingers,
strong heart to come so far alone,
home at last.
I held you, thinking of that elephant,
and wondered if my father watched over your flight.

Cher Holt-Fortin

"Homecoming" is a memory of my father taking me for an elephant ride when I was about five
or six.

J at 11

Dancing in your name
chalked beside the pool,
inside the J you turn,
tondu, arabesque, plie,
your boneless dancer arms
circumscribe the space around you,
as you pirouette away,
your hair a black cape
across your shoulders and back,
a small jete across letters.
I marvel at your grace,
feeling like the hippos in *Fantasia,*
astonished yet again
at the gift you are.
Did your Indian mother look like you,
that nameless, unknowable, woman
who is always there?
I imagine you with cymbals and ankle bells
dancing in another form —
wife, harem girl, street urchin,
prostitute.
You turn again at A, look back,
watch me watching you.

Cher Holt-Fortin

"J at 11" is for my daughter, who is a dancer, though she does not study any Indian dance forms.

Cher Holt-Fortin is an adoptee with three children. One is adopted. She lives in Georgia, where she writes poems to preserve and recover the past, teaches aikido, and makes quilts and dolls. Her publications include: "Raspberries and Rain," *Chili Verde Review*, April, 1997. "Black and White Kodak c. 1955." *Grasslands Review,* 1995. "Goodbye" in *Women and Death*, Ground Torpedo Press, 1994. "Sandi," *Karamu*, Spring 1993. "Thrift," *Earth Tones,* 1993/94. Selected untitled poems. *Literature East and West*, 1992. "Homecoming," *The Indian-American,* 1991. "The Doll," *Midstream: A Monthly Jewish Review,* 1989. "Atavism," *GSU Review,* 1989. "Ahab's Leg," *Gryphon,* 1988. "Of Archangels," *Rhino,* 1987. "Fibonocci's Curve," *GSU Review*, 1987. "Been Here a Long Time," *The Chattahoochee Review,* 1986. "Our Blades First Told It," *Japanophile,* 1985–86. "Mattie," *Sojourner,* 1986. "Red Peonies." *GSU, Review.* 1986. "Morning in January." *Blueline*, 1985. "Homesickness," *Bittersweet,* 1984. Book: *The Ayyam—I—Ha Camel*, Kalimat, 1987, a children's story about the Baha'i holidays and being of a different religion. Stories: "Dragons," in *The Cats' Meow,* Maine Rhodes Press, 1995. "In Our Mother's House," *Tender is the Net,* 1995, an electronic and printed anthology of work from members of CREWRT-L, Fly Neleth Press.

That First Night

for my adopted daughter Talia, from "Memory Box"

When I came for your mother
that first night, you greeted
me with giggles and snapping
gum and left me waiting.
From the hallway I could hear you
whisper, "He's here!"
into your mother's room,
trailing those giggles back
and forth until she appeared
in a special red skirt and blouse
that you picked out
to match my faded jeans.
Later that night, you showed me
how to blow into your flute,
and I promised, next time,
to bring my clarinet.

Talia, I didn't play with you
in your rainbow wading pool,
or rock you on your wooden horse
with your legs straight out,
or laugh when you stuffed your cheeks
with cantaloupe and honeydew,
or help you skip rope
with a long piece of seaweed,
but when we take out your memory box
of ballet tights and leotards,
knitted booties from Bubie Fanny,
a first book, *Where is Spot?*
a doll named Amy,
photos of birthdays I missed,
dusty drawings, dolphins and
other childhood relics,
you and your mom tell stories
and I am there.

Gary Imlay

Gary Imlay's poetry is published in *Raging Tea,*
POETS ON THE LINE, Art/Life and *Daybreak.*
He, his wife, and two children live in Ventura,
California. As a social worker, he works with
gang members and youth at risk. Through the
California Poets in the Schools, he uses poetry to
teach high school students Vietnam War history.
His wife Shelley Savren is a poet and full-time
instructor at Oxnard Community College. His
adopted daughter Talia Savren has won two
poetry awards in the children's category for the
Ventura Poetry Festival.

Beast Carolina
Laurel K. Jenkins-Crowe

I never told anyone about my other life. It would upset my parents. And I thought for a long time we all had one, just as I thought everybody was birthed by one set of parents and raised by a second set. Every time I say, "I have go, I'm late for my other life," people heard, "I'm late for the doctor." I realized this when I told a teacher I had to go to my other life and she said, "Which one, Hon? The allergist or the pediatrician?" She even asked me for a note. That was in the fourth grade. I did have to go to the doctor a lot as a child.

They must wonder about my doctor, because I stay away for days when I can. If anyone else thinks of my other life, they'd probably imagine me swaddled in bandages and bristled with tubes, with my head shaved and scars running over me like snail tracks.

My other life isn't like that at all. My name is not even Karen. I went to a hospital there once, and it was fun. Nothing had a needle or smelled like iodine, and the nurses wore their own clothes. When I say I have to get back here, they only say, "Goodbye, come back soon."

We don't discover it right away. We are born *there* and then we come here, and though we always know the difference, we don't know what the difference is. Then when we are old enough to tell a story, we might find the way. The story I could tell was the first one I ever heard, and there were no bears or Princesses in it, just me. It was called "How We Got You." In it I was not a scruffy little tomboy at all but an angel sent from heaven. It seemed a lot to live up to. I found my way after Mom took me to see Walt Disney's "Bambi." I was frisking around the carpet being Bambi. It didn't matter that he was a boy. Mom was Bambi's mother, never mind that she would die. I don't know how old I was, because I can't remember a time when I hadn't seen "Bambi."

"Let's play," I told Bambi's mother. She put her doe eyes over the top of the ironing board and looked down at the fawn gamboling there.

"I'm Bambi and you're Bambi's mother," I said. They always needed clues, these taller people.

"Bambi's mother is busy ironing right now," and she was. I never saw a more ridiculous sight than Bambi's mother balanced on her fine hind hooves at the ironing board, wrestling the iron up and down it with the handle tucked into the tiny space between fetlock and hoof.

I got out of her way. I couldn't figure out why I was so sad over this. I went along the forest floor with my head down, and none of my friends came to play. I think it was the sound of my forefoot in the leaves that made me realize I was in a forest and truly had hooves. I was best at being a horse, but I had never gone as far as this at it.

I was still sad. Bambi's mother answered all his questions and was never ironing. Not once in the film had she said, "Run along and play" or "not now." Maybe my *real* . . .

That's where the thought always stopped. I could not be disloyal. And if I had continued, Armadillo would have stopped me. He rolled up with his head and limbs tucked in like a cartoon, put out his forefeet to stop, and uncurled at my hooves.

"Hello, Faline," he said. His voice was quite clear, though his armadillo lips, if they were that, didn't move. Then he turned into a blond boy, a bit taller than I was in my usual body. He was filthy and his clothes were torn. The red and white shirt was too large and hung on him in rags. The jeans had their knees blown out. He had big ears.

"Jour mama give you away too?"

I winced. I felt the high hocks of my back legs sink and flex. Some kind of deer-human fight-or-flight reflex urged me to duck the question.

"You got to say something, then you'll change back. You ain't been here before?"

I shook my head. One ear went on flicking for longer than the head. A thousand smells clamored for my attention. I knew the water smell and the leaf smell, but what was that sharp odor, like a wet centipede . . . ?

"You got no watch," said Armadillo Boy.

"Ah cain't tayull tahm ye-et." And then I was me, a short-haired, grubby Carolina tomboy with leaves on my shirt. My nostrils were still searching, and I felt a whole world of scent dim and slide away like a symphony dying in the middle.

"You better stick with me," said the armadillo boy. "You're awful little to be here."

"Where is this?"

"This is the other place." He shrugged. "This is where we're from."

"I'm from Charlotte." I always said I was from Rock Hill, where I lived, but now I remembered I'd been born in Charlotte.

"You're from Scarlick," he said. "That's what it is here. That's where the king and queen live." He waited for me to react to *king* and *queen,* but I didn't. "They gave their baby girl away." He gave me a sideways grin. "You might could be her.

We all get here in the woods," he explained, "soon as we're old enough to tell a story and be an animal."

"Everyone can do that."

"Not like we can." And when I thought, that sounded right. My friends could be animals, but never the way I could. I always felt myself to be a horse and moved like one, but they only crawled on all fours and said "Raah." They never moved or spoke at all like lions or tigers at all. And my brother was good at it too; he was a cheetah. That made me panic for a second. Was he here? He wasn't born in Charlotte. I might never find him. But he couldn't tell a story yet. He never got the words right, although he knew what he meant to say.

I asked Armadillo his name. It was Armadillo. He lived in the wood and never left. He wouldn't go back home, where there were cars, and he wouldn't go into the other place to meet his other mother and father.

"They didn't want me." His hands were jammed in his pockets.

161

Sometimes I would go off in the woods behind our house and be Mowgli (a girl Mowgli) and sing songs about how stupid and cruel human beings were. Mowgli had no mother and father. There was the woman who said he was her son, but she was rich and the village agreed because of that. When I wasn't angry with her anymore, I'd go back to Mom and have my name again. Armadillo never went back. That was exciting and, since I was in this place where I didn't know if I ever could go back, a little scary.

"Maybe they just couldn't keep you. Maybe they . . ."

All I could think of was died, and I wanted Mom. I wanted her right away, and never mind this other mother, who might be a queen or might be dead.

I became a horse because that was easiest, and I wheeled and drove back the way I'd come, bumbling through the trees until I burst through something and found myself going hands-and-knees across the wooden floor in my own room.

Now I had another story, the one about where I really came from, but there was nobody I could tell. Even my brother wouldn't believe me.

When I went out to the den, Bambi's mother had finished the laundry. It was about lunchtime, and she fed me. She thanked me for staying out of her way for awhile and asked if there was anything I wanted to play now.

She thought I had been being *good*. I had been about to look for my other mother, the one they all called my *real* mother even though my real mother was here. It was the *other*, the imaginary one, about whom I knew nothing, except that she had long pretty hair. I didn't want to look at Mom or play anything. I wanted to cry, but that would make her worry, so I didn't. My head hurt low in the back near its base, as if I had a fever.

We drew. I didn't want to be Bambi anymore. I drew an armadillo that looked like a dirt hill with ears. Mom helped me draw the horse. She understood the joints of their feet and legs.

The next day I had an appointment with a new doctor because I sniffled a lot and stuff always dripped down the back of my throat. It didn't bother me the way it did Mom and Dad. I sat on the white paper table while the doctor stuck me all over the arms and back with tiny needles. I don't remember it hurting much, but I did get bored. There were so many needles, and the doctor tooked so long. I grew bumps all over where the needles went in and the doctor wrote things down. Then we went home and I wasn't allowed to roll in the yard anymore. I was allergic to the grass. I was allergic to just about everything.

I had to have shots. They smarted much worse than the testing but still not so bad I had to cry. I sat and waited in a back room at the pediatrician's. I stared at the clock, an orange cat wagging its eyes and tail every second for the rest of time. A nurse would come, pull a bottle from the refrigerator, and give me a injection of yellow stuff that smelled metallic and looked thick, as if there were more of the liquid than I could see. Sometimes she hit the bone of my arm with the needle. Sometimes I got a bruise but usually not.

My little brother always cried at the doctor's. He cried over the prickly little TB test and, if he ever had a real shot, he was just plain held down. Maybe cheetahs are made that way.

162

"You won't be allergic here." Armadillo had met me in the wood again. I didn't like his smile. Who taught him songs? Who tucked him in? Nobody. He couldn't read, and he was six, or thought he was. How would he know? Nobody to tell him it was say April and his birthday was coming soon and what kind of party would he like? He said he was an armadillo more often than not, and he liked it that way. He ate bugs. Lots of boys will do that.

He was right though. I never sniffled or sneezed there or woke with a sore throat.

"Still wanna go to Scarlick?" I had just quit being a pinto filly with improbable sky-blue spots. I squeaked out, "OK," before I could think too hard about Mom and Dad.

It was Spring. Last week it had been autumn here, but the woods were blooming. Many of the trees were sprouting tiny, bright-green leaves. Others bore flowers, baskets full of them, pink ones that rained gentle petals or white ones that shook their heads when there was a breeze.

"How cum it's Spring awready?"

"Time acts funny here. That's why you gotta tell time. You might be late back, and they'll think you're dead or something." He grinned at me. I knew he wanted me to cry because I still couldn't tell time, although I had mastered writing my first name and knew my address, ZIP code and all. I could read a book about a dinosaur. This was more than Armadillo could do.

"C'mon," he said. "I bet you're that princess."

"I ain't no princess." They weren't good for anything but getting rescued and falling in love. They had to wear dresses and stupid duncy hats. Who needed it?

But I discovered I was the princess of Beast Carolina, where all of us who could be animals liked to go.

My *real* mother cried. Her hair was pure blue-black and straight, as if she ironed it. It hung to her thighs, and when she hugged me, I hugged back and then struggled. When she put me down, I cried too.

Armadillo stood with his thumbs linked behind his back and waited until she shooed him away, telling him he'd get his reward in the kitchen. There was nothing Armadillo wanted from the world but food and breath and water. If you gave him money or a toy, he would throw it away.

I remembered watching TV and wishing I was Wednesday Addams so I could have Gomez and Morticia for parents. Pugsley could go live with Mom and Dad and take my place. Here I was in a castle, a house that was a museum, and I couldn't do anything but cry. Then my *real* mother the Queen sang to me. I don't know how she knew this little song, because there was no TV there, but she quietly sang in my ear the Addams family theme song.

And I broke out laughing. The smile on her face was like two suns coming out from behind two clouds at two dawns.

My father the King looked like Johny Quest's father Dr. Benton Quest. I had no doubt we'd go on adventures all over the world. He said there had been a pony waiting for me all these years. He smelled faintly of pipe tobacco, as if he had given up smoking yesterday and it was still in his hair and clothing.

Dad smoked Kools and smelled like stale smoke and after-shave.

"There's no kings and queens in America," said Dad. "We're a Democracy."

He told me why not for a long, long time and I didn't argue. He was right, and he talked so long I didn't often argue with him, even when he was wrong. I hid my other life, except to draw lots of pictures of armadillos. I drew the queen and king once, but the kindergarten teacher asked who they were. I said, "I don't know," and felt my face flush red and stay red. After that I quit thinking about them, whenever I could stop myself. It was wrong, it was ungrateful. What if Grandpa knew I was doing such a thing? Or Cousin Steven? . . . I would never go there again.

My brother was skinny and huge-eyed, and whenever a photo was taken of him, no matter the angle, his mournful eyes turned out red. I read later there's an invisible line dividing those of us who get adopted before six months and those after. He was after and everything scared him. He knew he was uprooted and maybe he felt it could happen again at any time. What could he trust? He wasn't big enough to hold onto anything. He was afraid of the doctor, dogs, the vacuum cleaner.

Sometimes when we were a bit older, I would sit and stare at him. I tried not to let him see. I'd think—Who is Ben? Who is he? He is my brother. Who is he? I could narrow my eyes and coast far away on this thought, not really thinking anything, but being in some other state. I think I was trying to ask myself who I was, only I dared not. If I asked who I was, the world would crack in half and bleed down the sky. Every child did it but us, who had most right. I heard *real* children howl out, because they knew so deeply it wasn't true, "You're not my *real* mother! I'm really adopted!"

I don't know how to explain how different these things make a person feel. For example, I have always wondered, do I love? When I have a strong feeling for someone and name it love, is it anything like what they feel and name love? If it is similar, then how? In quality, or in quantity or depth of feeling? Everyone else seems so damned sure about it. I never am. I believe I love. But I also believe I probably do it wrong.

Snow blows around the fawn. His ears are carried in the direction of the punishing wind. He cries out over and over. Surely it is just that she can't hear him.

"Mother!"

But it is the Great Stag who looms out of the snow at him, tall and stern as a cliff, offering no warm flank to curl against, no illusions about who will come back when. This is not Beast Carolina.

"Your mother can't be with you anymore," he intones. When he turns, the fawn follows. They turn to the slanting wind, lean on it, plant their stick legs to the knees and pull against the air.

Laurel Jenkins-Crowe is an adoptee born in Charlotte, North Carolina, in 1965. She is the author of "The Seventh Guitar," *The Vincent Brothers Review's* short story contest winner for 1996. "I got the idea for 'Beast Carolina' when I read about the elaborate fantasy lives some adoptees construct around their *real* parents. I don't remember doing that." Laurel works as a veterinary technician and lives in Memphis with her husband, actor Rick Crowe, two cats, two snakes, and a budgerigar.

From Dolpo to Boulder
Cynthia T. Kennedy

There is a soup kitchen near Boudennath, that most impressive of the Buddhist temples or Stupas, in Kathmandu, Nepal. Shaped like an upside-down bowl at the base, the Stupa has a cone-like top. In each direction the eyes of Buddha are painted to watch over the land. Bright-colored prayer flags are strewn from top to base, and imbedded in the base are hundreds of prayer wheels for the devout to turn. Each turn of the wheel, each wave of a prayer flag in wind speaks the prayer, and the illiterate can thus read without reading and benefit. Hundreds of Tibetan refugees huddle over their spread of trinkets to sell, mostly mani stones (stones inscribed with prayer), and woven bracelets.

For miles around, trails wind upward leading to the homes and camps of the Tibetan refugees. A number of ornamental monasteries also occupy the area and the air is full of the sound of brass horns and chanting of the monks. Following the directions on a hand-drawn map, we wended our way up dirt paths and finally, after many an inquiry, found Rokpa House, the home for homeless children set up by the Swiss. A Boulder woman, Jennifer, who spent several months donating her time to this home, asked us if we would take some things to a special child, Ram. We were delivering clothes, tooth brushes, magazines and crayons. A tiny smiling Nepali face opened the wrought-iron gate and the director, a Swiss woman named Leah, greeted us with a cold Coca-Cola. What a treat in a town with virtually no refrigeration!

She told us of Jennifer's undertaking to help Dorje Dolma:

"It was Monsoon a year ago," she said, "raining for weeks and coming down in buckets. Jennifer was working the soup kitchen near here—below the eyes of Buddha, the worst poverty."

Both my husband and I had commented on the irony at the Monkey Temple—a beautiful and historic place, under the care of the monks who most revere it, and yet covered with feces and filth. The monks don't assume the responsibility.

"This woman offered an explanation, 'They don't even see it. Urine is not something dirty.' But let me tell the story. Dorje is from Dolpo, perhaps three or four weeks walk. Her family saves for many years growing potatoes. Very poor. Many years. And they save to come to temple.

"To die well, a Buddhist must come to these places. They can not come before the rain because it is planting time. They cannot come after the rain because it is harvest time. And so they come in Monsoon.

"The youngest boy, a baby, is quite ill. They are in a strange city, this Kathmandu, and are directed to the hospital. The hospital takes their money, all their money, but does not cure the child. It is raining cats and dogs. I look up from my soup and I see this child, this Dorje, with her hair so dirty and uncombed it sticks straight out from her head—an umbrella that keeps the rain from her face. I think what a remarkable child, who can grow her hair in such a way to protect her from the rain. She is surely blessed. And what does she say? 'Eschole.' I want to go to school.

"Her back is misshapen with a great hump, but she smiles the smile of the gods.

"Our clinic could not help the baby. We fed the family, gave them enough to make the journey home. They didn't see their temples. The father places Dorje's hand in mine and says, 'She is no good to us.' He knows she cannot be married with this deformity. She cannot make her own way. For him she has been tending the sheep in the mountains, seeing sometimes four or five mountain lions in one day, sometimes losing sheep to them. She has no future. She will starve when they die. He signed the papers of abandonment, and yet I could tell they loved her too. What love.

"Then an American woman, this Jennifer, comes to our kitchen. She has money and she falls in love with Dorje's first smile. And now Dorje is going to America and will be adopted by this woman. They think maybe the surgery can be successful. Scoliosis they say can be helped, if the surgery comes before puberty. We are hopeful and she will get schooling."

We told her we were trying to adopt through Nepal.

"It is holy work," she said as we took our leave. "I have thirty-nine children. The thing about children is that the heart just grows; there is no end to the love one can give."

We walked away more convinced than ever that we would adopt, and adopt from Nepal.

Dorje lives in Boulder, Colorado, and is now entering the eighth grade. She's been here three years and her English is perfect. Many surgeries have straightened her back and, though she suffers pain, the prospects for her future are without limit. She has the open happy smile of her people. More than that, she is an exotically beautiful young woman with sculptured features and long, shiny black hair. Already she is selling her paintings here. Though her paintings tend to the abstract, if you look carefully you will find the mountains, the sheep and the mountain lions of Dolpo.

Dorje Dolma after her surgery with Jerry Kennedy
holding Bishnu and Cynthia holding Sunita.

167

Prayer flags in Nepal

Namaste

The seeds of
last year's pepper—
carcass crushed—
fall like
tiny aspen leaves

into the finger-
print pressed
pockets of
vermiculite—
one to a hole.

This ritual
I had so hoped
would be yours
and mine this year,

dark eyed child,

is mine alone.

Within the week
from each cube
emerges a shy
but confident
inhabitant
stretching its thin,

white noodle-neck
toward the light.
Leaf-tips
caught in
seed shells
reach like
little hands
held up
in prayer.
And more weeks pass.

I transplant the
seedlings and wait
as our dream seed
makes its way in
packets of
bureaucratic
paper work
through the channels
of two governments

and wonder what I will
say to you at our
first meeting.

Ah, but that's the
easy part. I will
say what all Nepalese
say upon a meeting,
chance or no.

Namaste. With the
gesture of the hands
palms pressed together,
and a slight bow.

It is what all
expectant mothers say
when the seed of
love has germinated and
they see their child's
face for the first time.

Namaste: I salute the
god within you, child.

Cynthia T. Kennedy

Cynthia T. Kennedy lives in Lafayette, Colorado, and she maintains her own law practice, with an emphasis on corporate, real estate, and bankruptcy matters. Her husband's mountain climbing adventures led them to Nepal where they adopted their two children, Sunita and Bishnu. Ms. Kennedy's work appeared in *New Mexico Humanitites Review, William and Mary Review, Oregon East*. She has works appearing in the upcoming issues of *North Dakota Quarterly* and *Eureka Literary Magazine*.

Daughter

On dark winter nights,
between the sighing of steam
from radiators, I have heard
your breath slip beneath
the door and fill up the bedroom
like a balloon which deflated
at the break of day.

Sometimes I have cradled you
in my arms before the fireplace
and rocked you asleep as logs
crumbled through the grate.

Coming home from work
I have tiptoed up the stairs
to find you still breathing
in the antique cradle
in the guest bedroom, stooped
over, and kissed you awake.

But your toys never littered
my study, your diapers never
fouled my bathroom. I never
held my breath through your
routine sicknesses, never had
to wonder how I would endure
your growing into the woman
some strange man would
take from my house.

But I have felt you, my
daughter, when the children
of those I love hugged me.
I see your lines in their
bright drawings I tape
to the refrigerator door,
hear your voice rise
in their chatter.

Ah, my daughter, I can
almost feel you reading
over my shoulder as I write.
Your harsh cry would have
been music to my night.

Norbert Krapf

171

When the Call Came

When the call came
I was about to cut the grass
for the first time. Wild
onion and dandelion were
sprouting across the lawn.
Sheaths of lily of the valley
bearing round green bells
were surrounding the lilac.

When the call came
the yellow marsh marigolds
were rising like the sun
against a boulder in
the flower bed. Bees
buzzed around bunches
of purple grape hyacinth.
The operator said, *I have
a collect call from Colombia.
Do you accept the charges?*
I replied, *Yes, I accept.*

When the call came
the leathery leaves
of bloodroot along the ledge
of the stone wall were
wrapped around stalks
like green sheets on which
white petals lay. Beside
the fishpond the fronds
of maidenhair fern were
unfurling in the sun.
A voice with a Spanish
accent spoke in my ear,
*This is a social worker. We
have a baby girl born eight
days ago. Will you accept her?*

When the call came
the white blossoms
of the wild cherry at the edge
of the woods were fluttering
on black boughs. The tips
of Japanese irises were
pushing through the soil.
Specks of bibb lettuce
lay like green confetti
on the upper level of
the rock garden. *Yes, we
accept her,* I said. *Yes.*

Norbert Krapf

Poem of a Crazy Man

As I pounded a wedge into the heart
of maple logs stacked outside our old
Long Island house on a hot sultry day
in August, my friends said I was crazy.

That day a child was born somewhere in Bogotá.

After one red-streaked beauty split open,
neither my wife nor my daughter, who was
also born somewhere in Bogotá, saw me
kneel on the patio to lick at the sap.

I would not claim to be a visionary.
I did not pause to consider the possibility
that along about then somewhere in Bogotá
a boy was being born. I admit I just
split my log and quietly licked it.

But I do know that because I am crazy
enough to split wood on a hot sultry
day in August and am not afraid to lick
maple sap, that boy born somewhere
in Bogotá is going to be my son.

My daughter and I have named him Daniel.
And if he wants to dream of lions instead
of logs somewhere in this old house,
there is no way we will ever stop him.

Norbert Krapf

Breathing in Bogotá

In a crib in the unheated
room above the empty street
where during the day
children lead burros lugging
supplies up the mountainside

you sleep sitting up strapped
in an infant seat, congestion
rattling your chest, as mist
from the humidifier drifts
toward you and drops like
clouds from the Andes above.

In my almost sleep I dream
you are coughing again.
When I count twelve I know
dream is no dream, sit up,
and lunge toward you.

Oh blue-eyed stranger
with the chestnut hair
and complexion fairer
than the climate of these
mountainous tropics,
I hold you, soft and warm,
and listen in the dark
to your rasping breath.

A kind of blind love
and longing and a flight
of thousands of miles
have earned me the right
to whisper these beautiful
words in the tongue
of your ancestors: Mi niño,

Norbert Krapf

Sun Also Shines

Wherever I walk
stars for which
I have no name
fall toward me.

Leaves drop and drift,
rain and snow fall.
But sun shines too.

People glide in
and out of my life.
A few swirl back.

Sometimes icicles
bar the windows
I look out of.

Two infants from
another country have
become our children.

I listen to them
breathe at night.

Rain and snow fall.
The children cry, yes,
but they also smile.

And light from
some other place
shines in their eyes.

Norbert Krapf

Norbert Krapf grew up in the German community of Jasper, Indiana. He is the editor/translator of *Beneath the Cherry Sapling: Legends from Franconia* and *Shadows on the Sundial: Selected Early Poems of Rainer Maria Rilke,* and editor of the revised and expanded *Finding the Grain: Pioneer German Journals* and *Letters from Dubois County, Indiana.* His German heritage also figures prominently in *Somewhere in Southern Indiana: Poems of Midwestern Origins* and *Blue-Eyed Grass: Poems of Germany.* He is graduate of St. Joseph's College (Indiana) and the University of Notre Dame, where he received his M.A. and Ph.D. in English and American literature. He has served as U.S. Exchange Teacher at West Oxon Technical College, England, and as a senior Fulbright Professor of American Poetry at the Universities of Freiburg and Erlangen/Nuremberg, Germany. He directs the C.W. Post Poetry Center of Long Island University, where he is Professor of English.

Clockworks

for Saul

Four years ago, Grammy Smith's once soothing
mantle clock ticked unbearably;
I stopped its pendulum
when the third of many pregnancies was lost
and moved it high and out of sight.
It stood silent above the living room
that long—watching, lifeless, as all our
fetuses died unborn
and our tears fed the endless nights.

Now the clock chimes
again on our mantle,
restarted when Saul came home.
God spoke in the boy's face,
from a snapshot and video
made halfway around the globe,
beamed through flickering lights,
his big ears suggestive of family:
"This is your son."
And so Saul came to us,
our second miraculous little one.

Born before the clock stopped,
not two years after Leah,
he is the second poem I could not write,
the second child that would not come,
and washed like salve of heaven
over ocean, rivers, ancient killing fields
to heal old wounds and new—
his own, ours, others'.

Angels knew early that Saul would come,
guided us even before we saw his face
to find new living rooms—
bigger ones, and fourteen stories higher.

The clock smiles again.
God and angels live with us—
jump with two children on our sofa,
laugh out loud as they play and kiss,
dance as light on pink stone counters,
dive with the peregrine past our windows,
surprise as noisy gulls and crows coast by,
bless our life as Jupiter and a full moon rise.

Alyssa A. Lappen
August 29, 1996

Imagine

Imagine our son, a tiny waif,
the first day he met us,
orphaned by his birthmother's
hasty retreat, after a year,
for reasons we can only surmise
stemmed from poverty, lack of work
and her own youth, her own
abandonment by a broken mother.

Imagine this frightened boy
smiling, shyly kissing us, wondering
who were these strangers—for we
were strangers then—where would
we would take him, why?
Yet he let us. Imagine how he beat
his head nightly on his pillow
in sleep, his motor-like cry
chasing demons only God
shares knowledge of,
since our Saul still will
not speak of Hungary, except
pretend. When I was in Hungary, he lies,
I flew on a jet, I lived in a palace,
I ate fruit every day, I drove a red car.
When I was in Hungary, my mother
loved me. And yet she must have,
that Anna, who left him,
never visited, but refused easily
to let go. For who could not love
his brightness, mischief, questions—
Es mios, "What's that?" His "Why?"
And how else did Saul manage
so easily to give his own
bewildering gift of love,
packaged imperfectly
like that of every child,
his unquestioning trust.

How he boasted in the Embassy,
to a room full of strangers,
"Ezek az én szüleim!"
"These are my parents!"

Imagine what's missing—
the memory, what happened
his first four years. Imagine
the loss of that Anna, who
unknowingly gave us a miracle.

Alyssa A. Lappen
January 10, 1998

Alyssa A Lappen graduated Phi Beta Kappa, Magna Cum Laude from Newcomb College, Tulane University, with a B.A. in English Literature. She has worked as a journalist for newspapers and magazines, including the *New Haven Register, Forbes, Corporate Finance, Working Woman,* and *Institutional Investor.* With *Institutional Investor* she has been a senior editor covering the investment management industry since May of 1993. Her poetry publications include a 1971 appearance in *The Harvard Crimson,* a 1975 appearance in *Best Poets of the Twentieth Century,* and a 1975 appearance in Notable American Poets. In 1998 she published two poems at Kudzu and one at Switched-on Gutenberg.

Another Mother, Another Woman

I.

It was simple in the beginning,
we couldn't have children
and we wanted them. I never thought
of the child belonging to another woman.
He would be our baby. I thought about me
and the best thing for that child,
the best thing meaning my husband and me.
I had to believe it, I wanted that baby.
I wanted him a lot.

Some women told me I was lucky,
I didn't have to go through the pain.
No post-natal blues, no sore stitches,
no reason to be tired, no stretch marks.

They didn't know what I went through.
When mothers talked about childbirth
I felt hollow and dry inside.

No milk.
I heard about an adoptive mother
who nursed her baby. She swore milk was there.

II.

Do you want him? the case worker asks.
Yes.

He arrived dressed,
bundled in blankets.
My husband and I were told we could undress and inspect
this being who stared up at us
with serious eyes, a cleft in his chin.

We gave the baby a new name.

We took him home
and while the formula simmered
I bathed him, powdered the new skin,
and oiled his head.

It was then I thought about the other woman,
what she was missing.
I wanted to say, *Thank you, thank you.*

III.

He always knew.
I practiced while I rocked him.
You've had three mothers,
the one you grew in, a foster mother,
and me.

Adoption, I told the case worker,
should be a common word like baseball.

I never told him I chose him. He belonged
here for himself and for me.

Once after watching a show on TV, he asked,
Why did she throw me in a trash can?
Who?
My mother, she threw me there and left me.
No, she didn't, I tell him, *she did the best she knew,*
she gave you a family.

Another time someone asked him,
Don't you want to find your real mother?
I live with my real mother.
I mean your real mother.
She is my real mother.

IV.

Now he's thirty-three, a man.
I look into those same serious eyes,
note the cleft in his chin now deeper.
I can't believe how, of all children,
he filled my life.

I think of Virgin Mary. She,
who Jesus called, *woman,*
knew he was not hers.

Diane Quintrall Lewis

Diane Quintrall Lewis is the adoptive mother of three children, now grown, married, and with families. She has nine grandchildren, is a poet and artist, and farms two and a half acres of avocado trees. Her writing has appeared in the anthologies *Cries of the Spirit* and *Women and Death,* and in several journals including *Alabama Literary Review, Mildred, Nimrod,* and *Borderlands.* She is editor of *Magee Park Poets.*

Big Girls Don't Cry
Hillary S. Liber

The day the sun stopped shining I must have been four or five years old. It seems strange now, but the day actually started out nicely. The sky was blue and the sun was brilliant. Daddy was home, and my sister Rhonda and I were getting ready for Cheryl Mitnick's fifth birthday party. She lived just across the alley behind our house. That day we planned to go the long way around the block, since it was a special occasion and we'd be all dressed up.

I was wearing my crinoline and was ready for Mommy to help me put on my velvet party dress, so I wouldn't mess my hair. Daddy called me downstairs. He was standing in the arched entry to the kitchen. He said, "I have something to tell you. You should sit down on the sofa in the living room and listen." I was excited. Maybe he was going to take me over to the party.

"I need to say goodbye," he said. "I won't be here when you get back from your party."

"Are you going on a trip?" I asked.

He cleared his throat. "No, not exactly. I'm moving out."

My eyes popped wide open and my heart pounded so hard I couldn't hear the rest of what he said. Something about fighting with Mommy and they weren't getting along and things would be better this way. It was all just lies. He and Mommy didn't fight. They got along OK. And things would never be better without Daddy. Maybe he was just kidding. I put my hands over my ears and shook my head. It was not true.

Daddy walked over, knelt, and made me look into his eyes. "Please don't make this harder than it is already. Be a big girl and give me a hug and a kiss goodbye."

Then I knew it was true. The tears came in torrents and my body shook. Daddy held me for a few moments. Then he rose and stood back. "It's time to stop crying now. You must go to your party. Cheryl is expecting you. Be a big girl and take care of your little sister for me."

I didn't want to go to any party then. I wanted to stay and make Daddy change his mind. There must have been some way to change his mind. Like . . . like . . . if he didn't want me to cry any more, I would wipe away my tears. And I would never cry again, not for my whole life, if only he'd change his mind.

So I stopped crying. It didn't work. Daddy left that afternoon. Over the next few months, Daddy came every once in a while. I was young and my time perspective not good, so I couldn't tell honestly if every once in a while was every day, every week or every month. But it wasn't often enough. I wanted Daddy to live with us so I could see him every morning and every night.

I loved Daddy. He was tall, handsome, and a great dancer. During the daytime, he sold furniture at Fradkin Brothers, and during the evenings, he taught dance lessons at Arthur Murray. Sometimes, he would come home and eat his dinner at the dining room table, and I would still be there drinking my milk.

My mother bought into the 50's philosophy that milk, not bread, was the staff of life, and we had to drink four full glasses every day. I detested the taste. By dinnertime, when I was up to that fourth glass, the thought of one more swallow made me gag. I would put off drinking my milk, until I had finished every last bite of my dinner. By then the liquid was warm and sour, even more detestable. Mother would clear away my plate, but she'd instruct me not to leave the table until the glass was empty. Sometimes I could get my sister to drink it, but often I just sat at the table until Daddy came home. He'd usually get me a fresh glass of cold milk, or sometimes he'd even get me off the hook entirely.

Looking back, I realize I was stubborn about drinking milk because I knew that dawdling would buy private time with my beloved daddy. Sometimes when I drank my milk quickly and Daddy was in a good mood, he'd give me a dancing lesson. I would select one of the 78 speed records in his collection, something by Perry Como or Patti Page, and Daddy would place it on the record player in the cabinet. We'd hurry to get into proper ready position. When the music started, he'd twirl me around the living room, song after song, until Mommy made me get into my pajamas and go to bed.

I cherished those evenings with Daddy. I was four. I had my turquoise corduroy dancing skirt. And Daddy was the love of my life.

That's not to say that I don't have any bad memories of Daddy. I can remember arguments we had over whether my temperature should be taken rectally or orally. And I hated him with a passion whenever he and Mommy gave me enemas. But mostly I adored him, and I cherished the fun times we had as a family, especially on holidays. So when Daddy walked out the front door that day, the sky turned gray and the clouds blotted out the sun. Life, as I knew it, came to an end.

Daddy told me he was leaving because he and Mommy fought too much. But as far as I remember, the fights didn't begin until he left. And then the fights were awful. It got so bad that, as much as I missed Daddy and wanted him in my life, I dreaded his visits, because they always began and ended with nasty screaming matches between him and Mommy.

Before Daddy left, Mommy always said nice things about him. I was sure she really loved him just as I did. After he moved out, she said terrible things about him. She said he didn't care about us. She said he didn't really want to see us. He only came to visit because the court said he should. She said he didn't love us. In fact, she said he never had loved us.

I didn't want to believe Mommy. Of course Daddy loved us and wanted to see us. He came, didn't he? But she made it very unpleasant for him to visit by picking a fight with him every time he showed his face at the door. Sometimes the battle would begin even before Rhonda and I could get downstairs. We'd cower in the second floor hallway, hold each other, and pray for the yelling to stop. As soon as it did, we'd fly down the steps, because one time the argument ended with Daddy walking out the door without even seeing us.

As time passed, I couldn't argue with Mother any longer. First of all, Daddy stopped coming. It was hard to understand Mommy's claims that Daddy didn't want us when he obviously did want to see us. Then Mommy began telling us how our father had stopped paying the bills for the house and how we could not afford to live there anymore. Finally, we moved to Grandma and Grandpa Fribush's house.

Although I spent the first year of my life in my grandparents' home, my only memories are of our life in the house on Wesley Avenue near Powder Mill Lane. That life ended permanently and irreparably the day we moved to the third floor flat in my grandparents' three-family house on Gwynn Oak Avenue.

People think that the worst thing that happened to me on Gwynn Oak Avenue is that I was regularly molested by Mother's father, but that wasn't the worst thing. The worst thing that happened on Gwynn Oak Avenue is that, for all intents and purposes, Daddy's good and loving soul disappeared in my life and was replaced by an evil and nasty spirit I came to know as Stan Mermelstein. Stan had the same name and the same body as Daddy, but Stan was frightening and detestable. Every night when I said, "Now I lay me down to sleep," I asked God to protect me from Stan, to keep him from darkening my doorstep, and to keep him out of my life forever and ever.

In retrospect, I realize Daddy didn't become Stan overnight. It took days and weeks and months of constant brainwashing by Mother for me to accept that Daddy was gone for good. By then, I had also been forced to believe his leaving was truly "for good."

I was a bright little girl and, stubborn though I was, eventually I conceded that it was doing me no good to continue loving my father. I'd be spending the rest of my life with my mother, and she wanted me to hate my father. So to stay on her good side, to survive life with Mommy, I hated him. I hated him with a passion. And I convinced Rhonda to do the same thing.

To this day, I have no idea what terrible crime Stan Mermelstein committed. I have no clue as to why he loomed as the most dangerous and heinous person in the world. I do know that I was terrified of his presence, and that I had nightmares about him showing up at our apartment. I even developed temporary, hysterical blindness when I thought I might have to see him again.

I saw him only a few times after we moved to Gwynn Oak Avenue. Mommy didn't want him near us, and she made every baby-sitter promise not to let him in. Once or twice, or maybe even a few times, Grandma Fribush and Aunt Barbara would sneak him in. I was afraid to get near him, and I was terribly worried Mommy would come home and find him. If she did, I feared she would kill him and kill us. Being with Stan meant certain death, either from his evil or from Mommy's anger.

Mommy used to tell us to be careful whenever we went out. She said he was sneaking around trying to see us. It was hard to believe a father would have to sneak around neighbors' houses just so he could peek at his daughters, know what they looked like, and guess at whether or not they were all right. I saw him once at Pantry Pride on Liberty Heights near Gwynn Oak, and I ran home to Grandpa for protection. I've been told that he once hid in the backyard of a family friend's house to watch us when we visited her children.

Another time, after we'd been adopted and my third sister Marcella was born, I saw him standing at the perfume counter in the Reisterstown Plaza Hecht Company. Mommy was at the cash register in the infant department, and Rhonda and I were wandering around picking out a present for baby Marcella. We were probably only twenty yards from our mother, but at least sixty yards from Stan. Nevertheless, I was panic-stricken when I spied Stan. I dropped the dress I was showing Rhonda. I grabbed her hand, ran, and hid behind Mommy so Stan could not look at us with his evil eyes.

I never told my mother, and I made Rhonda promise not to tell. Because as dangerous as I believed Stan to be, I knew speaking his name in my mother's presence was more dangerous. Long ago Mommy made it crystal clear to us that, in her mind, Stan was dead and gone. We were to pretend he did not exist. We even had to pretend he had never existed. To her way of thinking, I guess you could say Rhonda and I were born the day Stan died. We did not exist prior to his departure. Therefore, we were never, and I mean never, to mention anything about our life on Wesley Avenue.

It took me nearly thirty years before I could whisper Stan's name and over a year of therapy before I could find enough courage to tell this story. I still find it difficult to speak about the first ten years of my life with even my closest friends. And I am overwhelmingly terrified to even try to discuss those years with my mother.

In all my growing-up years to maintain a semblance of familial tranquility, there were rules of behavior to be strictly followed. When my friends were rebelling and breaking their families' rules, I didn't dare violate the laws of my household. I sensed the imminent danger inherent in the potential upset of the fragile balance the rules maintained.

Of all the rules, the strongest was the Stan Taboo. "Stan was evil incarnate. Do not speak his name. Do not mention his existence. Do not acknowledge that there was life before he left. To do so could bring on the direst of consequences. Anyone breaking this taboo will be shunned, ostracized from the family, and considered to be as dead as Stan."

Hillary Selese Mermelstein actually survived a number of heart attacks and strokes before succumbing to life by the rules. A part of me died the day Daddy left, another part passed on the day I realized he'd stopped visiting, and another part surrendered the day I agreed to accept my mother's view of the world. Miraculously there was still a bit of me alive in the very private, secret hope that one day Daddy might return.

Eventually, Mother remarried and her new husband gave his name to Rhonda and me. He seemed like a nice enough guy. If I couldn't have my daddy, Dave would be a good substitute. It'd be a lot easier to have a daddy, any daddy, than be the only kid in school without one. So I went along with the new rules. We moved into a new house in the suburbs. We started to call Dave Daddy. And when we registered at the new school, we told the principal, Mrs. Ruth Gosnell, that our names were Hillary and Rhonda Jacobs. She didn't like that much, and she wanted to know if we'd been officially adopted, but our new daddy told her that we were his children and we'd be using his name.

It felt funny to write Jacobs instead of Mermelstein, although I admit it was easier to fit Jacobs on the name line of school papers, and my handwriting was so big and sloppy that I cherished the loss of five letters in my last name.

Nevertheless, it was a while before I responded when the name Jacobs was called during roll and it was a good thing my first name was unusual. When she called out, "Hillary Jacobs," I might have thought the teacher was referring to another Hillary.

During those first few months as Hillary Jacobs, the most confusing thing that happened was my tonsillectomy. I had just turned nine, and it had been a long time since I'd seen the Evil Stan. Sometime after I was sedated, Stan appeared in my hospital room. He gave me a bead craft kit with instructions to make an Indian bracelet or necklace. I really liked it, but I was afraid to say so. Even in my grogginess I knew I was supposed to hate him, to be afraid of him. I worried I might say something nice and offend Mommy or my new daddy.

Stan said he loved me and he would come to see me after the surgery. I asked him not to. I was scared and confused, and I could see Mommy and Daddy were upset. Whatever drug the nurse gave me made it hard to think straight. I saw Stan standing in the door when I awoke in a haze after surgery, but I don't think he ever again came close to me.

During the following year, I learned to forget all about my life before Mommy remarried. Sometimes I heard her and Daddy talking about legal things like custody and visitation. I didn't pay much attention because it didn't appear to affect my life. As far as I could tell, Stan was gone forever, and I'd never again have to deal with the confusion and discomfort I felt in that hospital room.

Then one day there was a problem at school. Apparently Stan had learned that we dropped his name. He was furious with Mrs. Gosnell. A lot of phone calls followed and Mommy and Daddy visited an attorney. After awhile, they sat down and talked with Rhonda and me. They said since Mommy was pregnant and we would have a sister or brother (we all hoped for a boy and we referred to the unborn child as Marco), it would be a good idea to officially change our name to Jacobs.

"Wouldn't we like it?"

We didn't really care one way or the other, but we knew the expected answer. Yes, of course, that's what we wanted.

They told us it would be very easy to do. There was only one little problem. Before the court would allow us to be officially adopted by Dave, we had to see a psychiatrist. That sounded big and scary, but Mommy reassured us he would just talk with us, ask us questions, and make sure we were happy.

We got the message—be happy!

We dressed in our best clothes and we went for a long car trip. After the car was parked, we entered a tall, stone building and rode an old-fashioned elevator to a fancy office with dark wood on the walls, lots of books on the shelves and a big leather sofa.

The psychiatrist was actually very nice and grandfatherly. He let us draw pictures. I hoped we drew the right thing. I drew a house with flowers and swings that seemed to please him, but I wasn't sure he liked Rhonda's drawings. I crossed my fingers and prayed she hadn't blown it. I didn't think I could bear it if this man said no. Mommy would be so upset with us.

Several weeks later, Mommy and Daddy told us what the judge had decided.

The psychiatrist said everything seemed to indicate we were happy about our new family and the potential adoption. He recommended we have one last visitation with Stan, before the judge made his final decision. The way Mommy told it was that the judge said we could be adopted, but we had to "go through an ordeal of trial by fire" before the papers would be signed—we would have to spend an entire day with the evil man himself.

Rhonda and I were horrified. We cried and cried and begged and pleaded. Couldn't they get the judge to change his mind? Were they sure we had to visit Stan? Couldn't he just come visit us in our house? Wasn't there some way out?

As far as I was concerned, adoption wasn't so important that we should have to endure an entire day with the scary monster, and that our parents were unreasonable to expect us to do that. Didn't they love us? How could they risk our lives by making us spend an entire day with the unmentionable man?

Eventually, I saw we had no choice. We would have to do as our parents instructed. I remembered what Stan said four years earlier, "Be a big girl and take care of your little sister." So I comforted Rhonda and assured her I would protect her and it would be all right.

The awful Sunday arrived. We got up, had breakfast (I guess we had breakfast, but I'm not really sure), and got dressed. I was pretty chubby and my shorts were really tight, but Mommy insisted that Rhonda and I wear matching outfits. So we did. The doorbell rang. We gulped. I'd seen movies where pirates made their captives walk the gangplank. Now I knew how those captives felt.

As we got into the car and drove off, I tried to make polite conversation. Stan asked, "What do you want to do?"

I was tempted to say, "Go home." Knowing that was not an option, I told him, "We'll do whatever you planned." I think we went to the zoo or a movie. We must have gone bowling too, because I ripped my shorts when I bent over. We went to Stan's tiny apartment. It had a pass-through window from the kitchen to the living room. I thought the window was neat, especially when Stan passed us pink caramel popcorn.

He gave me a pair of his shorts to wear, so I felt less embarrassed about being too fat for my pants. A friend of Stan's came and took pictures. In all, it was a fun day. By the time we had to leave, I'd decided Stan wasn't half-bad after all. Maybe Susie Sandler was right—we could have two Daddies just like she did. Rhonda and I had a private conference in Stan's bathroom. We agreed we'd like to see Stan again and give him another chance. Stan was delighted. And everything seemed just fine. That is until Stan dropped us off and we walked in the front door of our house. Mommy greeted us. She was standing with her hands on her hips. "Where did you get those shorts?"

"They're Stan's. I tore mine, so he lent me these."

She stood with her arms crossed on her chest. "And just how do you expect him to get them back?"

I looked up with wide-eyed innocence. "I'll give them to him the next time I see him."

I don't know what happened to those shorts, because the bloodcurdling scream from my mother's throat paralyzed me. She yelled something barely intelligible about how we were awful children and we'd broken her heart and Daddy's heart and we were killing her. She disappeared into her room, presumably to die, and slammed the door.

Now I chuckle when I think of it, but at the time, I wanted to die. That was the last day I allowed myself to be guided by my needs, wants, intuition, or thoughts. Left to my own devices I had committed the crime of the century. Surely, I would be sent to the electric chair or at least to prison for the rest of my life.

Daddy followed Mommy into their room. I knew what I had to do. I took Rhonda by the hand, stepped out the front door, and started walking up the street. Tears streamed down my face. I knew I would never see the brother my mother was carrying. I would never see my school friends. I would never return to my toys, or my room, or anything familiar. I knew with certainty we had to leave. Mommy and Dave would have a new life with their new baby. We had to let them have it because we were just an abomination in their life. We had the wrong last name and the wrong father, and we could never have a normal life like other people. We were silly to think we could. I had no idea where we were going, but I told Rhonda, "I'll figure something out."

First, we had to put as much distance as possible between us and 3118 Betlou James Place. Then we could rest and think of a solution. Briefly I considered going to Mark Janney's house. No one would look for us there, because he was a boy and his family was Methodist, not Jewish like everyone else we knew. But his house was set back off the street. We'd be out in the open too long before we reached his front door. Someone might see us. We were better off hiding under the trees on the other side of the street. Rhonda wanted to rest. I found a hidden spot and we sat down. (When I met Mark at my 25th high school reunion, I told him how I'd almost run away to his house. He told me I should have come. Apparently, his parents harbored numerous runaways during his childhood, and they would have welcomed us.) Ironically, my intuition still functioned that day, but as time went on, I became afraid to trust it.

Soon Dad came in the turquoise-blue station wagon. I tried to get Rhonda to duck down and hide, but he'd already spotted us. He pulled up, rolled down the window, and ordered us into the car. I was tempted to run, but I knew Rhonda was scared and I really could not reassure her. Reluctantly I got in the car. Secretly I vowed to escape later that evening.

He lectured about how awful we were, how we'd devastated my mother, how we were selfish and stupid, and how we'd made a mistake and we'd never be forgiven. I don't remember eating dinner that night. I don't remember going to bed. I don't even remember seeing my mother. I just remember crying, crying, and crying, and praying to God I would go to sleep and never wake up. The only escape I could see from the terrible, awful terror I felt was death. I hoped death would be painless. I hoped death would be quick. But mostly, I just hoped death would come before morning.

God ignored my prayers. Morning came. I was still painfully alive. I looked across the room. Rhonda was alive too. What should we do? Not only had I failed to die, but I'd also blown my opportunity to escape during the night. Now I was stuck having to live one more day with people who hated me. Furthermore, today was Monday, so Dave was undoubtedly at work, and we were home alone with our mother, who found us so horrible and disgusting she couldn't look at us or speak to us all evening.

I don't remember what we did. I don't remember if our mother came into our room, or if we went into the kitchen, or if we ever had breakfast. I remember vowing that if there was anything I could do to turn back the clock and make things right again, I would do it. (I mean anything, which is saying a lot for a child who'd been sexually molested and had previously decided to set limits to what she would do to please adults.)

In fact, I remember suggesting we do what Mother told me to do the day I came home from kindergarten and told her I didn't like her any more because she had dark hair and didn't look like my mother—we should just walk out the door, start all over, and pretend the previous entrance and events never happened. However, this time Mother did not like her own idea.

"We can not start all over. I will never forget what you did yesterday, and I will never forgive you."

Only slightly daunted, the new Hillary rose to the occasion and cut to the quick. "Just tell us what you want us to do and we'll do it."

"Call Stan and tell him you never want to see him again and you want to be adopted."

I gulped. That wasn't what I wanted, but it didn't seem like I had much choice. I didn't know exactly how I would pull off the lie, and I felt terrible about how deeply we would be hurting Stan, after leading him to believe we liked him. But I knew I had to do it. Rhonda took the upstairs phone and I went to the basement. My fingers shook as I dialed the number Mother gave me. The phone rang only once and was answered immediately. There was no turning back.

"Hello," my voice quavered. I cleared my throat. It's Hillary and Rhonda." How could I phrase it?

"I know it's you. Would you like to be adopted by Dave? Would you like me to sign the papers?"

I couldn't believe my ears. Stan knew the bind we were in and he was offering us a way out. My entire body sighed. "Yes," I whispered. Then I remembered. "Yes, please." I wanted him to know I was polite.

I think Rhonda said yes, too. And I remember saying thank you. And then I said goodbye. I said goodbye to Daddy. I never spoke with him again.

Born on the East Coast and educated in the Midwest, Hillary S. Liber is a survivor of sexual molestation and an ugly divorce and adoption. She has pursued successful careers in public education and private Jewish education, sales, administration, social work, and fundraising. At thirty-eight she experienced a barrage of chronic stress-related illnesses from diabetes to depression. These forced her to deal with her past. Through the love of her husband Jeff and their two sons Reuben and Seth and the support of numerous caring friends, as well as the guidance of dedicated professionals, she recovered and is recreating life for herself and her family. She writes, paints, crafts jewelry, and is committed to volunteer work to help others, especially Jewish adolescents and young adults, achieve their potential. For the past twenty years she has found peace and happiness in San Diego's Jewish community.

The Chosen One

from a vast world of others

I came into your life

born of one frustration to soothe another

unwanted and wanted at the same time

created for a purpose beyond my mother's breast

incubated in her chambers for your sake

and mine

no regrets

just wonder

at the way God works

a sense of appointment

fills my being.

timing too great

for mere chance.

Jill N. MacGregor

Jill Noblit MacGregor is a native of Florida. Her work has been published, performed, and awarded in poetry, children's literature, essay, stage production, and musical lyric. This anthology piece stems from a profound understanding of the gravity of being adopted in a different way—into the family of God, through Christ. To be *chosen* by someone, or God, is the highest privilege and honor a person can know. It's undeniably humbling, filling one with an inexpressible and overwhelming sense of acceptance.

Birthday

As you always do
the day before Christmas,
you open the scrapbook
to a familiar headline
in an old newspaper clipping—
"Baby Jane Doe, a newborn,
abandoned at local hospital."
Beneath the caption, a picture of her
with tiny fingers reaching out,
her mouth a bawling circle.
You pat the face on the page,
as though to quiet the infant,
as though to reassure her.
The story still overwhelms you—
snowy footprints that holiday eve,
the surprised nurse who found her
in a box inside the back door,
the note pinned to her blanket.
You linger over the details,
longing for the lost pieces
in the puzzle of a life
that began thirty years ago.
You close the scrapbook
but the same questions haunt you—
if you ever find your mother,
will she want to see you?
Who are you?
Why?

John Manesis

194

II. Orphan Train

Nurseries Children
A company of twenty seven children
from the New York Nurseries
will arrive on August 7, 1859,
in Noblesville, Indiana,
and be presented to farm families
that afternoon and evening.
These boys and girls,
none above the age of twelve,
have received training and instruction,
are worthy of good homes
and may be taken on a trial basis
for a period of four weeks.

If all the parties are satisfied,
these children will be indentured,
the girls until they are 18,
the boys until the age of 21.
They are then to receive
two sets of new clothes
and payment to the girls of $50,
to the boys $150.
All who are interested are asked
to meet at the Christian Church at 1PM.
>*Mr. J. Macy, agent,*
>*Children's Aid Society*

We changed trains five times
after leaving New York City—
a journey that took several days.
We passed through Binghamton,
Dunkirk, and Erie, then hugged the lakeshore
to Cleveland, angled south and west
through Galion before crossing the state line
at Union City on our way to Indianapolis.

The country opened up before us
like a book of dazzling photographs
that we had never seen before—
the cattle grazing on the rolling hills
and golden wheat leaning in the wind,
the farmers bent in their fields,
wildflowers in bloom beside the tracks,

abundant rivers, pristine streams
and everywhere the color green.

On a warm and sunny day
we finally arrived in Noblesville.
As the train pulled into the station,
we pressed against the window panes
to obtain a better look of families
that had traveled many miles,
from Westfield, Arcadia, Carmel
and other surrounding towns.

I remember the wagons and carts,
the horses whinnying, the throng
that parted as we stepped down
and filed behind the chaperones
to the hotel a few blocks away.
After a large meal, they escorted us
to the church and arranged
our group of "little wanderers"
according to height on a basement stage.

There we stood, in a strange place,
our hands and faces scrubbed,
dressed in our best clothes
and ready to be reviewed.
The farmers crowded around
and scrutinized each of us,
a few of them even reaching out
to squeeze a shoulder or arm
in order to determine which boys
were sturdy and muscular.

I prayed we all would be among
the chosen and so it came to pass—
no one was left behind that day,
none suffered the ignoble fate
of being sent to the next town
and perhaps the town after that.
Mr. Butler, whose gentle look
allayed my innermost fears,
selected me for his family.

How foolhardy it would be
to maintain that each enterprise
was destined for success.
In later years I was appraised

of overwork, neglect and abuse
some orphans were forced to endure.
However, I wish to assure
the public that the "placing out"
experience served most of us well.

We boys and girls became
a part of our communities,
productive citizens with good names.
John Brady, who rode the same train,
went on to be the Alaska Governor.
There was no greater blessing for me
than the Children's Aid Society
and I am indebted to its founder,
the Reverend Charles Loring Brace.

John Manesis

Excerpt from *The Journey of Andrew Burke,* John Manesis, ©1998. Reprinted here with permission of the author. Andrew Burke rode on one of the orphan trains to Indiana in 1859. At the age of twelve, he became a drummer boy in the Union Army. Eventually he became the second Governor of North Dakota. The author's research on the orphan trains revealed the story of Andrew Burke. He has taken an imagined voice of Andrew Burke to tell his story in a chapbook length narrative poem to appear in 1999 as part of the hardback *Orphan Train Riders' Stories,* Volume 5, a publication of the Orphan Train Heritage Society of America.

John Manesis is a retired physician. Since 1974, he and his wife, Bess, have lived in Fargo, North Dakota. They have four grown children. His poetry has appeared in eighteen publications, including *Midwest Poetry Review, California State Poetry Quarterly, Wisconsin Review, Mediphors, Zone 3, Loonfeather* and *North Coast Review*.

Median Range

to Aggie for her story about Nikki

We are measured from the time
we first suck life,
enter the context of humanity:
apgar scale, numbered one to ten
skin color, breath, pulse, reflex.
There is a median range for everything—
crawling
  walking
    talking
      dressing one's self
        answering questions.
My daughter hangs below median range.

You write about her:
construct a breathy fear,
agile voice that glistens on her chin.
Not satisfied, you write her a twin
who saves turtle embryos,
who understands incubation.
One who you think she must be,
the other only grasps vaporous potential wishes.
Neither of these is my daughter.

Writing about another is like
pushing a camel through the eye of a needle
and expecting it to retain its shape.

But you are right:
        there are two children here.
The second one I pulled from the metal bellied plane
(female, brown eyes, black hair, 22 months, 17 lbs. 6 oz, 26 inches).
The bonding's been a slow draw.
We build by ripping pieces from each other—
bits of spine, thigh bone, eye
and heart muscle
held together with cell jelly,
toothpicks and glue.
She rests beside me now,
her breath, holy and sweet
rises from her open mouth,
her nostrils, her eye's
visible soul.

The first child I see ephemeral winged.
Five years of plying her with
body heat, love words
and still she only trusts in flashes,
elusive as the ruby cry of jungle parrots.
Quicksilver sparks this child,
the child she must write herself.

Martha Marinara

Martha Marinara directs the Writing Program at the University of Central Florida in Orlando, where she lives with her youngest daughter Nikki. She writes poetry and fiction. Her work has appeared in *Forum, The Manhattan Poetry Review, Maryland Poetry Review, The California Quarterly, Negative Capability, WILLA,* and most recently in *Southern Poetry Review, South Carolina Review,* and *Birmingham Poetry Review*.

A Letter from Your Birth Mother
Mary Marsh

February, 1998

Dear Kady:

Twenty years ago, on the 12th of February, I gave birth to a beautiful baby girl. She was born on a cold, snowy night, at Sacred Heart Hospital in Spokane. I named her Rachel. Her birth was the most joyous thing that had ever happened to me. Afterwards I lay wide-awake in my hospital bed so full of joy and awe and thankfulness for her safe arrival. The nurses scolded me for not sleeping. They were quite cranky actually. But how could I sleep? To give birth is life-giving and life-changing. My heart experienced a depth of love it had never known before. This child's birth, your birth, was no less than a miracle to me. Because hospital rules were what they were, I was allowed to hold you for a few moments after you were born and then had to wait till the next morning to see and hold you again. I waited as patiently as I could, my heart overflowing. I have never forgotten it. All these years I have held onto the memory of that joy and each year since then I have celebrated the birth of my first-born child, and daughter, on the 12th of February.

Because I placed you for adoption, it was decreed by the powers that be, we could not know each other. It was believed that knowing the mother who gave you life was somehow a threat to the mother and father who would parent you. So you could not know how much I have loved you, how much I missed you, and how often I have asked how you are. You cannot imagine what it is like to have been made invisible in the life of a child one loved and birthed. It was never what I wanted. It was simply the way things were.

Twenty years have passed and the world changes. You have grown from a precious baby girl to a beautiful young woman. Now you must make the decisions to know the parts of your life swept into secrecy under the banner of "the best decision for the child." A secrecy I never wanted. So in this, the twentieth year, I write to you—instead of to a folder in a file cabinet at Catholic Family Services. More than anything, I want you to know that I would love to hear from you. You are not forgotten nor unwanted. There is a place of welcome here for you. I am not presuming to replace the family you have now. I only want you to know the family that made your family possible still counts you among its members, despite this separation. I want you to know there are other letters and gifts for you, held in safe keeping at Catholic Family Services. What has gone on these past years is recorded there. Please contact them. Your parents have in their safe keeping a letter I wrote to you in the weeks after you were born. They were to give it to you when they thought you were old enough to understand that life is not always black and white. Have you received it?

To hear from you would mean more than words can express. To tear down the walls of silence and secrecy that made you and I strangers would be an act of justice. It would be as well, an act of great compassion towards this hopeful and trembling heart. Please call or write soon.

All my love,
Your birth mother,
Mary Jean

The 20th Year

Now I stand
before your door—
a stranger—
someone gone so long
you have no memory
of our
time together.

I do not know
if I was ever spoken of
or how.
If I was described
as ancient history or threat,
as whore or saint.

I wonder if the years
of this journey
cling to my being
like dirt
to the refugee?

Does my hunger show?
Are the scars on my heart healed enough
or will they split open?
Will my voice be clear
or crack under the weight
of so much feeling?
Will my words be right?
Will my face be welcome?

I have longed
for this moment
yet fear seizes my heart.
I cannot know for certain
if my knock
will open
to joy and reconciliation,
or the beginning of more loss.

Once long ago
I listened to fear.
And my daughter was lost to me.

This time
I will not listen.
Standing
at the door of my
daughter's heart,

I knock.

Mary J. Marsh
February 1998

Mary Marsh is a Seattle native. She relinquished a daughter born in 1978, while she was a college student. Ms. Marsh completed her B.S.N. in nursing in 1980, served as Jesuit Volunteer in Franklin, Louisiana, for two years, and is a founding mother of Birth Mother's Day. She is married, lives in Chehalis, Washington, and has a second daughter. Her reunion with her first daughter is on-going and has been a source of great joy for both. She continues to work as a hospital nurse, parent, poet, gardener, and community volunteer.

Waiting to Adopt

When you're waiting to adopt, everything becomes a sign.
Lynn Berg

No stomach-plummeting
heart-in-the-throat sensation
records my rises and falls
through Neville Hall.
Doors struggle closed
with coffin-lid finality.
Having chosen convenience,
I sweat, fearing eternal suspension
between two floors.
This is my future:
locked inside four walls
terrifying as a blank page
or a snow-covered Nebraska field,
a memory of squinting, without sunglasses
at slivers of splinters
of expanses of white
white as my eye-whites, inescapable
dizzying dazzling flashes
of sun on snow on snow
nothing but nothing darting and glinting.

But no: I will be calm,
as if, hanging in this balance,
I become my own daughter
who takes comfort in confined spaces
as she sprouts buds,
awaits fingers and toes,
frowns and fists and swallows,
the snow-blind panic of light.
I wait for what
I cannot take for granted,
the little miracle that portends all others,
a slow, creaking parting of doors.

Nancy McCabe

Nancy McCabe is originally from Kansas. Three years ago she moved to the South. Her work has appeared or is forthcoming in *Prairie Schooner, Massachusetts Review, Earth's Daughters,* and *Writer's Digest.* Her teachers' handbook, *Making Poems: Writing Exercises for the Classroom,* was published in 1988 by the University of Arkansas. She is a single mother who brought her daughter Sophie home from China in the spring of 1999.

Letter to My Daughters—Gardens

Even though the plants are only a foot tall,
you, our sixteen-year-old baby, dream them ripe
with fruit, the tomatoes scarlet in their fullness.
And you come flushed from sleep to tell this wealth,
how each night you root through rich soil
to reap the harvest of your first garden.
Nineteen years ago we dreamed your sister,
the child not of our own mating, although we tried,
who came to us, all rosy, at seven weeks
and slept cribbed in the room below ours.
Three times in those first days
we woke at night, eyes blind like moles'
against the lamplight, and groped the sheets,
palms flailing in the empty space between us.
We meant to find her when she cried, to make
her in that space of barren bed
our child, the fruit of love and holding,
before we opened to each other and the space
between us suddenly remembered empty, before we fled
the stair and soothed the dream
and counted soil for what it was
and took the harvest and felt lucky.

Judith Minty

"Letter to My Daughters—Gardens" was originally published under the title "Letters to My Daughters #10" in *Dancing the Fault*. Florida: University Press of Florida. 1991. It is reprinted here with permission of the author and the publisher.

Judith Minty lives in the woods in Michigan. She is the author of four full-length collections of poetry and three chapbooks. Her first book, *Lake Songs and Other Fears,* was recipient of the United States Award of the International Poetry Forum in 1973. She recently received the Mark Twain Award for Outstanding Contributions to Midwestern Literature. She and her husband have three children.

Standing in the Shadows
Eliza Monroe

I never thought I would be a farmer, especially when I had my son Kyle. Now I am and today I find myself doing a different kind of farming—putting seeds out there in the world, more like mining than farming, still lots of digging to find Kyle again after nine years. I have dirt under my nails, and my truck is double-parked outside. I'm farming a list and halfway through the A's. A woman in Los Angles told me over the phone how to find my son, but she made me promise to keep her method to myself. "There are groups," she said, "who don't believe birth mothers should have access to their children and are working to cut off all sources of information."

I can't think of Kyle without crying. And I think of him almost every day. I picture him at each stage of growth, even as an adult, though he just turned ten. Mostly I miss not holding him enough as a baby—soft skin against my arms, a giggle surfacing and rising like a bubble from his mouth to mine.

My first husband Martin and I were living in a condo in Modesto the day John Lennon was shot. We were depressed and broke our pact of seven years to never bring children into this world. All at once it seemed maybe the earth needed our child. Though Martin had a violent temper and no job, two characteristics which seemed to feed off each other, somehow we believed a baby could change him. Conceiving Kyle was a last ditch effort to save Martin, if not the universe.

The lab called me at work with the pregnancy test results. At first I felt awe at carrying life then fear about bringing up my child in less than ideal conditions. I stood in the salmon bathroom stall in the basement of my office building, the only place on earth where I had privacy and apologized in advance. I was the only one working, and role reversals were frowned upon in the Mormon Church. We were struggling to keep our membership. I don't know if Martin still struggles.

"I can't entirely blame the Church." Martin was already twisted when he was converted, fresh out of juvenile hall, and at a fireside where he ate cookies baked by fiercely optimistic virgins. And if it hadn't been for my meeting him at that fireside, I'd probably still be one of those virgins.

When I was pregnant and Martin was too nervous to go to school or get a job, one of his short-range goals became overseeing the production of the world's perfect baby. He spent his days preparing the perfect food, sushi. After work I swallowed big chunks of raw squid and tuna piled on rice or wrapped with seaweed.

I felt responsible for maintaining a buffer between the world and my baby's umbilical fluid. I didn't want to scare the fetus off before it gave us a chance to be parents. Inside me Kyle grew slowly, as if he knew what he was getting into but was coming anyway.

Martin's other short-range goal became coaching the world's smoothest delivery. He said a woman's pregnant state was just an extension of her non-pregnant state. The vast majority of pregnancy-related problems were psychosomatic.

Too scared to make him a liar, I tried to be a living confirmation of his statement. Besides, I still expected childbirth to be easy. "My mother easily gave birth eight times." My sisters all had numerous and effortless deliveries. More than one of my thirty-odd nieces and nephews were born with their mothers having no labor at all. I had no reason to believe I would be different. It was my heritage if not my religion.

Martin's only long-range goal was to stay home and care for the baby while I worked. We'd considered going on welfare, another non-Mormon concept, but I said, "I'd rather take the salary and benefits that come along with keeping my job."

I wouldn't mind leaving the baby with Martin. He hadn't hit me in two years, and most of the time he seemed satisfied about house-husbanding. The baby and I both needed Martin to decide on something. If house-husbanding was it, Kyle and I would work around it.

Round and waddling, I was content to come home to Martin on his good days. After all the times I'd seen him fail, it was refreshing to see him do something well safe inside our immaculate refuge, which he referred to as his cell. Sometimes he seemed to accept his role wholeheartedly and, I thought, courageously. Modesto was a conservative town and role reversal was hard to swallow. But I was proud of Martin. He was finally looking at what he could do instead of what he couldn't do. He was beginning to sound like a liberated, sophisticated, educated, American male but not all the time. Sometimes he looked up from the kitchen sink or above a pile of clothes he was folding and came up with ideas on how he could become the breadwinner.

The due date came. On September 17, the office gave me a baby shower then sent me home. I sat and waited. No money was coming in so we had garage sales. I sold the tiny, lavender earrings my father brought me from Cincinnati when I was a child. I sold the turquoise ring that had belonged to my great-grandmother. I even sold the baby presents from my shower.

I'd been working Monday through Friday, nine-to-five ever since Martin and I met, and for the first time we spent an entire month together. In between garage sales, we went to our Lamaze class and to movies, but all we talked about was money. I wouldn't receive disability checks until the baby came. He took me for brisk walks and bumpy rides to induce labor but the baby wouldn't budge. I wondered how long my pregnancy would last. Every day went by in slow motion. After carrying the baby a full ten months, I felt the first contractions.

During the evening of October 18, I realized I was in labor. By eleven, the contractions gnawed three minutes apart. I felt uneasy and hoped the worst was almost over. Everyone at work said that since my pregnancy was so easy my labor and delivery would be too. I believed them. Martin just plain demanded it. In our Lamaze class, we heard stories of women in labor cussing out their coaches. Martin warned me to control my tongue—mind over body. "Remember," he said, "there is no excuse for lashing out, regardless of your physical condition."

At one in the morning, he drove me to the hospital. My contractions gripped, then released. The doctor on staff told me to go home because I had not dilated yet. He doubted I really was in labor. But Martin was convinced that I was and he didn't take me home. We walked up and down the dark hospital halls, careful not to slip on freshly mopped tile floors, which smelled of antiseptic. I couldn't walk through the contractions anymore, but with Martin's help I hobbled between them. I still wasn't dilated, but finally I was admitted to Labor and Delivery.

Martin held my hand and blew with me. If blowing and preparedness meant anything, we'd have been in and out in forty-five minutes. But after twenty-four hours, natural childbirth was no longer an option. I looked at Martin. I hadn't even wanted to scream at him. I expected him to get irate long before and demand forceps, surgery, drugs, but he just stood by me. He was a quiet blur of patience and understanding.

He didn't even put up a fuss when we parted at the elevator, and at first I didn't want to be separated from him. I contracted and exhaled in the operating room, as I waited alone for the anesthesiologist. Even then, what saved me was the image of Martin blowing in my face. But after the anesthesia entered my body, relief registered in my brain and I was glad to be without Martin.

I felt no more contractions. At first, I felt nothing at all, except my body landing on the table when the doctors moved me. Then over the next seven minutes, I felt slight pressure as they unjammed my son's head from between my bones and pulled him out through an incision in my belly. He let out a low bellow. From a distance I could see his long, lean, healthy body and the tears in the anesthesiologist's eyes as she blotted my brow.

I envisioned a companion for Martin, a kitchen helper standing on a wooden stool, chopping celery while I was away at work. I began to cry. Then someone held him up close to me and I saw no one but myself in him. I was glad that Martin hadn't been included in this moment.

I was out of the hospital in five days and back on my feet in ten. My doctor gave me an extra couple of weeks on disability because of the surgery. And though the checks started coming again, Martin asked me to go back to work early. I didn't want to stay home unwanted, but I certainly wasn't going back to work sooner than I had to, yet I had no place else to go. So I stayed on stage without a role to play. Martin took over caring for the baby and the house. I could see what a good father he wanted to be and how he needed me to stand in the shadows.

I was afraid of what would happen to his soul if he failed one more time but I was not afraid of my own self-denial. I took a deep breath and garnered a strange brand of courage, not the down-and-dirty, stand-up-and-fight, recognizable-as-such brand that makes heroes, but the brand that to me now resembles cowardice. Other than pumping my breasts and freezing bottles of milk, I seemed to do nothing but crowd Martin's dark cell, and I was lonely for the light.

I rarely held or suckled the baby. When I did, it was from a distance as if I didn't have the right. I bathed or changed him only if Martin needed a break. Martin said that since he was going to be the house-husband, we might as well practice our roles now to make it easier for him and Kyle when I finally did go back to work. He added, "It will be easier on you too, Sonja. Then you won't get used to being home and taking over the mothering role. I'm already afraid of being an inadequate father. I don't need you around to steal any rewards that should be coming to me."

I had been as little bother as possible. All through the pregnancy, I had never been sick. I never got grouchy or deprived Martin of his sexual release. I never really lost my figure, and I never got stretch marks. And Kyle did his part too. He was an easy, quiet baby. He never fussed, and he slept all night. I still had to get up and pump at one o'clock every morning. Breastfeeding was the one thing I wouldn't give up, and I didn't always have enough energy to make love to Martin when he wanted it. One night after I'd been back to work two or three weeks and was very tired, I fell asleep right next to him, though I knew he was horny, uptight, and his reaction would be far from favorable. I woke up in the living room with the wind knocked out of me.

"Oh, I'm sorry, Sonja. I meant to just tap you on the thigh. It's dark in here. I didn't mean to get you in the solar plexus."

I was so tired that I just climbed back into bed and fell asleep again. Now that we had a baby watching, I figured Martin wouldn't do anything. But just as I was dozing off, he threw me out of bed along with a pillow and blanket. I put my head on the pillow again. Pow! I woke up to punches against my thigh and back. I was still curled up and coiled tighter while he hit me. I accidentally jerked my knee into my eye. Martin had finally gotten my attention. I was wide-awake. He went for ice.

"Oh shit, now you're going to have a black eye tomorrow at work." He applied the icepack, trying to get the swelling down before it started. "They're going to think I hit you in the eye and I didn't."

I spent the rest of the night listening to Martin devise an excuse for me to tell my co-workers the next day. By morning my eye was quite bruised, but I had my story straight. We were playing softball with another couple in the parking lot. I missed the catch and got hit in the eye with the ball.

When I came home that evening, he said I wasn't producing enough milk. I knew I was. I figured his real objection was not having my breasts attached to his body. He suggested that we start using formula. I was surprised he dropped it when I said, "No."

A few days later, Martin was bathing the baby and he raised his hand to slap Kyle for crying. I lurched forward. "Don't you ever come between me and the baby," he said. I backed off. After that I sat helplessly on my hands on the living room couch and listened to Kyle scream. Eventually he slept and Martin and I made love quietly in the darkness with the window open and a winter chill soothing our hollow bodies. After he came, he let me hold him completely and all night long the way I wish I could have held Kyle. Then he said, "I can't trust myself around the baby anymore." His large, hot tears rolled down my forearm as I wiped his eyes.

In the morning, he asked me to find a babysitter. I looked but I couldn't find one. During the next two weeks, he started leaving the baby home alone for a few minutes here and there, then for half-an-hour, then an hour. Once he left the baby unattended in his truck, then he called me at work. "I can't handle this fucking baby, Sonja."

I rushed home. When I got there, he said, "No violence ever happens when you're away. I want you to know that, Sonja. It only happens when you're home, because I know you're watching."

The following Monday night he yelled at Kyle again. I sat on my hands in the living room and grieved. Martin came out of the bedroom. "Sonja, I like the idea of having a son, but I'm not ready to be a father. And I won't allow you to raise him without me. We can't keep Kyle. I'm sorry."

I didn't whine or cry or patronize him. I didn't try to talk him out of it. I just grabbed his offer to let the baby go, hoping Kyle would be out of danger before Martin changed his mind.

The next morning I called L.D.S. Social Services, the Mormon adoption agency, and stated my case without mentioning violence. I talked only about Martin not being mature enough to care for the baby and my wanting the baby out of the house immediately. The agency was booked for interviews. When I said that the safety of the baby was at stake, the social worker agreed to stay late and interview us that night. He gave us the option of putting Kyle in a foster home for six or nine months, until Martin got a job and therapy. Martin said, "No. I don't want my son bounced around from foster home to foster home waiting for his father to get his act together. I want to break the chain right now."

I wanted the baby gone, safe, permanently away from his father and from my inability to protect. That evening Martin and I signed relinquishment papers—the thing that makes birth parents inhuman, incomprehensible, separate from the rest of society, and rightly so. I had to stop breast-feeding cold turkey. I slithered in pain, applied ice and took hot baths. Nothing seemed to help.

The agency didn't have any trouble finding a permanent home for Kyle. They chose a Mormon family in northern California with coloring, body types, and genealogy matching us perfectly. The father was a twenty-nine-year-old architect in business for himself and made good money even in the middle of the recession. The mother, also twenty-nine, was an artsy-craftsy homemaker. They had adopted an infant girl five years earlier. For two-and-a-half years they'd been calling the agency every week asking for a boy. Now their prayer had been answered. Their family was complete.

Martin and I said we felt happiness for Kyle and his new parents. We said we were also happy for ourselves to be rid of the child that perhaps we never should have had.

Martin was sure that no one would accept what we'd done. He told the neighbors the baby was in LA with his grandmother. The people I worked with assumed he was still at home with Martin and asked questions accordingly, until I finally broke down and said, "He's no longer with us." Word got around that the baby was dead and people stopped asking questions.

The social worker said a change of scene might help. I put in for a transfer to Sacramento and took the rest of February off to wait. Martin sold our furniture so we could move easier. Too ashamed to come out in daylight, we spent three weeks together in our empty condo and waited for a transfer. It never came.

In March I went back to work. Life went on. The pressure was off, but by the first of April Martin wanted the baby back. I felt as if I was living a reoccurring nightmare. I'd given up everything for Martin. The baby was gone. We'd let him go to a better life. Now Martin wanted him back. Hating myself as I lied to the attorney, I stood by Martin. The truth was I no longer wanted the baby. He belonged to some other people now. He had a different name, a different home, a big sister. I didn't want more problems. It was time to get on with life.

The attorney compared us with the adoptive parents and told us that it would be up to the judge, but the adoptive parents looked awfully good and would probably win. So we didn't pursue it. Martin finally realized he had to let go. I was tired and disgusted with myself then relieved. It was getting late and we couldn't very well try again to get him back.

By May a lot of the stress had blown over. We were stuck in Modesto and decided to buy new furniture. Martin signed up for a full class load. I enrolled in a management training program at work and enjoyed the recognition. I'd toned up and I could feel other men noticing me. During my long bus ride home every night, I cried behind my new sunglasses. I wished Martin would die. I hated myself for not having the guts to leave him. When I'd get home, he was always there—perfectly healthy.

Then I'd have to get into it. When we made love, I covered the reality of him with an opaque sheet of fantasy. I made up old boyfriends that I never had. I'd let them stroke my arm tenderly. It's not like I would leave him, I thought. But I did leave. That was nine and a half years ago. Though I've remarried, I have no other children. They couldn't replace Kyle. I knew.

As I stand here checking names and with the motor running, I know now I could have left with Kyle. I could have escaped, changed our names, managed as a single parent, until I found the man I later married and we made a life together on his farm. I could have kept my baby. I didn't know it then.

I've wondered if I'm healed enough to care for another child. I've considered adopting a baby and naming it Joaquin, whether it is a boy or girl, after this valley that has given me back my life. But adopted babies don't come from agencies, they come from mothers. I would always wonder about Joaquin's. I also wonder about the woman raising my son, but it doesn't stop me from continuing my search. Even on the most dismal days when I have nothing else to look forward to, I have the hope I will find him and he will accept me, not for what I was, but for who I am now.

"Standing in the Shadows" will also appear in *Ghost at Heart's Edge,* North Atlantic Press, 1999.

Eliza Monroe holds a Master of Arts in Creative Writing from Antioch University. Her stories have appeared in *Amelia, American Writing, Onion River Review, Pacific Coast Journal, Palo Alto Review, Rough Draft, Salt Hill Journal, SlugFest Ltd., Sonoma Mandala, Widener Review* and *Writers of the Desert Sage.* Her story "On the Inside" was anthologized in *Our Mothers Our Selves—Writers and Poets Celebrating Motherhood.* Ms. Monroe is a finalist for the 1999 Pushcart Prize. She won third place in the 1997 Salt Hill Journal Fiction Competition, Honorable Mentions from New Voices, New Letters and Asheville Writers'  Workshop competitions. She was a finalist in the Hayek, Chesterfield Film Company, Pen Syndicated Film Project, and Treasure House fiction competitions and won an Honorable Mention in the Dana Award in the Novel. In 1998 an audio version of her story "Clucking Them Home" was produced by Syracuse University.

Suzy
Barbara Moore

The *Detroit News* used to have a column called "A Child is Waiting" written by Ruth Carlton. On August 17, 1975, Ms. Carlton wrote about a little girl in an adoption agency that specialized in physically challenged children. Here are some excerpts from the article:

"Suzy is the princess of the hospital ward—a gay, flirtatious four-year-old who has something to say to everyone and enjoys making people laugh. In a children's convalescent ward where everyone else comes for a short stay and returns home, Suzy is the old settler. The hospital is Suzy's home. She's lived here all her four years. She was born with abnormalities. Suzy also was born with club feet . . . and sleeps in a brace."

Suzy has been my niece since 1976. Some years ago, I helped her write a letter to the *Detroit News* and Ms. Carlton to tell them what their article had meant to her life. Here is that letter:

June 13, 1990

Dear Editor,

I am "Suzy" in this 1975 *Detroit News* article. My real name is Barbara Ann Moore. I'm 19 now and just graduated from Centennial High School in Columbia, Maryland. My aunt and I were looking at old photo albums and souvenirs of my childhood and found this *Detroit News* article. I wanted to write and tell you this article is the reason I am here now in this place and with this family.

On August 17, 1975, a woman in Detroit read this article about Suzy, clipped it out, and gave it to her friend, Jackie Moore. Jackie had adopted a little boy, Shannon, in 1972, from Catholic Social Services in Detroit and now wanted to adopt a daughter. She was having a hard time because she was single and the adoption agencies preferred married couples. When Jackie read the article, she called right away for an interview. Six months and mountains of paperwork later, I was flown from South Carolina to Detroit to join the Moore family.

I don't remember that first year in Detroit. My mom says I had a South Carolina accent and no one could understand me. I couldn't understand those Yankees, either! I had never lived in a house so ordinary things like the refrigerator were strange to me. They tell me I would open the big door and stand staring at the racks of food while cold air blew over me. I wasn't hungry. I was amazed. I wanted to go everywhere. The first thing I said in the morning was, "Where are we going today, Mom?" and the last thing I said at night was, "Where are we going tomorrow, Mom?" Trips to the grocery store and the dime store were as exciting to me as Disney Land would be to other kids. The zoo was my favorite place. I loved animals and still do. I have a dog, two cats, a rabbit and a parrot, not to mention all the gerbils, hamsters, guinea pigs and gold fish that have come and gone.

When I was seven, my mom, brother and I moved to Columbia, Maryland. I went to school, joined Girls Scouts and sold cookies, and went to day care centers after school because my mom worked full time as a Pediatric Nurse Practitioner. I rode my bike, learned to swim, went to summer camps, and participated in competitive horse back riding.

As the article about Suzy says, my feet and legs were not formed properly for walking. Doctors from the University of Maryland and Kernans Hospital tried everything to straighten out my legs so I could walk. I had four operations. Most of the time one leg or the other was in a cast. Finally when I was thirteen, they said they couldn't fix my legs. I have used crutches and a wheel chair ever since. My other physical challenges remain and have caused me some painful problems but I have recovered from each operation and try to live as normal a life as I can.

At our graduation ceremony, I walked across the stage on my crutches to receive my diploma. It was a great moment! I've had wonderful teachers and counselors and my mom to help me through some hard times growing up. Sometimes I think about the things I can't do and it makes me angry and sad, but I realize that the world is accommodating itself more and more to allow disabled persons to do all that we can do, and we can do a lot.

I wanted to share this with you and thank you for printing Ruth Carlton's article fifteen years ago. Because of that, I got a family, a normal childhood, and have a future full of potential.

Sincerely yours,
Barbara "Suzy" Moore

Formula For Success
Rose Morand

When Karl and I first adopted our infant daughter Grace, I joked to friends about wanting a bumper sticker that would read "I'd Rather Be Breast-feeding." We'd laugh, but inside I could feel myself wince a little. When you're unable to breast-feed, when you're not given the choice, the idea of actually providing your baby life-giving milk from your body seems a thing of miracles.

Back when we were trying hard to get pregnant—timing cycles, visiting doctors, and injecting my aching backside with fertility drugs—I often focused my thoughts on what it would be like to breast-feed. Karl would bring our little bundle to me in the deep, starry night, and I would hunker down under the blankets to stroke the silken head as the baby drank.

Instead, after the adoption, we found ourselves shivering as we stumbled across frigid linoleum to measure, dilute and heat bottles of formula poured from a can. We were equal partners with equal responsibility for feeding our new daughter, and my breasts held no more significance for the baby than Karl's did.

I still carry in my mind an abundance of breast-feeding wisdom gathered during the waiting years and, along with it, occasional sadness. In *Your Baby and Child,* a book I studied in preparation for parenthood, Dr. Penelope Leach writes, "Breast-feeding brings the two of you as close as it is possible for a mother and baby to get . . ." *Wince.*

Television commercials for formula constantly blared, "Of course, breast milk is best, but if you use a formula " How could I escape feeling that somehow I wouldn't be able to do all I could for my child when even the people selling the stuff say it isn't as good?

My sister, a member of La Leché League, once asked me to consider that maybe I could breast-feed after all. "Other adoptive mothers do it," she said, adjusting her son Bruce as he nursed. "It takes a lot of work and patience but it can be done. You start while you're still waiting, then you're ready when the baby comes."

"What if we don't get a baby for a long time, or never?" I asked, watching the easy exchange between mother and child and marveling at Bruce's utter contentment. "Can you see me expressing milk every single day for five years just in case?" She was silent and, I could tell, sad for me.

As it happened, we had six days' notice that Grace was coming. She had been born five weeks earlier and was living with a foster family. Quick as a phone call, we had to burst into action with a long list of tasks before us. We had to go to the adoption agency for background information about the birth parents, call our families and friends, give a final cleaning to the nursery that had, thank goodness, already been decorated, then see the baby for the first time at the foster family's home.

On the morning we met Grace, the foster parents, Harry and Linda, let us hold her while they described how she liked country music and cooed when Harry talked like Donald Duck. I looked at this baby, this stranger. Her long fingers, reddish-brown hair and sanguine complexion were not at all what I'd pictured. I wondered if this child really, finally could be mine. It didn't seem possible, and I half-prepared for someone to burst in and tell us that it was a mistake, that she was someone else's after all.

At my suggestion—I was still so nervous—Karl held Grace first. As he cradled her on the family room couch, Linda motioned for me to follow her into the kitchen. She moved quickly from refrigerator to sink to stove as she showed me how to prepare a bottle of formula. "There's a lot to look out for when you do this," she warned. "Too watery, and the baby doesn't get enough nutrition. Not enough water, and she develops too much mucus. Oh, and you have to sterilize the nipples," she added. I nodded as I furiously scribbled the instructions in a notebook. Then I watched as she tested the temperature of the warmed formula on her arm.

The bottle read, Linda invited me back into the family room and to an easy chair. Karl stood carefully and brought the sleeping Grace to me as I sat down. I squirmed a little, feeling that it was very important to get adjusted just so. I finally settled with my elbow resting on the arm of the chair to support the baby's head. Karl placed Grace in my arms. Linda handed me the bottle, then she and Harry went into another room to give Karl and me some time alone with Grace.

I watched her sleeping face for a few seconds, trying to memorize the moment. Impossible! My heart was pounding too hard to concentrate. Slowly, I brought the bottle toward Grace's tiny rosebud of a mouth. A drop of formula touched her bottom lip, and she stirred. Her eyes fluttered open briefly, and I worried that the only thing I might accomplish would be waking her up. What if she cried? What if she could sense that I was not good at this, that it wasn't natural?

Then, in one sudden movement, she opened her mouth like a baby bird and reached hungrily for the nipple. I watched her carefully, waiting for her to discover the imposter and howl, but instead her enthusiasm settled into a strong rhythmic pull and her breathing alternated with little grunting sounds as she swallowed.

I sat back. I breathed in deeply, held the air, then let it out slowly. I looked up at Karl, who smiled. His eyes shined with wonder and love and a kind of light that had never been there before.

I smiled, too, and looked back at Grace. Suddenly, this felt good. It felt right. I felt like a mom.

Rose Morand is a freelance writer living in Brighton, Michigan, with her daughter, Grace, now five, and her husband, Karl. She graduated from the University of Michigan and works as an advertising copywriter. Morand has published essays in *The Baby Connection,* and the Detroit Free Press and, most recently, a short story in the literary journal The MacGuffin. "Formula for Success" appeared in *The Baby Connection News Journal.*

Journey Home
Jill Ann Mortell

I wake with a knot in my stomach and my heart palpitating. I reach over and touch my sleeping husband's shoulder. His warmth is comforting. For a moment, I know I will be all right. I watch the light on the window shade turn gray then yellow, as the sun rises. I think about the day ahead and begin to cry. My sniffling wakes David. He holds me tightly, "You'll be okay."

"I know I will. I've just waited so long, wanted this so much. I used to think this would happen in heaven, but I'm getting the chance now. I'm so scared." I sit up in bed and say out loud, "Today is Saturday, July 13, 1996. I am thirty-eight and I am going to meet my mother for the first time."

My knobby six-year-old legs dangle from the side of my mother's bed. I watch her back. She leans toward the mirror to apply makeup. "You were a very special baby," she says without turning around, "because we chose you. The couple that had you couldn't keep you. Your daddy and I wanted a baby very much, so we asked them if we could have you. We were so excited when we got the call telling us you were born. Then, when you were six days old, you came to live with us. You see?"

I sit on my hands and nod. In my head, her story doesn't add up. They didn't choose me. They arranged to adopt me before I was born. They chose some baby they didn't know and only because they couldn't have their own. That doesn't sound very special. I wonder why my mother is lying to me, why if I'm so special, my real parents didn't keep me? I stare at my feet and bang my heels rhythmically against the side of the bed.

I put on my blue-denim skirt and the "Sisters" T-shirt my birth sister Kate sent. My birth sisters Irene and Kate will be wearing the same shirt, when I see them for the first time at the airport in Binghamton. I love being included this way, being a part of something. This is new for me. All my life I have felt like an outsider. As I dress, I shake. My palms sweat. I look at myself in the mirror. I am surprised when I see myself. I ask my husband six times, "How do I look?" I want to be pretty. I want them to love me.

I'm eight and at my grandmother's house. I'm fighting with my cousin Lizzy, two years younger than I. We are jumping on grandma's bed. Lizzy says, "You're dumb to play with Barbie dolls. You're a poopie head." I lunge at her, pushing her off the bed. She lands in a heap on the floor. "Mommy," she yells, "Jill pushed me and hurt me." My Aunt Elsie runs in from the other room, grabs me by my arm, twists so hard I feel it burn. "What's the matter with you? You're just a trouble-maker, that's what you are. Just a bad seed. Where'd they get you anyway?" She picks up Lizzy and carries her from the room. I tell myself I will not cry.

At night I'm afraid of the dark. I plead with my mother, "Don't leave me alone." I refuse to close my eyes, to go to sleep. My mother gives me a radio for company. I find a call-in talk show. I like listening to the people's voices. The show is "Party Line" hosted by Ed and Wendy King. Every night for years Wendy King's high, sweet voice, with a touch of southern twang soothes me, makes me feel less alone.

On the way to the airport, we are quiet. David holds my hand. When we get to our gate, I sit in one of the brightly-colored plastic chairs. I feel as if I'm in the doctor's office waiting for a shot. At intervals, I cry. People around me seem to be trying not to look at me. I want to jump up and say, "This is the most important day of my life. I am meeting my mother today." Instead, I just look away. With my left hand I press my fingers to my lips and with my other hand alternately dab my eyes and shred Kleenex.

I am twenty-eight and very pregnant with twins—the result of fertility drugs. I find my infertility confounding. I always thought I would have no problem getting pregnant. After all, my mother had me by mistake. I lie in bed and watch the lump of a tiny elbow move across my naked abdomen. Someone is rolling over. I wonder how anyone could give up a child that has been a part of them like this.

I adore the smell of my baby girls Amanda and Kate. When I feed them, I hold them close under my nose and breath in the smell from the tops of their heads. I wonder what they think of my smell. I remember how I always hated the smell of my adoptive mother. Like an animal, I could tell by her scent that she was not mine, I was not hers. I think about the book read to me when I was little— "Are You My Mother." It always made me cry.

In the air, I cannot concentrate on the book I brought. I stare out the window at the thick, gray clouds. I cry. I shred Kleenex.

I am thirty-one. The social worker calls. I think maybe it's the news I've been waiting for. She says, "I've hit a dead end. I will have to close your case." I tell her, "I don't understand. It's been two years, since we started this. Why is it so hard? The county appointed you to help me find my parents and the county knows who my parents are. The county has the records. Why don't they just show you the records?"

She says, "The records are sealed. This is the way it's done. I'm very sorry."

I am on the phone with a man from the New York State Bureau of Vital Statistics. "I am researching my family tree and I am trying to obtain a marriage certificate for a woman named Sandra, who married a distant relative of mine named Stashinski." It is illegal for me to be an adoptee looking for my family.

He says, "All vital statistics in New York State are confidential unless you can prove you are next of kin, or unless the person you are looking up has been dead for at least fifty years."

In the past six months, I have committed several crimes—wire fraud, mail fraud, forgery, lying to a government official. Who knows what else? Still I have little to go on. All I want is to know who I am and no one will tell me.

Nights I get up and pace like a caged animal. I go over every fact. I sit at my desk and reread every paper, looking for clues I might have missed. I jot down a list of phone calls to make in the morning. When I can no longer think, I go back to bed and finally sleep.

We touch down in Binghamton. All the other passengers leave the plane. It's pouring. The rain is rolling down the windows. I'm sitting in my seat crying and rocking back and forth, like a rabbi praying. My husband stands next to me in the aisle, holding our carry-on bags, looking down at me, waiting patiently. After nine years of searching and a lifetime of wondering and longing, I know that my sisters are waiting in the terminal just yards away. My mother is waiting just across town. I cannot move. "You can do it," my husband says.

I can do it. I stand up and walk down the aisle, down the stairs, and into the terminal.

I have been reluctant to contact anyone except my parents, because I don't want to disclose private information. But, I cannot find them. In desperation on the Saturday before Thanksgiving 1995, I call Kate Manzone, a woman listed on next-of-kin records as my paternal grandfather's adopted daughter. I think this woman is adopted too. Maybe she'll understand. I say to her, "Bear with me while I tell you who I am." My voice shakes. My mouth is dry. I feel so close.

She lets me finish, then slowly says, "My God. I'm not your aunt. I'm your sister!"

The phone rings. "Hey, honey, are you sittin' down? This is your big sister Irene!" We talk for an hour. She tells me, "We love you darlin'." I cannot believe I am part of a family.

What if they aren't here? What if we don't recognize each other? Then I see them. Kate and Irene are smiling and crying and squealing. I smile and cry and shake. I hesitate for a moment then look into their eyes. I see myself. I let out an animal sound—relief, pain, joy. I start to collapse. They hold me. Our tears mix on my shoulders, on their shoulders. I step back and look at my sisters again. They are beautiful. They look like me. I am beautiful. I look at David. He is crying.

My birth mother calls. She tells me, "I love you." I cry for two days.

We drive up the driveway. Through sheets of rain on the windshield I see a tall, blond woman waiting just inside the shelter of the open garage. "It's my mommy." I open the car door before David has stopped. I run to her. She gathers me into her arms. We cry. She rocks me from side to side.

"Oh, I thought you would never come," she says through tears.

Later, we are alone. She looks into my eyes and tells me, "I know you are trusting me with your heart. I promise I will not let you down again."

220

The next morning I wake. I think about how unknowingly I named one of my daughters after my sister Kate. Then I hear my birth mother's voice ringing clearly in my head. She is telling me something about her garden. Or is it Wendy King's voice? With a start, I realize they sound the same—sweet, high, with a touch of southern twang. For years each night I've heard the soothing sounds of a voice like hers, a voice that lulled me to sleep as I listened to the radio my adoptive mother gave me.

Jill Ann Mortell (left) with birth sisters Kate and Irene

My First Word Is Light

I don't remember the smell
of my birth mother
or the sound of her heartbeat
strong above the wash
of amniotic fluid in my ears,
but I know she is not here.

It's not about what is.
It's about what is not.

I develop a fear of the dark.
One day it has a name—dark
and I say, "No Mommy,
don't turn out the light."

It's not about what's under the bed or in the closet.
It's about losing what's there when it's light.

Before the light goes out,
the lamp is there,
the pink wallpaper, the white bureau,
and my mother in the doorway.
Where do they go in the blackness?

It's about tearing flesh from bone.

My husband reaches to turn out
the light on the bedside table.
"No," I say, "not yet."
I drink in his face.
Will he be there in the morning?

Jill Ann Mortell

Jill Ann Mortell is a writer and editor. She teaches
technical writing at Penn State University's New
Kensington Campus and works as a consultant to
business and industry. Her articles have appeared
in local and national publications and her recent
poems can be found in the *Comstock Review*. She
lives in Pittsburgh, Pennsylvania, with her
husband and three children.

Our Daughter

She began in your yes,
that melting instant of your drinking in,
that merging,

then, like the point of a compass,
your spinning into an unplanned course.
Were you hurt, angry, ashamed
when you pressed your face against the cold glass
of the next nine months,
and folded your plans
like yesterday's laundry?

I don't even know your name
or how much you poured out
with your choosing,
whether any shawl comforts the ache
of milk that once filled your breasts,
if any sleep lets you forget
the surprise of her first kick,
or if you see, even now, the shadow
of your consent on that black line,
hear her cry in the cold shift of wind,
or imagine her face in the rain,

but I wish you could hear her laugh
and understand
how much we thank you.

Ginger Murchison

From One Hand to Another

She put you in the clothes
I brought and carried you, pink
blanketed,

and at the end of
a soundless mile of marble floor and unopened doors
    —not even a dust particle impinging on stark, even planes—
      just like in Florence where the hall exploded and the sky announced
        David,

Perfect, she said.
I heard the word
in the place of no breathing,
and she gave you to me,
my mouth mountain-climbing the words,
Let's go home.

Ginger Murchison

Gemstone

She was our first.
It's not important how
we found her, who gave her
up, or even why. We didn't hesitate,
said yes, wanted her
like you'd covet something priceless,
a strand of pearls, perhaps,
know it would feel good
against your skin,
take color from your eyes.

We brought her home,
pink and round,
but there were flaws.
She never crawled
didn't walk,
said no words. We called
the experts. They appraised
the imperfections, speculated
why,

but we didn't know
gemology. She felt good
against our skin,
took her color from our eyes.
Radiance and luster
count, of course,
with pearls.

Ginger Murchison

Disappointed that teaching English left so little time for her own interests, Ginger Murchison quit teaching in May of 1977 to write. She is published so far in *Laughing Lions, Maelstrom, Seasons, The Penwood Review, The WolfHead Quarterly,* and *tri di-verse city,* the anthology of the 1999 Austin International Poetry Festival. Married and the mother of Arienne, 27, her adopted daughter, and Jason, 25, her natural son, Ginger divides her time between Atlanta, Georgia and Sanibel Island, Florida.

Birthday in Milwaukee

Holding your breath

in the darkened bedroom,
bathed in secret silver light,

you watched
with teenaged eyes

as her head
cleared the darkness.

The midwife wrapped her
in newspaper,

taking her somewhere else,
recycling your child.

Jacqueline Newman-Speiser

Jacqueline Newman-Speiser lives in New Jersey. Her poetry has appeared in several publications including *Devil Blossoms, Defined Providence, Poetalk, Erratica,* and *Blind Man's Rainbow.* She is the mother of two daughters, who bring her infinite pleasure.

In the Garden of My Womb

In the garden
Of my womb
No flowers grew.
I failed to germinate
My lover's seed.
With the liquids
Of my body, its grains
And tendrils, I did
Not water it nor nourish.

In those seasons
When I should have
Swelled, the pod
Of me should have
Risen from flat
To full, I did
Not fructify.

And when my lover turned
From me, I said:
Oh, wait! there will be
An unwanted boy
Left at the base
Of a leafless tree.
Let us take him
As our own, bring
Ourselves to him, that
Small and squirming yield.
Let us give to him, together,
Our air and light
And you, my love,
Will watch me open
Like a tight-bound
Blossom in the sunshine
Of his need.

June Owens

Poem to a Peruvian Street Child

Child of three,
I have filled this poem
With colors.
Can you see them?
Or has the world already
Turned your dark eyes
To stones?

"Hold still and let me
Tie your shoe,"
Is not enough.
Has no one said to you,
"Roberto, look! Balloons!
And kites! Hammerkops
And ibises?"
Has no one said to you,
"Oh, Roberto, listen—
Miles Davis and Pavarotti,
Skylarks, pianos and marimbas?"

Have you never smelled the sea
Or apricots, snow before it snows?
Has no one shown to you
Fossils and seashells,
Armatures and eclipses?
Or let you feel what a kiss
Is like or an embrace
Or love or trust
Or anger or anguish?

Child of three,
Come be my boy.
Give me your hand.
We have a way to go.

June Owens

First appeared in *Prize Poems,* 1992, Pennsylvania Poetry Society, Inc.

Between Tree Roots: Finding My True Father

Father, who gave me up
To well-meaning aunt and uncle
When my mother died,
Who went off to Greenland
As empty, bewildered, disowned as I:

I have come to find out.
I want to know
How much of you is left
Beyond icy callings
Of the heart or flourishes
Of your rage and loss
Fisting papered plaster walls
In all the freezing houses
Of my imaginings.

I want to know that you
Are not yet gone to dust.
I know there cannot remain
Leather, cloth, or flesh.
Too many snows.
Too many river-seeking rains.
Too many seismic struggles
In the earth have gone
Into your final rendering.

But, surely, bones are there,
Between the blasphemed satin
And the rotted wood broken into
By thieving roots of trees
Looking for your sustenance.
I could build upon them,
Your good, long bones,
Drop tears turned to gemstones
Into your eye sockets,
Bring you up out of your
Cold house, into the sunlight,
Whole.

June Owens

First appeared in *The Reach of Song*, 1992–1993.

A native of New York City, raised in northwestern Pennsylvania, June Owens now lives and writes in central Florida. Her poems, book reviews, and non-fiction have appeared most recently in *Amelia, The Blue Moon Review, Blue Unicorn, Iowa Woman, Manoa, Mid-Atlantic Country, Orbis, Snowy Egret, Spillway,* and more. Her award-winning collection of poetry, *Tree Line,* Prospect Press, will be out in 1999. Six of her poems are included in the anthology *The Muse Strikes Back,* Story Line Press.

Julie
Marian Parker

From the first moment I saw her, I knew she was destined to be a part of our family. Her name was Veronica. She was nine years old, and probably a little tall for her age. Her blond hair, streaked with brown, was in braids. She brought her yarn and knitting needles with her. I suppose that was in case she was bored with her visit, or perhaps knitting had become her security blanket. Our first meeting was at a designated place chosen by the case-worker. After our initial introduction, and if she agreed, we could bring her home to meet the rest of the family. That is exactly what we did.

Our children, my sister and her family, and my mother were at our house waiting anxiously to meet this new person that just might become a part of our family. I asked my mother if Veronica reminded her of anyone. She said she didn't think so. I was a little surprised because I thought she looked quite like I did at that age and I was sure at least my mother would recognize the similarities. Same complexion, freckles, same color of eyes and hair, and braids, just like I wore at that age.

Our daughter Lisa, who was six at the time, took to her immediately and didn't let her out of her sight. Our son Neil, who was three, probably had no idea what was going on, nor did he care. For the past couple of years we had been foster parents, so I knew my family would have no trouble accepting her and loving her. Taking in foster children was kind of a prelude to the adoption process, at least for us it was.

We adopted our daughter through the state. We tried a private agency and a church agency and were rejected or at least put on hold. The adoption process takes awhile. From start to finish it was about three years.

The time frame was longer for Veronica. She had spent the last three years in foster homes. The parents in her most recent foster home had planned to adopt her and her brother, but the family changed its mind after a year. She had changed families three times in the last three years. She had also changed her last name, changed locations, which meant changing schools, and even changed religions. The state had a policy that they would make every effort to place a child in a home with the same religion as their biological parents, unless the parents listed

 no religious preference. In this case there was no preference listed, so she was placed in a Catholic home, a Jewish home, and a Protestant home. Also when a ward of the state was placed in a home with adoption being considered, the child took the name of the adopting family. It would be hard enough to cope with just one of these changes, but imagine being taken from your home and your parents and having to make all of these changes. Doubts and insecurities would become a part of her life and will probably never leave entirely.

231

I'm sure her biological parents loved their seven children very much. The parents were fairly young, uneducated, transient, probably because the father was often unemployed. The parents separated on many occasions but always drifted back together, with another child being born as the result. There were three boys and four girls, each about a year apart. Our adoptive daughter was the second oldest.

The two oldest children started school at the same time. The explanation for this was the mother needed the older children at home to help care for the younger children. It was through the school that the state became aware of the children's home life. The children missed a lot of school and, when they did attend, they were often dirty, poorly dressed and hungry.

Taking children out of their home and putting them up for adoption is not something the state does lightly, nor without working first with the parents to help them make a better life for their children. The younger children were easiest to place and adopted first. The youngest boy and girl went to one family, the next two youngest girls were placed together in another home, the middle boy was never adopted and stayed in foster homes until he was 18. The oldest two, Veronica and her brother, stayed together in foster homes. After the third foster home did not work, the children were split up and placed separately. Before any of the children were permanently placed, a picture was taken of all of them together. The picture, a snapshot, was given to Veronica. She hung on to that picture and took it every where she went. The parents had two more children, a boy and a girl. After finally divorcing, the mother raised these two alone.

Veronica and her brother made a pact that they would love each other and always stay in touch, no matter what. The separation of brother and sister was probably the most difficult adjustment they had to make. We knew this was a difficult time, at least for Veronica, and so the brother was invited to visit us. It was during the summer and what should have been a very pleasant experience turned out to be the opposite. This boy had so much hate and resentment. He was rude to everyone, especially his sister, and couldn't wait to leave. I think he was afraid we might like him and ask him to live with us. I think that was probably what his sister had in mind also. He made it quite clear that he did not want to live in the city.

Eventually a farm family adopted him. He never came to our house for a visit again, but we visited him on several occasions. Brother and sister kept in touch pretty much until we moved to California. Veronica continued to write to him and occasionally tried to call. He stopped writing to her and never had anything to say on the phone. She told him she would like to find their parents and their sisters and brothers. He made it quite clear he did not and would not have any part of them. To this day he continues to be a troubled person and rarely has anything to do with his sister.

Usually a child stays in a home about a year before they can be legally adopted. At about nine months, we were told we could go ahead with the adoption. However, an incident just before the adoption postponed it. The girls became very angry with their brother, and Veronica decided she and Lisa were going to leave home. When I asked where they planned to go, they said they would call the case-worker and she would find them a place. It never went that far, but I was concerned. I mentioned the incident to the case-worker, who laughed, and asked if I ever threatened to run away as a child. I said, "No. Never. My concern is that perhaps Veronica really wants to leave." We decided to wait the full year.

I asked the case-worker, "Could I do all the paper work without an attorney, since the state had done all the other requirements?"

The case-worker said that this would be acceptable but added, "I will tell the judge your plans and see first if he has any objections." He had none.

When I went to the court house to pick up the papers, the clerk said, "You can't have the papers. It simply isn't done that way." When I asked why, she said, "For one thing the biological parents have to be listed and then the child will know her name and parents."

I told her the child was ten years old, and for those ten years, she had her parents' name. "Besides," I added, "I have permission from the judge." With much reluctance, she gave me the papers.

Before the final adoption, Veronica decided to change her name to Julie but kept her middle name Sue. She discussed this with the case-worker and was told it would be all right. All adoptions were done one day a month in the judge's chambers. I wanted to make this a memorable occasion. At first Veronica/Julie didn't want anyone else at the adoption but the three of us. I convinced her that the adoption should be a family affair and that her adoptive sister and brother wanted to be part of the ceremony. On January 17, 1973, we all dressed up in our finest and proceeded to the County Court House. We sat in a waiting room with other adopting families and their attorneys. When most of the families had been taken in and we were still there, I asked the clerk when she thought it might be our turn, "Oh," she replied, "I forgot all about you. You see, this is just another reason for having an attorney."

The clerk's statement pretty much set the tone for the rest of the day. Julie was told the judge would probably ask her questions and she was looking forward to it. These would have made her feel much more important. But the judge never spoke to her. In fact, he barely noticed her. He paid a lot of attention to our son and asked him questions. The judge gave his usual memorized speech about the law, the do's and don'ts, and stated that a new birth certificate would be issued naming us as Julie's birth parents. However, the birth place was unchanged and the original birth record was impounded (making it inaccessible) by the State of Wisconsin, Dept of Health and Social Services in Madison. The children didn't seem to be too disappointed, but the whole process certainly disappointed me. The children got a day off from school and we had dinner at Julie's favorite restaurant.

I would like to say, "The rest of our lives went very smoothly." Unfortunately they did not. The move from Wisconsin to California was particularly hard on Julie. She was a teenager and starting her first year of high school. Everything that could go wrong did. She refers to those years as her rebellious years and says every child needs to experience them. It was easy to make excuses for her behavior, because I understood why she did many of the things she did. That, however, didn't make it easier. But, we survived.

When Julie was in her teens and we were living in California, we tried to find her parents and brothers and sisters but never succeeded. Much to our amazement, many years later her brother, then an adult, found all of the brothers and sisters, and they had a family reunion in Wisconsin. Of course, Julie brought her picture taken of the children before they were placed for adoption. One of the parents enlarged the picture to a 5 x 7 and gave each sibling a copy. They also took their picture again as adults and standing as they had in the original picture. Julie suggested they contact a local newspaper and perhaps the newspaper would do a story on them. At the time, the two youngest were still minors, and their parents did not want any publicity for fear the biological parents would see the article.

A few years later the seven children found their birth parents. In 1993, while in Wisconsin, I met Julie's birth mother. I was told her mother was very apprehensive about the meeting, but I think it went very well. She thanked me for raising her daughter when it was impossible for her to do so, and I thanked her for giving me that opportunity.

Julie's main goal in life was to be married and have a family. She has been married for 19 years and has two teenaged boys. She would like to have had a daughter. She even considered adoption. But after trying foster children and learning that her husband and sons were not very receptive, she gave up the idea.

Today we all live nearby and enjoy our close family. Julie and I love to shop and do arts and crafts. She is very talented and creative and makes many gifts. She is caring, loving, and has a great sense of humor.

Julie continues to stay in touch with her parents and brothers and sisters. Three sisters have come to California to visit.

Marian Parker was born in Wisconsin. She met her husband in high school. In 1976 they moved with their children from Wisconsin to Ventura, California. They are now retired and continue to make their home near all of their children in Ventura. They have three grandchildren.

What I'm Proud Of

When I searched for my birth family
I found ten or eleven generations of ancestors

including real Pilgrims (capital P)
and Revolutionary (capital R) soldiers

and my farthest back known female ancestor
Rachel Bouton whose name means Black Button

and someone who founded the farthest west
Chapter of the Daughters of the Confederacy

and someone in the Arkansas Legislature
when they voted to become a state

and Michael from Monaghan who
fought for the Union and settled in a sod house

and a doctor whose heart
was broken by a land scam

and a Superintendent of Schools who
almost died when his grandson was

kicked out of school for a hole he drilled
between the boys' and girls bathrooms

and someone beheaded by a buggy when he
stuck his head up out of a man hole

and the President of the DAR for the
State of South Dakota

and so on but I want you to know I'm
not bragging about these ancestors

I've done nothing to deserve them
or not deserve them

and I might have liked these folks and
they might have liked me or not

I'm bragging about not going through my
life not knowing about these ancestors

that I got out from under the shame
of being a bastard

that I got out from under my fear
of my parents feeling abandoned

that I got out from under my fear
of maybe not finding anybody

that I got out from under the law that
withholds my original identity from me

that I got out from under inertia
(even pathological passivity)

that I got out from under all this
is what I'm proud of

Penny Callan Partridge

Memory

My brother
            loans me a tape
                        for improving memory.
Somewhere under
            this gurgling water
                        subliminal messages.
But what will
            they help me
                        remember?
Someone I
            haven't thought of
                        in years?
Something I
            promised to do
                        and haven't?
That day in
            that other world
                        when the bottle
fell from the
            fridge onto my
                        mother's toe?
Will I remember
            everything we
                        need at the store?
To relax my
            shoulders? The
                        poems I hope to
memorize?
            What I decided
                        we are here for?
I need no help
            remembering
                        the first thing
my brother
            ever said to me:
                        This is Bill
Duckett from
            Hope Arkansas
                        and ah never
knew ah had
            a sister but
                        ah love you.

Penny Callan Partridge

238

The Adoptee's Kite Fantasy

I know just how I got
this fantasy. I was on
the beach with one of
those two string kites
you can wave back
and forth across the
sky. And then I
read an author's
thank you to her
mother for keeping
her anchored to earth.

Now I am out here
over the waves
with just the right
tugs at my corners
to let me dance
like the world's
best dancers while
back on the beach
each holding a string
and looking this way
are my four parents.

They must have
met in heaven
all white-haired
and blue-eyed and
dressed all alike
by J. Crew!
in sky blue
Oxford cloth shirts
and baggy white
pants rolled up
their white legs.

They must be here
to help me soar like
none of them ever
did for long. Each
had a taste but there
was so much waste
in each of their lives.
Maybe they thought

that with all four of
them helping I might
soar for all of us.

I do love them
all pulling for me
together. So
knowing they can't
see these gold
sparks flying up
off the dark wheels
of water below me,
I send them the sight
through these delicate
strings attaching us.

Penny Callan Partridge

The three poems of Penny Callan Partridge first appeared in her book *Pandora's Hope*.
Reprinted here with the author's permission.

Penny Callan Partridge has been active in
the adoption community for over twenty-
five years, having co-founded Adoption
Forum in Philadelphia in the early
Seventies. In 1980, she became the first
elected President of the American Adoption
Congress. She now lives in Massachusetts,
where she is involved in ABC (Access to
Birth Certificates). Both an adoptee and
adoptive parent, she has two print
collections of her poems and stories about
being adopted; and R-Squared Press
recently produced an hour long audiotape of
Penny reading "Pandora's Poems" (from *An
Adoptee's Dreams* and *Pandora's Hope*). Penny takes pride in her identity as the
daughter of four parents and as a poet of the adoption community.

The Last Confession
Royal Phillips

"Ah, now you're truly a sight for sore eyes. A real vision of loveliness, you are." Father Michael stood at the bottom of the plane steps. He took my hand as I stepped into the desert night air.

"Help me, Father. This trip around the world was a nightmare. Mother was drunk the entire time. My brother is putting her in a sanitarium in New Jersey." I looked down and struggled with my cosmetic case.

"Here, let me take that for you. Calm down there. It can't be as bad as all that." I stared at Father Mike. He seemed more handsome than I remembered in his Bermuda shorts and monogrammed black shirt—not at all like a priest. Immediately I felt embarrassed. I dismissed the thought and hoped he couldn't tell what I was thinking.

"You've got to help us. She said you gave her special permission to drink wine instead of water in foreign cities. Her Catholic pledge went out the window before we took off in LAX."

"Ah, now, you can't be blamin' me for her drinking. You're tired from traveling." I felt dismissed. I needed someone to help me. There was no one else.

"Put it out of your mind now. I've signed us up for a breakfast ride at dawn. I'll even let you use my western saddle this time." He directed the porter. "Put this luggage on that black T-bird."

I enjoyed Father Mike's Irish sense of humor. He often came to our house and entertained us with his tales, and his visits did make life not so lonely, after Daddy died. Mother disliked my college boyfriend. She had asked Father Mike to intervene to save my soul. So here he was meeting me at the plane just like my father would have done. I could use the wisdom of this older man right now.

During mother's stay in the sanitarium, Father Mike kept me busy. I loved the attention, as I waited for my final college semester to begin. He took me to all the Palm Springs social events and country clubs. Often his drinking pals would pat him on the back and say in passing, "Another one of your nieces, Father Mike?" At the time, I wondered about his nieces. I had never met any of them.

I hadn't seen my college boyfriend Dirk in five months. I missed our closeness, and I had so much to share with him about the world I had just seen. After the sobering observations of starvation in places like Calcutta, college parties seemed frivolous and I began to enjoy the more mature discussions with Father Mike. I began to trust him even more over this period. We talked about many things. One morning we went on a horseback ride to Taquitz Canyon. The desert was especially beautiful. A purple carpet of wildflowers greeted us as we walked his thoroughbreds to the falls for a cool drink. We then went to our Ranch Club for lunch.

"You look like a model, you do," he said. "Waiter, please bring Kim Novac and me two double vodka martini's."

The liquor fueled my bravery. I wanted to confess my sins, things I had never told anyone, to Father Mike. "Let's go, please," I begged.

"Hop into my chariot and I will drive us to my open air office."

On the ride I began to feel giddy and my vision played tricks on me. I thought I could see heat waves shimmer across the shiny black Thunderbird's hood. I tried to figure out what was happening to me and gradually became very quiet.

"A penny for your thoughts." Father Mike said, as he stopped the car and reached to secure the brake.

"A penny?"

"Why is your blue-eyed angel face so clouded today?"

I swallowed. My mouth felt dry. I looked down at my hands. "I'm not an angel, Father." He slipped his arm over the back of my seat. I felt his warmth as the scent of English Leather cologne filled the car.

"You're safe with me. Tell me what's bothering you?"

"Well, to begin with I truly wanted to murder my mother on our trip."

"I've thought of that myself, my dearie darlin'. She's quite a queenly handful." He laughed.

"No, no, I mean I really wanted to kill her. I'd look at her passed out, and I'd think about smothering her with a pillow."

"That's understandable. So young, you've been through a lot." He smiled.

"I have other sins." I took a deep breath. "Well, its about Dirk."

"Go on."

I looked down at my hands again. Perspiration formed on my forehead and began to dampen my hair. "I love petting. At times I'm full of lust."

He hugged me more tightly. "Well now, that's interesting. I am too."

"What . . . what do you mean? You're a priest!" I went stiff. I looked up. His face was now very close to mine.

"Priests aren't made of stone." He paused. "I'm a man. I have feelings— feelings of desire." He looked into my eyes. "I've been fighting this since I first laid eyes on you." He began to stroke my hair. "I'm sure you've no idea how much I love you, my beautiful angel. I want to take you in my arms as a man. I want to kiss away those tears. I can't bear to see you crying."

He lifted my chin and began to cover my face with light kisses. Reality started slipping away. I was confused. His warm fingers were unbuttoning my blouse. Then he slipped my bra strap off my shoulder and began kissing my breasts. My thighs began to feel moist.

"With time, you won't be shy. With time, my darlin'. I'll know you perfectly." He slid his hands under my crinoline petticoat.

"She's back, Greta. Get ready," I yelled. The German housekeeper ran to the foyer. I looked through the glass peephole. Sunglasses askew and wearing an embroidered blue Matthew's suit and matching pumps, Mother staggered from a Yellow cab. Greta and I opened the door.

"Listen, you son-of-a-bitch, I paid you enough. I don't care if you did drive all the way from L.A." Then she noticed us.

"Greta, take care of this jackass." She lurched forward. I smelled sour Scotch and stale smoke as she lurched through the door. "They locked me up! I told them I'd sue them and shut their doors, if they didn't let me out. They took all my things away. They locked me up, Royal!"

I ran to call Father Mike. He arrived promptly, his tires screeching on the circular driveway.

As he rushed in the front door, he shouted at Mother. "Jesus, Mary and Joseph! Madge, do you know what worry you've put your daughter through? Do you have any idea the harm you've caused in her life?" Angry red arteries bulged on his forehead.

No one ever spoke to my mother like that. He was the priest. He was like a father. And by now he was my lover. At that moment, he also became my hero. I adored him.

Mother's arrival made it more difficult for Mike and me to have our love trysts. She began to suspect. One day she announced, "You're not welcome in my house any more, Father Mike. And furthermore I'm switching donations to the Indian Church."

"Do you think I care about your bloody money? My parish makes the most money in all of Southern California. And you won't be getting those padded tax write-offs anymore, will you now?" Father Mike's face reddened.

I wanted to throw my arms around him. Mother saw how strong my feelings were for him. Her suspicions grew.

I became pregnant. "What do you want me to do, Michael? I can get an abortion."

"Oh, my God in heaven, no. I'm a Catholic priest. There will be no abortion."

"So, what do you propose I do?" I began to feel powerless. I stood there looking at him for a while then added, "Look at my crazy mother!" I knew what she was capable of doing. I saw her operate many times over the years.

"I told you before, I've loved you since I first laid eyes on you. I want to leave the priesthood and marry you. Yes, I want to get straight with God and leave. I've wanted to leave for so long and live truthfully. We'll go away and start a new life."

I was surprised. He'd give up all he had known and developed in the church for me?

"We'll go to Europe. You must be ready to give up your American life of privilege."

I returned to college, while we made plans. We met in Arizona, New Mexico, and California. Confiding in only one trusted sorority sister, I packed a steamer trunk with maternity clothes, a cookbook, children's books and baby clothes. During spring break, Mike and I escaped to Spain. At first we traveled like honeymooners, seeing all of the sights and relishing just being together in freedom. Then we settled in a tiny, white house near the sea in Torremolinas. An Army buddy who owed Father Mike a lot of money supported us. Our life became idyllic.

Mike often thought of surprises for me. One day he said, "C'mon, little mother, I have a surprise for you. We're going to town to buy you paints, canvas and brushes." My heart leaped. I missed painting, my studio, and courses. He knew that. But then he added, "And for me? I'm having a plate of squid."

"Ugh. Now that could make me have my first morning sickness."

About this same time, he began to call our baby Deirdre. "You're healthy, Deirdre's healthy. Why, you're glowing!" He rubbed my belly.

"How do you know it's a Deirdre?" I smiled.

"Why from such a mother this baby could only be an Irish princess."

I was beginning to look very pregnant by now and wanted to be officially married, as we planned. "And will this baby princess have parents who are married soon?" I bit my lower lip and looked directly at him.

He hedged and his face darkened. "It's better if we wait a bit. Besides how can a Catholic priest marry in Spain?" There was something in his voice that made me uncomfortable but I dismissed my feelings.

Then not long after, the cleaning lady found his clerical collar behind a bookcase. She laid it on a small table where I found it. "What's this for?" I demanded, holding up the collar. "I thought you'd left your priesthood behind." I saw Mike's face redden but he quickly recovered.

"Well, I have it just in case one of my family dies in Ireland. I couldn't be going home as anything but a priest now, could I?"

"But you told me you wanted to leave the priesthood and live truthfully."

Mike took several steps away from me. "Don't start with me. I can leave you at any time. What would you do then?"

I was shocked. He was threatening me. I started to cry. I felt trapped, helpless, and vowed to myself to keep all negative thoughts inaudible. Soon after that he told me we were going to have to go back.

"What do you mean go back to the states?" I yelled. "I made a complete commitment to you. What about my mother? Are you crazy?"

Mike waved a letter in my face. "My old army buddy says in this letter that your dear mother has been getting drunk and calling Bishop Buddy and making all kinds of trouble for us."

"Where would we go, for God's sake? I love it here." I chewed my lip.

"I think Arizona . . . maybe Phoenix. You'll get better medical care there."

"Isn't it summertime? Isn't it over a hundred there?"

"Now don't you be worrying. You know I want what is best for you and my Deirdre. I love you both so." He hugged me tightly.

The Italian ship Michaelangelo stopped at Gibraltar and we booked third class passage.

"We're returning so I can work out our finances. My old buddy isn't sending me money. Guess he thinks while the cat's away he doesn't have to pay."

"You warned me about my life-style changes. What matters to me is that we're together. I love you so. Feel Princess Deirdre kick." I placed his hand on my stomach.

In New York customs I struggled with my painted canvases while Mike mopped his brow with his handkerchief. Settling in blistering Phoenix, we had one set of sheets, one pot, one pan and two library cards. Several times a day I swam in the apartment complex pool. As the desert sunset streaked across the sky, we played Gin Rummy. One night Mike lost and angrily threw the cards across the room.

"There is no way that you can keep this baby!"

"What on God's earth do you mean?" My jaw dropped.

"Because your mother will haunt us until the day we die, and she would never accept the child."

Stunned, I thought, this can't be true. He can't be saying this. I'm in a dream.

"I'm taking you to a Catholic doctor, who will see you as a charity patient at St. Joseph's Hospital. You'll take the bus. Afterwards we'll go to the Catholic Social Services to make arrangements for adoption."

My head spun. "Did you say adoption?" I paused in disbelief then distracted myself by adding, "I've never been on a bus!"

"Remember if you make trouble, I can put you in a Florence Crittendon home for unwed mothers. I don't have to stay with you." I noticed his fists were clenched.

My eyes widened. "But surely there is something you can do. Get a job or something? I would, if I could. I'd do anything to save our baby. I'll never give her up for adoption. Never!"

"People don't hire Catholic priests." He paused for a moment, as if he was searching for something. "Besides, we can always get married later and have more children."

Never for a second did I think I would have to give my child up for adoption. We had no more discussions because I lived in fear that he would abandon me. I just believed some miracle was going to take place. Swimming kept me sane. I swam back and forth in the apartment house pool for long periods each day.

One morning early just as the pink and orange sun stretched across Camelback Mountain, I woke to hear a dull popping sound and feel warm liquid oozing between my legs. I lay there for a few minutes, then I woke Mike.

"I think something's happening," I whispered.

"Do you think the baby's coming now?"

"I'm having cramps and I think my bag of waters popped—there's liquid coming out of me."

"I'd best get dressed and go down to the manager's apartment to call the doctor then," he said. He sounded concerned.

"While you're there, do you think you could ask if he would give us a ride to the hospital?"

Mike rushed around nervously, brushed his teeth, pulled on a pair of Bermuda shorts, and grabbed a shirt.

I called from the bed. "Wait awhile please. Come over here and just hold me. Hold me tight, Mike. I'm frightened."

"There, there, Royal," he said, patting me while I nuzzled my head against his chest. "Women have babies every day. You're going to be just fine."

I heard his heart thumping rapidly underneath his black shirt and knew he too was afraid. Coming to childbirth with little knowledge and so few ideas of what to expect made my experience a raw one, unshaped by preconceived ideas, beauty-parlor patter, or old wives' tales.

The manager's car had no air-conditioning and with each contraction I struggled to breathe. "I really thank you . . . Mr. Garcia . . . This ride means a lot to me," I said.

"Think nothing of it Mrs. O'Donohoe. It's not every day I get to deliver precious cargo." He smiled and winked at me. "Don't worry about a thing. I'm the last of thirteen children, and my mother, gracias a Dios, never had a problem."

Mike blurted, "She's not going to have any problems." He grabbed my arm. His hand was sweaty. With his other hand, he mopped his brow. Repeatedly he tried to reassure me. He whispered, "Royal, believe me, everything's going to be all right. I'm going to take care of you. I think we'll go to San Diego after this. I know some people there who can help us to start over."

I smiled at him. I thought about his idea to give up the child. I said nothing, but I refused to accept it. I was determined some miracle would occur and I would keep the baby.

"Believe me when I say we'll have a life together," he continued.

The first part of labor lasted all day, and Mike stayed with me. Contractions came and went, but I was able to talk with him and play some Gin Rummy. By afternoon I was starving and begged him to smuggle in something to eat. He left and returned with four oily cookies and one pink carnation. I stared at the carnation. I picked it up and smelled its spicy sweetness. "With your next baby, you'll have a room full of flowers," he said. Tears filled my eyes. I knew future flowers would never mean as much as this single carnation.

The pains increased. The contractions seemed to engulf my being. I felt vulnerable and afraid, as my body opened wider and wider. Over the screeching pain, fatigue, and fear, a song of jubilation rose within me.

Suddenly, there was a flurry of activity. I was lifted to the gurney. Mike appeared. My body was twisting with pain. I cried out, "Help me, Mike. I feel like I'm dying." They wheeled me to the delivery room. Mike hung over the gurney rail, sputtering, "My God, my God, my dearie darlin'! My angel! Don't worry! Don't worry about anything! I swear to you, don't worry about a thing! Oh, my God, my angel . . ." Then everything went black.

As I emerged from anesthesia, I saw an unfamiliar face over me. "You're not my doctor." I said hazily, "Who are you?"

"I'm Doctor Stuart. I'm the doctor on duty."

"Oh, excuse me," I said, fighting to keep conscious, "but what did I have?"

"Girls like you don't need to know," he replied coldly.

His remark cut through me, but I pressed on. "I do want to know. Do you think you could just tell me if it's a boy or a girl?"

"It's a girl."

"Is she healthy?"

"Yes, she's healthy, and that's all you need to know." Our Deirdre, I thought, then I sank back into a drugged twilight.

After the birth, Mike managed to get me a semi-private room. My roommate, Elise, was twenty-six, and a fifth grade schoolteacher in Phoenix.

"Hello. I had a boy yesterday. What did you have?

I swallowed. "I had a girl. She's healthy. Her name is Deirdre . . ." I was in a haze but continued to talk. "Deirdre was to be killed at birth to save the kingdom. But she lived and news of her perfect beauty spread throughout the land."

Elise added, ". . . and the Druid prophecy was that Deirdre would be forced to marry a king. I know that legend. It's sad, but lovely. But what a beautiful name. You seem tired, maybe you should rest."

"Thank you. I am tired. It must be the drugs." And I fell asleep.

"Good morning, Royal," Elise said. "Are you feeling better now? They just brought breakfast and it was horrible. I don't think you missed anything." She laughed. "You talked in your sleep last night."

"Oh, what did I say?"

"Well, you kept repeating that you hadn't signed the papers yet. You seemed worried about it. Can I help you with anything?"

"Uh . . . those drugs. They confused me."

"By the way, while you were sleeping Deirdre's grandfather came by."

My heart jumped. "How did you know her name?"

"Last night we talked about the Celtic legend of Deirdre. You don't remember?"

"Oh yeah, yeah I do. But, grandfather? Was he an older Irish man with gray at the temples?"

"Yes."

"Did he call himself Deirdre's grandfather?"

"No. I just assumed."

"Well, Elise, that's Deirdre's father, and we have a big problem."

"I'm sorry I didn't mean to assume, or to pry."

"Oh no, that's okay. Since he's so much older, my mother refuses to accept our marriage. He has convinced me that for the welfare of Deirdre, we may have to give her up for adoption."

"Oh dear, I'm so sorry. I hope you get to keep her."

She understood my pain and asked if it would bother me to see her nursing.

"Oh no, I think its wonderful you're nursing. I just wish I could nurse my baby. With all my heart I do."

Mike came at appointed visiting hours. He was quiet and withdrawn. Unlike other couples, we weren't walking to the nursery to see Deirdre. Nobody came to tell me anything about our baby. From the tension and withheld emotion, I started chewing the insides of my mouth. I was fighting to hold myself together. I never cried. I was terrified Mike would leave me if I fell apart. There was no counseling or tranquilizers—nothing. My breasts filled, and I still hadn't seen my baby. I didn't even know where she was. After four days, the Catholic social worker came. I said, "Could you tell me what happened to my baby, please?"

"Oh, your baby! I think it went home two days ago," she mumbled, shuffling through some papers on her clipboard.

"Went home where?" I asked in alarm. "What home?"

"The babies go to a foster home first, and then . . ."

"But I haven't signed any adoption papers," I interrupted.

She looked flustered. "Oh, you haven't? Well, didn't they tell you the babies go to a foster home before they are adopted?"

"I don't remember that," I said.

"Okay. I'll be right back. I'm just going to check on this." She nervously retreated.

I was astounded. I thought, this is a human being. This is my greatest gift to the world, and they don't even know where she is?

A few minutes later the social worker returned. "Your baby is still here," she said sheepishly. "You didn't get to hold her yet?" I shook my head. "I'll bring her so you can hold her."

"No!" My heart was pounding. "No, you may not bring the baby in for me to hold," I couldn't believe what I was saying.

"What?" she asked, surprised.

"Don't bring my baby. If I hold her now, I'll never let her go, and you'll never have her." I began to realize I was making some kind of decision.

All along Mike refused to look at Deirdre, saying he didn't want to carry her image with him the rest of his life. I understood and I also hated him.

Just before I left the hospital, I asked Elise to accompany me to the nursery. She took my arm and together we made the painful journey down the tiled hall. From behind a glass window, I saw my beautiful eight-and-a-half-pound Deirdre Dawn O'Donohoe. She was lying on her side, facing me, swaddled tightly in a peach-colored blanket. She had a cherub face and blond fuzz for hair. She had the Phillips dimple in her left cheek, and she was perfect! She worked her little lips as if she were hungry or preparing for a kiss. Then she opened her eyes and they seemed to lock on mine. I wanted to smash the glass. Grab her. Hold her. Smell her. I bit down hard on the inside of my mouth. Despair and yearning heaved in my breast. I felt torn from head to toe and joined to her by an invisible magnet. How could Mike even consider giving her up?

Elise's hand tightened on my arm. "She's beautiful, Royal, like you." Then she slipped her arm around me. "I think we'd better go now."

As I turned from the nursery, I saw tears on Elise's face, but my eyes were dry. I thought, how strange. Part of me was standing outside myself watching all of this.

After my release from the hospital, I was desperate. The lease on our apartment was about to expire. We were out of money. Deirdre was in a foster home, pending adoption. I still hadn't signed the papers. I had milk in my breasts and no baby to nurse. I was weak, depressed, and filled with unreleased emotion. Broken dreams, betrayed trust, hopelessness, and fear, all surged inside and were knotted together with a cord called survival. I went day to day, simply placing one foot in front of the other. Sleep walking.

Finally I came up with a last-ditch, desperate attempt to keep Deirdre. I would call my mother, though Mike was vehemently against it. I banked on her sense of "family blood" and pride I knew was part of her Southern mentality. I thought maybe she'd change her mind about Mike and me and help us stay together, if she knew there was a baby, her own flesh and blood. I had nowhere else to turn. I dialed the familiar number. Mother answered.

"Royal, where the hell are you?"

"I'm in Arizona, Mother,"

"Is that son-of-a-bitch with you?" she snarled.

"Yes, he is."

"Are you pregnant?"

"No, I'm not. But I must tell you I love him and we want to stay together."

"Well, you may love him, but as long as you're together you'll never be a part of my life or get any help from me. And I can assure you he'll never again be a part of any life in Palm Springs. I've seen to that. He's nothing but a dirty liar." There was an icy pause. "Listen Royal, I can't be bothered by your problems. I have a new husband, an elderly gentleman Mr. Hamilton, and I will not upset him. You've done enough. You've caused me nothing but pain and sorrow. I have a new life and I won't have it disturbed by your stupidity."

My heart snapped shut. I thought, you cold bitch, you don't even deserve to know about your own flesh and blood.

"You must want something. What is it?" Her voice was shrill. At this moment in the sweltering glass phone booth, I realized the family I was born into had nothing to offer me except material goods. I decided to stop fooling myself by expecting more. I knew the only thing I could do was go home. I'd utilize Mother's spiritless offerings.

"We've run out of money. I need a ticket home."

There was a short silence. I could hear Mother relishing her triumph. "I expected this," she said. "You can come here on the condition that you come alone and do nothing, and I mean nothing, to upset Mr. Hamilton or our household."

"Of course, Mother."

Mike let me take a taxi to sign the adoption papers. The one thread of sanity holding me together was, despite the nightmarish circumstances surrounding our lives, I had accomplished something worthwhile—I had given the greatest gift to the world.

"This is a healthy, special baby I'm giving you," I told the tight-lipped social worker as I signed the papers.

I turned and walked slowly out of the office and down the long hall. Many thoughts ran through my mind about the past months. I never had any intention of giving her away. I just believed that some miracle was going to take place. I talked to her and loved her, loved her, loved her. I cherished her to the very end. I had no guilt about rejecting her because I never did.

Mike returned to the priesthood, claiming that it was the only way to get his finances in order.

I was so frustrated that he could come up with no other solution to our tragic predicament than to return to the hypocrisy we had left behind.

"In Blythe I have a friend who will put me up, until I contact the Bishop. I'll probably be required to go on retreat at Via Coeli Monastery in New Mexico."

"How do you know?" I asked.

"From my former experience of re-entering the priesthood. Remember I'm an old hand at this," he said sarcastically. "I'll have to do penance to cleanse my soul."

"An old hand? Is that true?" I looked at this man, this priest, this father of my child then added, "Cleanse your soul? Do you really believe that?"

"Now Royal, don't be startin' with that again."

We took a small plane, a puddle-jumper, out of Phoenix. Mike got off in Blythe; I got off in Palm Springs. My mother's first words were, "You're as fat as ever. You look like s.h.i.t." She laid down the rules of my re-entry. "Now, Royal, you will have to behave correctly around Mr. Hamilton. You must respect him at all times as he is an older gentleman."

"And how old might that be, Mother?"

"That's none of your business, young lady. And another thing . . . I don't want you playing your music loudly on your hi-fi."

"Oh, you mean to say, I still have a hi-fi?" I asked.

"Watch that tone of voice, Royal. I won't put up with that. Wipe that smug look off your face. You no longer have your MG. I sold it as soon as you left."

She had rebounded from my disappearance by marrying Mr. Hamilton, donating a stained glass window to the Church to wipe clean her slate, and buying a new Cadillac.

Mother created a new façade to go with her new husband. When sober, she was in total denial of the past. As usual to the outside world, we were going to pretend that nothing had happened.

She forbade me to mention Mike's name. "That S.O.B. has cost you your inheritance," she told me. "What has happened is over, Royal, and I don't want the shameful incident mentioned again in my home. I'll know the whole truth soon enough when I get the detective's final report."

I told only one sorority sister about my baby. Mike made me vow I would never tell anyone else. Her existence was to be our sacred secret. I hid my grief from everyone. For Mother, part of washing away the past was insisting I go to confession. She made a private appointment. My inner reaction was this is ridiculous, a sham! She was relentless. Finally to appease her, I gave in. I was frantically reaching for some kind of help in my confusion and grief. On some level, the confessional was better than nothing. She took me to the smallest of all the Catholic churches in Palm Springs, one attended mostly by Agua Caliente Indians. She had donated many of the church's stain-glass windows.

I went alone into the church, where I was greeted by calm and the familiar smell of incense and candles. I walked to the statue of the Virgin and lit a votive candle for Deirdre. Kneeling in the dark confessional box, I began timidly, "Bless me, Father, for I have sinned. My last confession was . . ."

"Where is he? Are you pregnant?" The priest's voice boomed from behind the mesh screen. I was stunned. Having nowhere else to turn, I had given the Church one more chance. This priest only wanted to rat on Mike to the Bishop.

At his words, a cold curtain fell across my heart. I reclaimed my soul. I arose and said loudly, "To answer your questions, I'm not pregnant, and I don't know where he is." I added bitterly, "And thanks for hearing my confession, Father." Fighting back rage, I stumbled into the glaring sunlight where Mother was waiting in her new Cadillac.

The following days were a blur. I alternated between numbness and unbearable despair. I wondered if Mike really loved me. When drunk, my mother seized every opportunity to remind me I was good for nothing.

One day the black steamer trunk arrived. I unpacked it, and to my raw cheek I pressed the pink baby blanket I knitted. Then I thought about how I would kill myself.

Letters for Dierdre
Royal Phillips

I.

May 14, 1993

Connie Mitchell ACSW, CISW
Executive Director
Catholic Social Service Adoptions
1825 W. Northern
Phoenix, Arizona 85021

Dear Connie Mitchell:

As you requested, enclosed is proof of my identity. I want to update my September 1961 adoption file with the CSS. I am not searching for my daughter but have always kept my file in current order, in case she wanted information or wanted to contact me.

Times have certainly changed and I thank God! Can you imagine all the years of therapy I have had just to cope with the shame and humiliation?

Please place the enclosed letter to my daughter in our file. Thanks for your help.

Very truly yours,
Royal Phillips

II.

Dear Deirdre Dawn O'Donohoe:

This is the name your father and I picked for you. Perhaps you will never know it. Every few years I update my file, just in case you are curious about your birth mother and father or wanted to find me. I never wanted to disrupt yours or your adoptive parents' lives by finding you. The Catholic Social Services of Phoenix assured me you were going to be adopted by a loving, wonderful family. I see by my correspondence with them that you are the eldest of three adopted babies.

When I signed those papers in 1961, I felt as if I was giving the greatest gift in the world—you—to someone. I was! Never for a moment did I not want you. Never for a split second did I not love you.

Your Irish father was a Catholic priest, 28 years older than I. He died as a result of alcoholism on August 9, 1967, at the age of 53.

252

The forbidden circumstances and close-minded era of your birth trapped me in a situation I had no control over. Please always remember that never for a moment did I not want you. I did everything in my power to keep you. Thank God, today's woman has more freedom and choices in the realm of adoption. I married and gave birth to three special cherubs. I dedicated my life to the spiritual and mental health and the well being of children. The recovery of my mental health after the trauma of your adoption has been a long journey.

I hope your adoptive parents have provided a warm upbringing, spot lighting your individuality. I already know you are quite beautiful! Every year on September 16th I say prayers especially to you. Feel my love around you at all times. As you grew in my womb, so also did never-ending love grow in my heart.

Truly yours,
Your birthmother

"The Last Confession," as it appears here, is a shortened version of Ms. Phillips' memoir, *The Last Confession*. An excerpt from "The Last Confession," as it appears here, won the 1999 Santa Barbara Writers Conference award for best non-fiction.

Royal Phillips was born on Valentine's Day in Chicago. An alumnus of The University of New Mexico and an accredited montrice from the American Institute of Family Relations, Los Angeles, she has been an international childbirth instructor since 1970 and made the joy and dignity of parenthood her life's devotion. She has taught and lectured in the United States, the Middle East, Central America, Europe, and Indonesia. She has produced an educational video, *The Complete Birth,* and audiotapes with Steven Halpern: *Birthways, A Parental Relaxation Guide; The Father Connection, Bonding With Your Child. Her books include: Life Itself, A Parenting Experience; Waiting; Pleasant Avenue.* She is a photographer, world traveler, avid SCUBA diver, as well as a columnist for the *Montecito Journal.* She is the mother of three, birthmother of one, and grandmother of two.

Postcards From The Arctic

1.

Put out for adoption at birth, now
you send me a trio of polar bears:
the mother, dark muzzled, leads
two cubs over the floes. Her feet
stand square on one raft of ice.

The camera caught the first cub
in his mother's wake, front paws
on her float, his black nose
close behind her white tail,
like Babar's procession of elephants.

His back feet stretch from the floe
slipping away behind and he is about
to belly flop into the drink—
His twin stares toward the lens as if,
when he's grown, he would eat it.

Floes shift like lily pads in a summer pond.
Drifting islets of ice extend
toward polar infinity, will freeze
into solid crust when the Wise Crone
snatches away the sun in a cat's-cradle.

2.

Ignorant of your parents,
no offspring of your own
(one learns to be careful),
did you choose this card
half-aware of an inner longing?

Or did you sense that like Mother Bear,
I still try to guide my progeny
through dangerous passages—
even in our more temperate zone,
the world can be slippery. Cold.

3.

I picture you trudging across urban snow
into a brick municipal hall. You seek
a sign: *Origins Information Centre.*
Day after day, you wait in line,
snowy boots paddle into dark seas,
questions leave more question marks.
Like navigating through Arctic straits:

icebergs surround you, blizzards engulf
your charts scratched on ice, what you
hoped was safe harbor is icebound.

4.

Children irked with imperfect parents
imagine: I was adopted, my real dad
is the Storm King, my mother—the Snow Queen.
Yet we are all scions of princes
raised by the shepherd's wife.

Locked in the vault, our crowns await us.
Minions will rush with welcoming roses.
Our kingdoms stretch rich and green.
Meanwhile, we tend royal sheep
whiter, more woolly, than polar bears.

Elisavietta Ritchie

Reprinted with permission of the author from *Amelia,* 1993 "Amelia" Prize; *Kairos,* 1993; *The Arc of the Storm,* Signal Books, ©1998 Elisavietta Ritchie; prose version absorbed into essay "Re-inventing The Archives," *Gifts Of Our Fathers,* Thomas Verny, editor, Crossing Press, 1994.

Elisavietta Ritchie lives in the Washington, D.C. and by the Patuxent River, Maryland. Her publication credits include *Flying Time: Stories & Half-Stories,* 1992 and 1996 (four of the stories won PEN Syndicated Fiction awards); Re-inventing the Archives just won a competition to launch the new Washington Writers Publishing House fiction series and will be published in Spring, 2000. Poetry books: *The Arc of the Storm, 1998; Elegy for the Other Woman: New & Selected Terribly Female Poems, 1996; Tightening the Circle Over Eel Country,* winner of the Great Lakes Colleges Association's 1975–76 "New Writer's Award;" *Raking The Snow,* winner of the Washington Writers Publishing House 1981–82 competition; and chapbooks *Wild Garlic: The Journal of Maria X* and *A Wound-Up Cat & Other Bedtime Stories.* Edited *The Dolphin's Arc; Endangered Creatures of the Sea.*

When the Robin Comes in Spring
Nancy and McDonald Robinson
for our daughter Ehren

> *You asked me to write your story and I said, "You will have to write your*
> *story. I can only write my story."*
> *"Will you?" you asked.*
> *"I'll try."*

We had this conversation several months after I met your birth mother. I'm
not sure, but you may have been thinking about the three women wrapped
together around one life, yours. Since we talked, my thoughts have been flooded
with memories.

I remember you fresh from the delivery room, perspiration across your
forehead, cradling your first child in your arms. You said, "Mom, I knew I would
love him, but I didn't know I would love him this much." Your voice was filled
with awe.

All I could say was, "Now you know how much I love you."

You were very wanted. We
planned a family after your dad
finished his doctorate. The
adoption agency started the
home study on my twenty-
eighth birthday. In barely three
months they called, "Can you
come down to the agency? We
have a baby for you."

September 25, 1967, fall in
Boston, tinges of autumn in the
air: we dressed in our best
clothes and went to the agency
about 10 A.M. The social worker Hannah Lynn was nervous. You had cried all
morning and I think she wasn't sure how we would react. You were dressed in a
Carter's yellow jumper, white blouse trimmed to match, and yellow corduroy
booties. You were small for three months. Your tiny legs and arms were
extremely thin. Your nose was bright red and tears pooled at the edges of your
eyes. I wanted to gather you up and hold you against my chest, pat your small
back, brush the palm of my hand across your blond, fuzzy head.

I held back. There would be a lifetime for us. I could imagine myself
scooping you up and becoming totally immersed, while ignoring your father. I
looked at him—always quiet, studied, careful in showing his emotions. I wanted
him to make a connection with you first. "Go ahead, pick her up," I said. He did
and placed you on his shoulder. You immediately vomited on his suit. Mrs. Lynn
rushed about getting something to clean up the mess and tried to explain, "She's

256

been doing projectile vomiting. The doctor checked her carefully. There doesn't seem to be a medical explanation but she has been slow to gain weight."

I looked at the medical history she gave us. In your first three months, you gained only three pounds. "She probably needs to be placed," I said.

Already you had been in two foster homes. You were very aware, extremely sensitive to sound, and startled at the slightest abrupt noise. I knew as soon as we got you home and comfortable, you would flourish.

On the way home, I cradled you in a soft blanket. Slowly I took in the unforgettable sweet baby fragrance. You were quiet. You kept looking first at me then at your dad, as we drove through the streets of Cambridge toward the Watertown Arsenal, where we lived and where Dad was stationed in the Army. I knew everyone at the Army base would be peeking through windows, waiting for us to arrive. The entire contingent of twelve or thirteen young officers and their families living on the base was as excited as we were about you.

We needed some time before driving through the gates and greeting everyone. We stopped at a park and placed you on a blanket under a huge, spreading tree. You looked around at the tree, the birds, and us. Your large blue-eyes grew even bigger as you took in the world that day. You felt so right to us, as if this day and all it held was written long before.

Among the beautiful moments that morning were some funny ones. Because the agency said you were already on whole milk, we stopped at the store to buy some. At the checkout, you kept watching your dad. The cashier laughed and said, "She sure knows who her daddy is." We laughed too and gave each other a knowing look. She never knew how recently Dad acquired his title.

Right away you responded to our love and warmth. The next week at the base pediatrician's office, the scales showed in our first week together you gained four pounds.

However, because of those first three months, there were some things to work through. I wanted to hold you while you drank your bottle, but you had already established a pattern. You liked to be in your crib with the bottle propped on a receiving blanket and the bedroom door closed. I knew you were probably fed this way in the foster homes. So we began with your established routine. At first if the door was open even a little, you cried. Eventually, I left it open and gradually increased the size of the opening, then I stood in the doorway. Finally I stood beside your crib and talked to you. By the time you were six months, you would let me give you the bottle.

I wasn't always comfortable with having adopted you. Sometimes I feared something would go wrong and we would loose you. Once when we traveled in western Massachusetts near your birthplace, we stopped at a Howard Johnsons for dinner. A waitress fitting the description of your birth mother stood for a long time at our table looking at you and asking all sorts of questions. I never felt such fear or panic before or since. Dad didn't understand what was going on in my head. I couldn't eat and gave the waitress very short answers. When we got in the car, I said, "I couldn't wait to get out of there. Did you see how that waitress looked—just like the description of the birth mother." Dad dismissed my feelings and said it was probably just a coincidence.

Sometimes other Army wives where we lived were over solicitous of us. Everyone wanted to hold you, but you were very selective. In fact there were some loving people you simply did not like. You screamed whenever they came near. One of the women had recently lost a baby. She lived in the apartment just below us and was always trying to make friends with you. You would have nothing to do with her.

The three of us had a lot of fun that first year. As soon as we heard you in the mornings, we brought you into our bed to play. Dad bought a backpack and we took you everywhere—hiking along the Concord River, walking in downtown Boston, around the Boston Common and the lake with the swan boats, and even skiing. You loved skiing. Dad said carrying you on his back improved his skiing, made him turn more rhythmically. Whenever he skied with you, he never fell.

Everyone at the Army base had one child and we all shared a common play area, so there were a number of other children sharing the sandbox each morning. You loved being with the other children. You didn't like sitters, however. If you woke and found a strange person caring for you, immediately you began to do projectile vomiting. After one or two attempts to go out in the evenings, we decided to devote full time to you. We didn't leave you with anyone until you were much older.

The day arrived for your formal adoption. The social worker called and said, "You must bring your daughter with you." Then she laughed in her shy way. "They must have the evidence."

During that first year I seldom thought about the pending legal formalities. I decided this formal court day would be a celebration. At the same time, I decided never to celebrate the date again. I knew eventually you would wonder about the three months between your birthday and the date you came to us. Perhaps you would also wonder about that first year when you were not legally ours. I wanted to erase all trace of any gaps when you didn't belong to us. I wanted this court day to feel like a party. I wanted those early memories to be of being in a beautiful dress and going with us to a big room filled with other children and parents, a room filled with gaiety and love.

I dressed you in a blue voile dress with a matching, filmy coat trimmed in lace. Your grandmother sent the dress for your first birthday. I bought white patent-leather slippers and anklets trimmed in lace. I brushed your baby-soft blond hair and stood you in front of the mirror on the dresser. "Look, sweetheart. How pretty you are!" You beamed. When I put you on the floor, you began to run around, twist and turn, purposely falling on the couch, and delighting in being dressed-up.

At the court, children and adult voices created a din in the crowded room. Mrs. Lynn sat next to us on the walnut bench. You slipped down from the bench perhaps two dozen times, while we waited for our names to be called. "That's why God gives children to young people," she said. "No one else could keep up with this energy."

The judge called the court to order. When he spoke, he was warm and caring. "It always gives me a great deal of pleasure to preside over this court. So much of law deals with society falling apart. Today we are celebrating putting society together." He began to call the individual families. He read the adoption papers and affirmed the legality of each child's place in a family. When our name was called, Dad picked you up, held you, and we walked forward with Mrs. Lynn. The judge asked a few questions. Dad and I struggled to hold back the tears, nodded, and Mrs. Lynn answered. On that fall day when you were declared our daughter, you already had been for an entire year.

During those early years, frequently you cried out at night. The cry was haunting, lonely. We went in, but though you appeared awake, you were asleep. Nothing we said or did stopped these crying periods. As you got older, you walked and talked in your sleep and appeared to be awake. You seemed to be in an unconscious world working out various aspects from your life. You said and did funny things. Sometimes the things were very serious and gave us insight into what you did not verbalize when you were awake. Your first encounter with Halloween sent you into a series of frightening walking/talking sleep adventures. One morning you announced, "I can't go to school today because of Halloween. There will be ghosts and monsters." You refused to wear a costume. I encouraged you to go to school so you would overcome the fear.

However, all your childhood years you suffered from a recurring dream that someone was going to come in the night and steal you. As you became older, you talked about it a great deal. You always wanted to be sure the doors were locked. I don't know when that dream went away. When you went to college, you were still having the dream.

Physically you were very advanced. You crawled shortly after six months and walked at ten months. Soon you were climbing on the couch, up into your highchair, and up and down stairs. But your verbal ability was slow. From the beginning, we talked a lot to you and sang. Still you never babbled or tried to imitate our sounds.

When you were around eighteen months, we became concerned about your speech. You followed simple directions, so we knew you could hear, but you were almost silent except when you cried. We took you to the speech department at a local hospital. After a great deal of testing, the speech pathologist concluded you could follow directions, but you had difficulty reproducing sounds. The sounds you made were actually syllables of words, but they were out of sequence. Doorbell was bell door for years.

In time, the nature of the problem became more obvious. At that point in time, speech therapy was not very sophisticated about solving your type of problem and rehabilitation was a long journey. The specialists thought you might have experienced oxygen deprivation during birth and that affected your auditory sequencing ability. However, no one really knew how the problem began.

We decided to start you in a Montessori nursery school where the approach might be helpful. Every day as I drove to school, you cried. I thought you didn't want to go, but I knew it was important. One very snowy day we failed to receive the call saying school was cancelled. As I drove, you cried the entire way. When we arrived and found the school closed, you were disappointed. You said, "No school? No school? I cry no more." And you never again cried. Apparently all your crying had become a ritual for my benefit!

You loved and enjoyed other children, were often concerned when someone else was crying or unhappy, and you asked to have neighbor children over all the time. Frequently you grabbed your daddy's beard on both sides, held his head firmly and looked right at him saying, "I need a baby."

We, too, wanted more children. Since we had moved from Massachusetts to New Jersey, we had to begin again with a new agency. The abortion law had passed and the social climate had changed. Women were now keeping their babies. There were few children available for adoption. We went through another home study, paid our fee, and waited for a child to become available. Several years went by and I became pregnant, lost that baby late in the pregnancy, and became pregnant again. After our second daughter's birth, we withdrew our application with the agency.

By the time you were in first grade, you had a sister and a brother. We always told you that you were adopted and you readily shared that information with others. You thought it was one of the most wonderful things about you. One day when you came home from school, you rushed into the living room, dropped your school bag and said, "Mom, what does real mean?"

I was sitting on the couch nursing your brother Adam. Your sister Shannon was still napping. I didn't understand exactly what you were asking. "Real can mean lots of things. What are your talking about?"

You stood beside me, looking at your brother, your wispy, blond ponytails, slightly disheveled from the school day, brushed the shoulder of your blue jumper. You reached down and slipped your index finger into Adam's palm. "Real, Mom. You know, what makes something real?" Your enormous blue eyes had an urgency and expectation. You dropped Adam's hand and scooted up on the couch next to me and snuggled in as close as possible. I knew something was really troubling you.

I reached my free arm around you and kissed the top of your forehead, "I love you tons."

"I love you tons too," you mumbled. "Mom, the kids at school say you are not my real mom. What does that mean?

"When I told the kids at school today I was adopted, they asked me who my real mom was." Your voice trailed off. "You're my real mom, aren't you?" You studied my face.

"Yes, I'm your real mom, but I understand what your friends are thinking. They think that because you are adopted, your real mother is your birth mother. You actually have two real moms, one gave birth to you and the other one takes care of you."

You were very quiet for a long time that afternoon sitting next to me on the couch. We watched the chickadees and nuthatches at the feeder hanging outside the large living room window. A robin flew up to the window ledge and hung there for a moment studying us. There was no need to ask you about your school day.

Finally I broke the silence. "Your other real mother loved you very much. She wanted to make sure you would have a mother and a father. Real people are the ones who love you very much."

That day was a turning point in your awareness. You didn't immediately stop telling people you were adopted. People often commented to you, "You don't look like your brother or sister."

At first, you responded, "I'm adopted." Over the years you stopped telling them, but people never stopped saying that. Finally one day I heard you say simply, "That's right." You added nothing more.

I asked you why you changed your response and you said, "I'm tired of that."

When you were in fourth grade, you came home and said, "Dad, I have to do a family tree. Your face had the same expression you wore on the day you wanted to know what real meant. Your book bag slid out of your hand and you climbed into the chair in Dad's study. You had seen Dad's family tree that goes back to King Egbert and 775 AD and heard my father talk about Abraham Bailey, a Revolutionary War veteran, and Lady Hope and John Bell, who were given land by the King of England for a plantation in Virginia. But you were certain your family tree had to be different because you were adopted.

Dad asked, "How does your teacher want you to do your family tree?"

"She told us to start with our family and go back as far as we can. I don't know why I should do it. Don't you guys have different relatives than I do?"

Dad's logical mind kicked in. "That depends whether you are talking about genes or the family you grew up in. However, I'll bet if we go back far enough, we would find that you and we have common ancestors in the gene sense too."

"But Dad!" A comment you frequently made when Dad started in with his numbers, graphs, and explanations. "How would anyone do that?"

"Well, let's think about it. Everyone has two parents and four grandparents. Since each grandparent had two parents, you have eight great-grandparents and sixteen great-great grandparents."

Your eyes started to glaze and you slumped in the chair. Dad hardly noticed. He was having a grand time pursuing his idea.

"You can turn that into a simple formula that says if you go back a certain number of generations, let's call that N—the number of people in that generation is two raised to the power N."

"Dad let's just do the family tree. I'll just take Mom's and your relatives. OK?" However, you knew Dad was on a roll you couldn't stop. So you gave up trying to stop him, listened, and tried to figure out what he was doing.

"It's not so hard," Dad encouraged. "For example, your great-great grandparents are four generations back, and two raised to the fourth power is sixteen."

"Dad, are we doing multiplication tables again?"

Dad nodded. "Yes. It's that simple. If people have children at an average age of say twenty-five years of age, there are four new generations each century. Let's figure out how many people you are related to who lived say eight hundred years ago. At four generations per century, that would be thirty-two generations. Two raised to the thirty-second power is more than four billion people, way more than the population of the world at that time." Dad smiled.

"Come on, Dad. I'm not really related to that many people." But you didn't stomp out of the room. Somehow Dad captured your imagination.

"No, but not just because we came up with such a big number. People lose track of relatives more distant than second or third cousins. Every time someone marries a distant cousin, they create two paths to some of their children's ancestors."

"Dad, come on. Stop. I have to do my family tree."

"The point is, we all do in fact have so many ancestors that the chance is very high we are related by blood, especially since your gene-ancestors and ours both came mostly from Europe. Come, I'll show you the family tree your great-aunt Analydia put together. A couple of branches go back more than eight hundred years, so you are almost certain to be genetically related to them."

Dad pulled his family tree from the file drawer and unfolded it on the dining room table. "Here we are. You can start here. When your are finished with this, Mom has hers."

I don't know if you were convinced, but you did your homework. In fact you always did your homework. While school was never a breeze, you worked hard and did reasonably well. You were excellent in athletics and won two awards one year in high school—Most Improved Player and Most Valuable Player. And you could ski faster and better than anyone but Dad. When you began English riding, I was impressed with the way you related to horses. You had a special ability to communicate with animals. And you were funny. You could always make us laugh and never allowed us to stay too serious for long.

Remember how we always sang? When you were to be married, you asked Dad to sing all the songs we sang to put you to sleep each night when you were little. When you asked him to sing "Where Are You Going?" or maybe it is named "Turn Around" at your wedding, Dad said, "I don't know if I can get through it." In some way, you will always be his little girl, the golden-blond little girl who first called him Dad, who was tiny, and when he turned around, you were grown.

In no time you were off to college, married, and having your first child. I believe having your first child encourage you to search for your birth parents. I remember one of the first things you said to me after Brandon's birth was, "Mom, I don't understand how anyone could give a child away."

We always told you that we and you, when you were twenty-one, had the right to open the sealed records in Cambridge. I remember telling the social worker at the time of the adoption, "I want the top part of the records covered, when we come to sign." I didn't want a name to think about. I had a sense you were always meant to be our daughter. You just had to find an atypical way of getting to us because there was a roadblock.

However, I knew one day you might want to learn the rest of your story. Knowing who your birth parents were seemed natural and very much a part of finding your identity. So when you called that day to tell me you had found your birth mother, I cried, not because I was sad or felt threatened but because things were as they should be. Your first day at school, leaving you at college, your wedding all flashed across my mind's eye. Here was another step in your becoming. You sounded incredibly mature in the story you shared, amazingly thoughtful, and very much the loving daughter you have always been.

By coincidence, when you went to visit your birth mother Veronica, I was back in New Jersey finishing a graduate degree. The two of you drove from Massachusetts to Pennsylvania to meet one of your birth mother's sisters, who you apparently resemble. You stopped in New Jersey so Veronica and I could meet.

Over the years, I never thought about meeting the woman who gave you life. Intuitively, I knew she did not forget you, but I had no reason to search for her. That day in New Jersey the past and the present joined. As you introduced Veronica to me, your voice had a soft quiver. I looked at this beautiful woman, a few years younger than myself. I reached to shake her hand, but she looked like family—like you—and I hugged her instead.

"It's wet out there," she said.

I stood looking at her and at you. She was taller, had the same hair and skin color, the same thick, black eyelashes, the same bone structure around the eyes, but her fingers, arms, legs and body were longer and thinner.

You looked from Veronica to me, weighing the moment and pulling at your wet jeans, and I knew you were hoping everything would be all right. "We thought we would just pick you up and go to the Black Horse Inn for lunch," you said.

"Sure. That sounds great." I nodded.

"My car is warmed up. I'll drive." Veronica said and I saw the same 'I'm in charge' manner you have always possessed.

Once we were inside the restaurant and ordered our lunch, Veronica said, "I was so nervous to meet you. Ehren said that was silly. She said there was nothing to worry about with her mom."

I studied Veronica. She began to relax as we talked. Life had given us such different experiences. I could only imagine how difficult relinquishing you must have been. I noticed a glow about her. She was warm, poised, and thoughtful. We talked more than two hours in the wood-paneled restaurant with rain falling outside. It was the same restaurant we frequented on Friday nights with you, when you were growing up.

Veronica told us about the Catholic unwed mother's home. She described her difficult and lonely delivery—the nuns' refusal to call her parents until after your birth. She shared how insistent her father was about the adoption, and how the birth father had been unresponsive to her calls and letters.

"Did you give Ehren a name?" I asked.

"Yes. I named her Robin. A robin made a nest outside the window of my room in the maternity home. She laid her eggs. They hatched, and the babies flew away the day I left."

And you grew up Ehren Robinson, I thought. My husband's sister's name is Robin Robinson. For a moment life took on a surreal quality, but I said nothing about the coincidence.

"Why did you call her Ehren? Didn't they tell you she had a name?"

"We didn't ask. I suppose they would have told us, yet they didn't volunteer the information. Ehren is a German verb. It means to cherish."

I looked over and noticed the waiter taking down the buffet. We were the only ones left in the restaurant. The afternoon had slipped away.

"Will you take our picture?"

"Sure."

I handed him the camera, and we smiled while he unknowingly recorded our private celebration

We drove back up the familiar, winding mountain road in the rain—the road you took every day to and from school—to where I was then staying with an old friend. Our conversation seemed natural, casual, like family or good friends. After hugs, you and Veronica let me out at my friend's driveway and drove away.

That day back in my study with my books closed, I sat looking at the rain washing the summer dust away. Images of your smile and incredible buoyancy floated across my memory. I thought about the unexpected afternoon with Veronica and you. I thought about how connected we all are in a much larger family.

At the end of the summer, I went home to Santa Barbara and began work on my thesis. That Christmas you asked if I could put together an album of your school pictures for Veronica. In January I sent Veronica the album, but I didn't hear from her for a long time. Finally three months later when everyone was gathered for Adam's twentieth birthday celebration, she called, unaware that the date was anything special. I was putting the finishing touches on dinner when the phone rang.

"Hello, Nancy. This is Veronica." At first I didn't recognize her voice. I moved a pan of vegetables off the stove and forced my mind to flip through the Veronicas I knew. Then I realized who she was. "I've been wanting to call and thank you for the pictures you sent. They mean a great deal to me."

264

We talked for forty-five minutes. She was warm and funny, like you. We talked about our families and about you. At the end of the conversation, she said, "Nancy, I want to be completely honest with you. That's the way I want our relationship to be, and so I want to tell you something."

"Sure."

"When I saw those pictures of Ehren, I felt so jealous of you. You had what I could not have. You had what society took away from me."

A long silence passed across the 3500 miles of phone lines connecting us. An ache rose in my stomach. "I understand." My voice was a whisper. I could never explain to her how much I felt you were our daughter, how many of your qualities were like mine, nor how quickly I forgot you were adopted as we lived our life. Veronica's understanding and experiences were different from mine. I knew the intimacy of your childhood. I cared for you in illness, enjoyed your friends, encouraged your education. You helped me grow and understand so much. You are so deeply woven into the fabric of our lives and our family. She was left with an enormous question mark and a sense of loss.

"I hope you're not angry," Veronica said. "I can't help it. I'm jealous. Maybe someday I won't be."

"I'm not angry and I do understand. It's a perfectly natural way to feel. You know I am really glad you called, and I am very happy I had the pictures to send you."

"You are very easy to talk with."

"Well, Veronica, you are too. Thanks so much for calling." I hung up and tried to imagine what Veronica was thinking. She had given this incredible gift, not knowing who we were or how we would care for you. I wondered if Veronica felt relieved to learn you enjoyed a loving home, siblings, a beautiful childhood, you had grown up wondering about your birth parents but not angry, and you simply wanted to get to know them and offer your friendship.

That night I reheated Adam's birthday dinner. He tossed me a tender glance as we sat down to the table. After, we sang "Happy Birthday," had our traditional cake, and Adam opened his gifts. I watched the delight and joy spread across his face, and I thought about how it must feel each year on your child's birthday not knowing what the child looked like, where she was, or what her life was like. I thought about the fine thread connecting all of us, stringing the events of our common human experiences. As I picked up the wrapping paper and cleared the dishes, I felt privileged to experience the gift of birthdays with all three of you children.

We watch you now with your three children and we marvel at all you do. Coming for each of your children's birthdays and experiencing the love in your family give us tremendous joy and satisfaction. When I see you act silly with them, I see myself twenty-five years ago. I hear the same expressions of love and tenderness I used with you. Your attention to details at birthdays and holidays reminds me of times in our home when you were growing up.

It is spring as I write. Easter will be this Sunday. If the robin is the first sign of spring, if spring is nature's reminder of rebirth, if your birth mother named you Robin, and you grew up Ehren Robinson, your place in our lives is a reminder of the power of renewal in the human spirit. As I reflect on the last thirty-one years, I am convinced a force leads us and connects us in ways we cannot always comprehend in our finite form.

McDonald and Nancy Robinson were childhood sweethearts. They graduated the same year from the University of California at Berkeley and were married the next day. Mac holds a Sc.D. from MIT in Materials Science. He is the Chief Technical Officer of Lawrence Semiconductor Research Labs, where he develops new materials for semiconductor businesses. Nancy Robinson holds a M.A. from Drew University, is a former teacher, and is a writer and editor. The Robinsons live in Santa Barbara, California. They enjoy sailing and skiing with their children and grandchildren.

Veronica's Story
Ehren's Birth Mother

The day I received a letter from Ehren, I was at the beauty shop fixing someone's hair. The mailman came with a registered letter for me. I had never received registered mail, so I didn't understand what it was. I signed for it. All my co-workers asked, "What is it? What is it?" I had no idea. No idea.

I opened it and saw three pictures of Ehren in her bridal dress, one of Brian in his tux, and one of Brandon as a baby. As I looked at Ehren, I saw a faint resemblance to my sister Cindy. I opened Ehren's letter and the first thing I saw was June 25, 1967. Immediately I knew who she was. I started to shake, to get very warm. I went into the shop's backroom and began to cry. I couldn't believe I was finally looking at a picture of my daughter. All those years I wondered where she was, what she looked like, was she happy, did she look like me, was she tall, short? Now here her picture was right in front of me as a beautiful bride.

My co-workers kept talking through the door trying to find out what was wrong. I finally gave them some flimsy answer. Since it was a Saturday, I had many customers still to do. When I finished, I called my mother and told her about the letter. She couldn't believe it. She planned to come in that afternoon, and now she wanted to see the pictures.

I must have read Ehren's letter fifty times that day and fifty times I thought about calling her. I didn't know how my husband Robert would react, so immediately after work, I went to Mother's to make the first phone call to Ehren. Ehren's husband answered the phone. He knew I was calling. There was whispering in the background. Ehren came to the phone. "Ehren, this is Veronica."

"Well, hi!" She tried to sound casual.

We had a wonderful conversation. Ehren was full of questions. I think she was shocked at a lot of the answers. Though I was still in a state of shock, I was thrilled to be talking with her.

That night Robert and I had a dinner dance to attend. I was not in a mood to go, but Robert insisted, "We can't miss it. We paid good money for those tickets." So, we went. A group of our close friends were also there. All evening I felt as if I was in a dream and could not focused on the social life around me.

During the evening, a friend began telling us a story about a neighbor. She had just been reunited with her son. I listened to the story. Thoughts whirled through my head. I said nothing. Robert kept looking at me. I had not yet talked with our children about Ehren and the letter and didn't want to say anything.

The next morning when Robert was playing golf, I called our children Janet and David into the living room to tell them. Easy going David said, "Oh that's good. Okay, I'm going out to ride my bike." Janet did not handle it well. She was very upset but has accepted it over time. When Ehren and her son Brandon came to visit, Janet really enjoyed Brandon. Now she is comfortable with the knowledge that she has a half-sister.

Janet, David and Ehren enjoyed each other during the two visits they have had. I think if we lived closer, their friendships would develop but a two-week visit out of a year isn't long enough for them to develop a friendship.

Everyone shares stories about reuniting with a child. Few share stories about relinquishing a child. I want to tell you what it was like.

When I realized I was pregnant and I had to tell my parents, I felt such shame. I knew I had disappointed them. Of all my siblings, I was the one who got in trouble. My father was very upset and definitely wanted to go after Hal. One way or other, Hal was going to be made responsible for the situation. He repeatedly said, "How could you do this? I thought you were smarter."

Immediately I was put into The Guild, a home in Westfield, M.A., run by nuns for unwed mothers. Since I am not Catholic and was not accustomed to being around nuns, I was petrified. The home was very regimented, but it was not as bad as I thought it would be. I made friends. Some of the nuns were friendly, some were not, but that is the way with most people.

I spent four months there. Another girl went into labor the same night I did. We were put in a room together and the nun checked us periodically. Eventually she said, "It's time to go to the hospital." At the hospital we were put in separate labor rooms because they said girls from the home needed to be separated. My labor was so intense that I called to the nurse for help. The nurse came in and said, "Would you please keep your voice down?" Then she pulled the curtain around my bed.

"Have you called my mother?"

"No. It is the middle of the night and I don't want to wake her." She left and returned with the doctor. He broke my water and gave me a shot.

The next thing I knew I was in the delivery room. I said to the nurse, "Please don't let me fall back to sleep. I want to be awake."

I knew it was a hard delivery, but I was so drugged that I remember only when she was born. The nurse said, "You have a little girl." The next thing I remember was the recovery room. Then I was put in a room at the end of the floor because I was from the "Home" and had to be separated from the other maternity patients. I was told by the staff, "Do not walk out of your room during visiting hours."

I was in the hospital five days and saw Ehren during her bottle time. I knew seeing her would make giving her up harder, but I decided that even if I could not have her for the rest of my life, I could have her for these five days. She was a beautiful baby. She never cried. I fed her, changed her, and washed her. On the fifth day, the social worker came. Ehren was brought to me for one last visit. I sat on the end of the bed and looked at her. I wanted to remember what she looked like, but I could not focus on her through the tears.

They took her away. Mother was in the hall. She was crying. Immediately I had to go down the hall where witnesses were and sign the three papers surrendering my child for adoption.

This was one of the worst moments of my life. I felt such shame and I knew I had to give her up. I had embarrassed my parents and I knew I had to do what they wanted. I left the hospital, drove away, and stared out the window. I felt some consolation because the social worker told me, "Your baby will be leaving the hospital this afternoon. She will go right into the arms of her adoptive parents."

Twenty-three years later when Ehren found me, I learned the social worker lied. My baby did not have a good start. She had bronchial problems. She was in two different foster homes. If I had known this at the time, I would have kept her. I would have gotten her back. But I was deceived. Today they would not be able to deceive the birth mother.

My parents did not support my desire to keep the baby. They did not want to raise another child. Life was very hard for me for many months after surrendering her. Believing that she was with a family that desperately wanted a child was what helped me get through this period.

Her first birthday was one of the hardest days. I kept saying, "This is the best thing for her." Now I know why it was the best thing, though it still hurts and I have never recovered from relinquishing my child. Ehren feels that finding each other after all these years makes everything all right. Sometimes it feels like relinquishing her was yesterday. Tears fill my eyes and emotions flood my mind as if the experience just happened. The pain never goes away.

I am very happy with the family who raised Ehren. I think they are very good, loving people. I am pleased with the way she was raised. She is a wonderful, beautiful person, and I thank God everyday that she is in my life again.

Veronica's story is a transcription from a tape. Her real name and those of her family are changed at her request. Her story is printed here with her permission.

Insomnia

Midnight. Tiger. Rain. Clouds
entangle street lights. Walls.
Paw my daughter's sleep. Her
blanket rises, falls with each breath.
My wife, asleep and I'm awake
wondering about my mother. Outside
tires peel rain
like strips of newsprint.
Headlines: Forty-five campesinos
massacred in Acteal, Mexico.

What is my mother's name? Is she
poor? Homeless? My country. America.
I always noticed poor people, Homeless
people. Mowing lawns at the Federal
Customs House, sometimes I'd
have to move them. Sometimes
I'd imagine an older woman,
brown skin, black hair. Five foot
one. Something in my blood
would recognize her.

The rain. Hasn't stopped. Faster now.
A drum beat against my roof.
I imagine a car horn blaring,
some dead person required to move.
How many people die with each
drop of rain? I wish I could sleep.
In cities across Mexico. Six and seven
year-old kids. Run. In subways.
On busses. Down restaurant isles.
Sing. Play guitar. Sell gum and
ceramic pigeons. Four pesos.
In Cuernavaca. A homeless lady.
Gray hair. Dirt-red blouse
hiked above her waist. Pissed and shit.
Huddled between brick and walls.
A baby slept. I wish I could sleep.
Write a poem. I know
my birth mother is out there.
Does she know I am here?

Does she sleep? What thoughts of me,
in night, come to her?
Rain falls. Faster. Fingers tapping
on a key board.

Mark Sanchez

Mark Sanchez is an M.F.A. candidate at Colorado
State University and editor of an on line journal
Nieve Roja Review for the English department. As
a Chicano writer, he explores self-identity by
wondering about adoption. This allows him
freedom to cross borders and create an identity tied
to historical and biological Mexican ancestors as
well as one connected to the people surrounding his
daily activities. At this time, he does not search for
his birth mother.

Birth Mother

You named me Ilene twenty-five years ago.   It's funny
I didn't turn out to be   Ilenish at all. Not that it's not
a nice name.   I just called to let you know   I'm OK.
I thought maybe you needed to know that. Maybe sometimes you stay
awake, look out over the patient blue lawn, and wonder.   I'm happy.
As happy as anyone. Who has insomnia, yellow skin. Pale eyes, an urge
to wander. As a child I thought I was Native American, whispering leaves
instructed me to follow the seasons, name myself Prancing Pony.
When I was told you were Jewish, I settled for Sephardim davening
in dusty Mediterranean moonlight.   Roumania? So that's where all
this hair came from, the flat cheekbones. I suppose I should ask about
cancer, diabetes, heart disease, any?   I never thought this day
would come. I have a great family. Never wanted for anything
anything but   what you did   it is the most   selfless act
anyone ever. Even when I was three and I spent the entire afternoon
crying in the Dunkin' Donuts parking lot begging my mother
to tell me why you didn't want me. Even then I had a sense of the love
behind the courage it took.   I imagine when I kicked you hummed
lullabies tangled in stained cheeks and crow's feet. I just wanted
to tell you   we have each other. Even though I've never touched
the hems of your dresses or the ridges of your spine   I can only
smile because your full lips. You can only dance on my flat feet with
delicate ankles.   Sure, maybe we'll write

Lauren Schiffman

"Birth Mother" is reprinted here with permission of the author. It appeared in *Cipactli* and won third prize in the 1998 Browning Society Dramatic Monologue Contest.

Lauren Schiffman is a M.F.A. candidate in Creative Writing at San Francisco State University. Her publication credits include poetry, fiction, and nonfiction in *14 Hills, The Noe Valley Voice; the San Francisco Bay Guardian, Barnabe Mountain, Cipactli,* and *SOMA*. She also edits and publishes the annual literary journal *crack*.

How Much I Would Understand
Kathlyn Scott

Unlike a lot of adoptees, I never wondered about my birth mother. I know that sounds awful. If I am involved in a discussion with another adoptee and mention this fact, I never hear the end of it. I've been called not only selfish but also heartless and an emotional cripple.

How could I not wonder about where I came from or who I looked like? How could I not want to meet the woman who gave birth to me and know who I was? How could I ever feel whole?

I do feel whole. Mostly. Maybe I didn't know where I came from biologically, but I know myself pretty well. It took time, maturity, and yes, some therapy, but I like who I have become. I am strong and intelligent, self-reliant and funny. I also enjoy knowing there is no one else like me in the world.

Aside from one very dark period of my life, I consciously avoided thinking about my birth mother. I focused on the future not the past. Perhaps I did not want to deal with the potential rejection. If I never wanted to know my birth mother, if I never allowed myself the hope that she might want to know me, then I never opened a door, which might well just slam in my face. But sometimes when I tried on silly hats or played with new makeup techniques in the mirror, I wondered if there was someone else in the world who did these things too and what else we might share.

Then one day I received a letter from my birth mother. Just like that—no endless searching, no anxious trips to the mailbox waiting for correspondence that might come. I came home from work one night and on my bed was the letter, tossed there by a roommate along with a last chance to win the Publishers Clearinghouse Sweepstakes and my Amex bill. As I would jokingly comment later to one of my friends, "It didn't even glow."

Hello.

I have been thinking lately that you are at an age where you might be considering marriage and starting a family of your own. As a result, I have completed the enclosed forms for the Agency and requested they forward them to you. I hope you find this information useful.

Sincerely,
Linda

Neatly clipped to the letter were forms listing various medical conditions from frequent headaches to Alzheimer's disease. Next to each condition was a box for yes and one for no, and most of the no's were checked. At the end of the forms there was a space for comments, and penned in Linda's handwriting was the sentence, "There is no information available on the biological father." A note from the agency caseworker stated that Linda was not interested in a reunion and did not wish a reply.

I had absolutely no idea how to feel. Here was someone I had tried not to think about, but she thought about me and wanted me to know something about me. Wow! This was more than I ever thought I would have. Suddenly I had an actual medical history. I sat on the porch with my cat and read the letter over and over, sipping wine and hoping that more words would magically appear on the page. When my roommate came home later that night, he found me there looking dazed and out of sorts.

"What's wrong?" he asked.

"Nothing," I replied, shaking and holding out the forms. Breast cancer did not run in half of my family.

Unfortunately for the caseworker one taste of this woman, whose genes made up half of my DNA, became an addiction. Once I had a little information, I wanted more. I wrote to Linda in care of the adoption agency. Briefly I sketched the quarter century of my life and offered her photos. I included my address, phone number, and let her know I would be happy to hear from her, if she wished to call. Then I placed the letter in the mailbox and joined the ranks of those anxiously anticipating the mail. I didn't receive a reply immediately, but I never stopped hoping.

Each time I moved, I let the agency know my new address and phone number. I tried not to get my hopes up and never consciously believed she would actually call. Still a shard of hope remained in the back of my mind.

On a rainy Sunday four years later, she called. I was trying to hem the new curtains in my living room. "Hello," I said. No answer. "Hello? Hello? Is anyone there?"

"Is Kate available?" a soft, shaky voice nothing like mine.

"This is she." More silence. Then a deep breath.

"This is Linda. I received your letter from the agency? It had your phone number."

"Oh my God . . ." I sank onto the floor. The curtain material draped around me. This is what I wanted. Wasn't it? I wasn't sure what to say. Taking a deep breath, I started with hello. In the tense conversation, we tried to gently tiptoe around any emotional depth charges. She was guarded, hurried. I asked neutral questions about innocuous things like favorite movies and books. We both liked "Casablanca" and had traveled extensively. To my delight, I found she too enjoyed spending days wandering around the British Museum. My favorite exhibit was the extensive book collection and second was the Mummies. Her favorite was the reverse. We both wore reading glasses and never had to have braces as children. We both loved cats.

Was she relaxing a little? I was. Maybe this wasn't so hard to accept—in the world there was this woman, who carried me around for nine months then gave me up, but now she wanted to know me. Maybe there was a chance . . .

"I was raped." Her voice was almost inaudible. My eyes filled with tears as she told me of the man who was my father. She trusted him. One night she went back with him to his room, and he had gone too far.

Was she crying too? I couldn't tell. Her voice became measured and steady as she continued.

"It wasn't your fault," I said, hoping she believed it as much as I knew it was true.

"I can't discuss this any longer. I just wanted to call and say hello, to see how you were. I've wondered about you. I hope you know that. And I think about you often."

"Call me back." It was more a plea than a request.

"I'll try, when I can. Good-bye, Kate." Then she was gone, leaving me with more questions than answers. At least now I knew how she sounded when she said my name.

The call was almost three years ago. Somehow I always thought she would call back. Was there something more I could have said, something to make her stay on the line? Lots of things I suppose—that I graduated with honors from college, trivial things—I liked hats and Hanna Barbera cartoons. Then again, maybe nothing. I regret the one thing I should have said when she said, "I think about you often."

I think about you too, Linda. I do.

In my freshman year at college, I walked home late one night from the library. Someone I could not later describe grabbed me and violently raped me. Shaking and constantly looking over my shoulder, I made my way to the local hospital.

Did you go for help, Linda? Did you sit in some hospital waiting, shivering even though it wasn't cold? And did you look around to make sure no one you knew was there, because even if you knew you had done nothing wrong, you still didn't want people to see you there?

I waited a long time while the more "serious" cases were treated. I told the receptionist, "I've had an accident." I couldn't say the word rape. But in privacy, in the stark-white exam room and alone with a kind nurse, I stammered the truth.

The following events made me feel detached from reality. My body became the provider of evidence to be collected and cataloged. Photographs were taken and swabs obtained. My body was examined and my torn shorts and underwear placed in an evidence bag. In some ways the exam was more of a violation than the rape. As I numbly placed my feet in the stirrups, the nurse asked, "Do you want me to hold your hand to make it better?" I don't recall if I replied, but my look made her recoil slightly. She didn't understand—nothing would ever be better.

Did you call the police?

Many date rapes go unreported.

If you reported yours, I hope the doctors and officials were kind.

What they say makes you feel more safe and, in a way, brings you back to earth. Though, you can't quite believe them, you want to. But the entire scope of your life has shifted irrevocably. My officers were male and gruff. They insinuated I should have known better than to walk alone at night. They asked if I had someone who could come and get me.

Did you have someone?

I want to think there was someone for you, they put you to bed, and maybe they made you some hot chocolate liberally laced with brandy.

Were you able to tell anyone?

I imagine a sympathetic friend, who sensed something was not right and

*wanted to make you feel better. Maybe they tucked you in, asked if you wanted the
light. Maybe even if it was on, you still couldn't close your eyes, because you
never knew who might be in your closet or under the bed.*

After taking a statement, the police took me home. I didn't want them to
drive up to my dorm. There would be on-lookers and I didn't want to answer their
questions. The police let me out near my dormitory and I practically ran to the
front doors. I couldn't get in. When I was grabbed, my bag opened and I lost my
ID. I had to fill out forms at the dorm desk and then have my roommate sign me
in. I was thankful that one of the nurses gave me a pair of scrub pants so the
bruises were not visible.

Were you actually able to find water hot enough to burn off his touch?

I couldn't, despite the hours I spent in the shower long after my roommate
went back to sleep. I kept lathering myself with soap and rinsing in the scalding
water. For years I could not get clean enough.

Since my periods were irregular, I waited three weeks before I took a home
pregnancy test. The results were negative. For the first time in a long time, I
thought of you. In my thoughts, you walked beside me every minute I waited.
During those weeks, I often found myself rubbing my stomach and wondering.
Six weeks later the lab test came back negative. I did not have any venereal
diseases and was pronounced fine. The nurse was young and I thought I could
relate to her. However, her forced, cheery disposition conveyed her discomfort.
My requests for another test and an HIV screening met resistance. I knew the
serum test was more accurate and the AIDS test seemed important as well. I
wasn't sure the rapist had worn a condom. I wanted to be safe rather than sorry.

The nurse didn't see it that way. "We don't have the facilities for those kinds
of tests here. I can give you the address of a place that does." She scribbled a
name on a paper and shoved it across the table. Before she left the room to get
the lab technician for the pregnancy test, she said, "I don't see why you have to
overreact like this. You don't need an AIDS test. You're fine. You just need to put
this behind you and concentrate on enjoying college." From her I learned the way
my rape would be regarded by those who had never experienced anything like it.

*How did you feel when they told you that you were going to have a baby?
Did you even consider pregnancy as a potential outcome of what happened?*

I used to wonder if I was wanted. Now I know I wasn't, at least not then.

I admire your decision to carry me and also know in the 1960's there weren't
a lot of options. I don't think that I could have gone through with a pregnancy,
even though I am very uncomfortable with the idea of an abortion. I support a
woman's right to choose, but I never want to have to make that choice.

What did your parents think?

I hope that they were understanding and supportive, that they never blamed
you, that they thought you were brave. You were. I know you took a semester off
from college. I imagine you spending time reading in your favorite chair and
taking long walks with your mother in the woods someplace. In my mind, she
told you that you were doing the right thing, that she loved you, and that none of
this was your fault.

Did she tell you that we would both be better off separated? And did you believe her? Or did you half-heartedly nod and concentrate on the sound of the leaves crunching beneath your feet.

That sound must have seemed like the loudest possible in the world.

How did we spend our time together? Did you talk to me?

I have a lot of friends, who have children, and we spoke to their stomachs all the time they were pregnant.

I've decided that you read aloud to me *To Kill a Mockingbird.* The first time I read the story it had a sweet familiarity, as though I had heard it many times. I've always felt you gave me my passion for books. Since you knew there wasn't anything physical I could take with me, you were going to give me the gift of words.

Did you get to see me after I was born, or did they take me away immediately? Did you even want to look? Did you wake up in the hospital as though from a bad dream and decide not to look back?

I know about that feeling. No mater how hard I tried, I could not complete my education where I was raped. I tried, but I suffered horrible nightmares and retreated to the safety of my bed. Once I was away from the campus, I gained some distance and began healing.

More than anything, I hope you have found some peace. I know there is not complete peace. Memories of being raped live with you forever. You think you are past the feelings, then someone touches your arm or moves toward you too quickly. All of the feelings of vulnerability, anger, fear return like a flood.

I wanted to write this so you will know what I have been through and how, in some ways, you and I traveled a similar road. I realize my very existence is a reminder of a most painful moment in your life—something indelible you might wish to erase.

When I heard the building where I was raped was to be torn down, I flew thousands of miles to the campus and watched. Even packed a lunch. I must have looked strange to passersby—a twenty-something woman, sometimes smiling, sometimes wiping away cold tears, sitting on the grass, watching intensely as an old building fell.

I wish I could erase the past for you, but that would mean erasing myself. And I don't want to do that. My life has not been perfect, perhaps not even enviable by some, but it is mine and I am proud of what I have overcome. Now I know where I get my strength, and the knowledge fills me with pride. Every day that you get up in the morning and talk to people, every night as you go to bed with the light off, you take back some of what he tried to take from you, and you win.

Perhaps you never will call again. I accept that. But please know if you ever want to talk about what happened to you, you can give me a call. Maybe we can come together as survivors first and as something more later on, if it feels right. You have the number, and you might be surprised how much I would understand.

Originally from the Midwest, Kathlyn Scott now lives in San Francisco. In her spare time she writes fiction and searches for Bigfoot in Golden Gate Park.

Real Mother

I didn't conceive you in desire,
although I wanted you
more than any lover.

My limbs weren't split apart
like a wishbone to admit you,
the most glorious wish.

Your birth rendered me
vulnerable to pain
after I stripped my life
to accommodate yours.

I wanted a baby more
than anything in the world,
a child becoming
everything in mine.

I didn't make you, son,
but you made me a mother.

Mary Scott

Kitchen and Kin

I'm making brownies from scratch.
My teen-aged son George takes over,
assigns me the task of reading the recipe.
I assemble ingredients he adds to the bowl.
Batter turns bittersweet brown and glossy
with cocoa, the color of his hair.

Nearly a man, George becomes again
the small child I baked cookies with,
arranging cutters on floured dough
and coloring warm impressions.

As he stirs and sifts and pours,
I watch this blending, wonder what
my son, adopted at birth, gets from me.
A teenager, he's naturally a stranger,
and it's difficult to nurture a boy
living with his father in another city.

We're at home in this kitchen, not
the room he remembers from childhood
but one we share this summer afternoon.
While the brownies bake, George types
my recipe to take home with him,
lets me lick the battered wooden spoon.

Mary Scott

Adopted at Birth

My world focused on you
as your universe opened.
Eyes like indigo didn't fade
but intensified with time.

I absorbed you,
your skin like the fine
graininess of a ripe pear.
A milk blister on your lip
response to first friction.

Umbilical cord fell off,
severed physical connection
to your birth mother.

She relinquished you,
denied herself pleasure
of seeing you grow

from this plummy bud,
fragrant as vanilla.

We developed together,
filled each other's needs,

mine infinitely greater.

Mary Scott

Decree

The judge declared you my son
but didn't know you already were.
He never witnessed our first meeting,
when only the nursery window
came between us initially, then
nothing to disrupt our bond.

Only I recalled the half-slumbering
middle of night when you suddenly
pitched me awake. Enchanted
I watched your eyelashes grow.

I promised to raise you as my own,
but you, my child, already were.

Mary Scott

Mary Scott writes a weekly poetry column for the *Ventura County Star.* She has
been the associate editor of *rivertalk,* a poetry journal published by the Ojai
Center for the Arts. Her poems, articles, short stories and photographs have been
published in more than sixty magazines, newspapers and anthologies.

Summer
Anne Seale

Last year when I was ten, I used to sometimes wish my real mom had kept me so I wouldn't have to think about being adopted. It's not that I didn't love Momma and Libby—I loved them to bits—but when I'd wake up in the middle of the night, it was hard to keep from thinking about real moms and dads and stuff like that.

This year I have other things to think about in the middle of the night, like wishing it was last year. This year, in June, Momma got cancer.

They told me on a Saturday morning. I know it was Saturday because it was the day Libby had a new haircut when she picked me up from my piano lesson. I told her she looked like my friend Jessica's Schnauzer that had been trimmed for hot weather. She made a sour face and said she'd been intending to take me to meet Momma at Butterchurn Park for a hike, but now she was having second thoughts. She took me anyway, of course.

When we got to the park, Momma was waiting, sitting on a swing but not swinging. She stood and hugged us, asking, "What did you learn today, Summer?" like she always did after a piano lesson, then handed me a bottle of water in an insulated bag. I strapped it on my belt and we all headed for the nature walk as I hummed for them my new practice piece, "There's Music in the Air."

Momma and I had been hiking the Butterchurn nature walk for as long as I could remember. In early spring, wearing boots and ski jackets, we'd search for yellow crocuses poking their way through the snow. Then every week or so until school started, we'd go back to check on what had sprouted or bloomed since we were last there.

Sometimes my friend Jessica would come with us, and sometimes Libby would. Sometimes we'd bring sandwiches, sitting on rocks to eat them while Momma read poems about nature from a little book she kept in her backpack. Then we'd finish the walk, reading for the umpteenth time the plaques on the wooden signposts that identified the plants. I'd run my fingertips over the little Braille bumps below the words on the signs, wondering what it would be like to be blind and have them mean something.

That Saturday we hiked almost halfway around the loop before stopping in the woods whose sign said it was The Pinetum. Once I told Momma and Libby that when I build a house I want it to be in a spot like The Pinetum where it's shady all the time and the air always smells like Christmas. Libby said I'd better get a good-paying job then, so I could afford the fire insurance. Momma told her to stop being so darned practical.

Anyway, it was in The Pinetum that Momma told me she had cancer. We were sitting on pine needles, Momma leaning against Libby and me leaning against Momma. "It's in my liver, Summer," she said. "I'm going to have some treatments, and we are all going to hope for the best."

I pretended I didn't hear and looked up into the branches to count birds, but I didn't see any. So I picked up all the pinecones I could reach and lined them up.

There were ten long skinny ones and two small round ones. I arranged and stacked them in every way I could think of until Momma said, "Come, my loved ones, it's time to go home."

I had a stomach-ache the rest of the day, and it took me a long time to fall asleep, even though they let me stay up to watch a movie that wasn't over until ten-thirty.

The next morning I was surprised when Momma woke me up and said to put a dress on, we were going to Mass. It wasn't that we'd never gone to Mass before—I'd even made my First Communion—but Momma had decided there was no point in it and we'd stopped going. Once when I wondered why, she said she had become a sinner in the church's eyes and was having a whole lot of trouble bringing herself to regret it.

I was even more surprised when I saw Libby, dressed in her good shirt and slacks, waiting for us in the car. Libby hadn't been Catholic ever in her life.

We sat in the tenth row and were the fourth, fifth and sixth people from the center aisle. I thought everybody would stare at us because we hadn't been there for so long, but they didn't. They even shook our hands at the Sign of Peace. I went to take Communion, but Momma and Libby stayed in the pew.

After we got home and had dinner, Momma went to lie down for a while and Libby said it was a nice day, how about going for a ride with the top down? I said "Sure!" because without Momma along, I'd get to sit in the front seat and look cool. Then I felt bad for thinking such a thing. I'd a hundred times more rather have Momma go with us.

We'd been riding for a while out in the country, when Libby reached over and turned down the radio. She looked at me and said, "Summer, I've been thinking about what will happen when . . . if . . . your Momma has to leave us."

Leave us? Momma wouldn't leave us, how dumb! I concentrated on the flapping of a tarp that was on the back of a truck a little ways in front of us. I was trying to count how many times it flapped each minute by watching the dashboard clock.

"What I came up with, " she said, "is that I could start proceedings to adopt you, with your Momma's permission, of course. What do you think about that? You could stay with me in my house, go to the same school. Otherwise, I don't know what would happen. Maybe your Aunt Laura would want to raise you."

The tarp was flapping too fast to be counted. I waited for some bales of hay that were coming up on my side of the road.

She squeezed my shoulder. "In the two years we've all been together, I've come to love you, Summer, a lot. I want you to stay with me, be my daughter."

There were sixteen bales.

"Well, you think about it," she said, and turned the radio up again.

Even though I didn't want to, I did think about it. Momma was going to get well again and that was all there was to it! But the thought that someday I might have to go live with Aunt Laura and Uncle Jeff kept popping into my head. We used to go over to their house for dinner sometimes when I was little, but I hadn't seen them in forever. We all stopped speaking to each other about the same time Libby came into our life, and Momma and I stopped going to Mass.

One day when Libby had gone to the store to get something for supper, I went into the living room where Momma was lying on the couch watching the news. I stood and watched with her until a commercial for frozen pizza came on, then I said, "Momma, you aren't going to die, are you?" She sucked in her breath and stared at me. "Good," I said. "I didn't think so."

Momma sat up, took my hand and pulled me down next to her. "Oh, Summer," she said, "We should have talked about this long before now. I guess I haven't quite come to terms with it myself."

"We don't have to talk about it." I said quickly. I'd realized that the answer wasn't going to be anything I wanted to hear.

But she kept on talking. "The truth is, Sweetie, I suppose I might die a whole lot sooner than I'd planned on. Oh, I'm not afraid of dying, but what I'd like is to stay here with you and Libby, and have us all grow old together. She held me close and I felt her kiss the top of my head. Her breath moved my hairs as she quietly said, "If I should die, Sweetheart, I want you to know that I'll be with you in my thoughts, wherever you are and wherever I am, and that I love you very much." I kept my eyes on the TV screen where they were laughing like crazy over something I couldn't see because my eyes were all bleary. Momma and I watched the rest of the news and the weather and even the sports without moving a muscle.

Two weeks later Momma stopped going to work. She stayed home all the time except for treatment days, and then she'd go right to her room when she got back and not come out for supper. She started wearing a kerchief over her head all the time, even when nobody was around except us.

Then one day when Libby and I were playing Scrabble, a priest came to the door. He was carrying a black briefcase. I told Libby, when she got back from showing him to Momma's room, to do whatever had to be done in order to adopt me.

"I've already filed the papers, darling." she said, and took hold of me tightly. I started crying and so did she. We cried for a long time, getting each others' shoulders all wet.

Momma died on Monday August 15, in the middle of the afternoon. Libby and I were with her, sitting on the bed on either side. She didn't say anything, but she smiled at me like everything was okay and she wasn't going to die after all, and then she did.

Aunt Laura and Uncle Jeff came to the funeral home and stared at Momma for a long time, crying. Then, without saying a thing to Libby, Aunt Laura took me from the room. Uncle Jeff followed us. She sat on a carved wooden chair in the lobby, looked into my face and wouldn't let go of my hand when I tried to pull it away. "You poor thing," she said, "I didn't know Theresa was sick or I would have been there, you know I would."

I watched Aunt Laura's mouth as she talked. It moved like Momma's, and her chin was like Momma's too, sort of pointy. I pulled really hard and got my hand away.

"Summer," she said, "Uncle Jeff and I want you to come live with us."

"No thank you." I said. "Libby's adopting me. I'm going to stay with her."

She looked at Uncle Jeff and then back at me. "I don't think so. She's not a proper parent for you. You need a real family."

A basket of flowers had been set by the door to the room where Momma was. There were twelve long stems of gladiola with five pink flowers each, actually a couple had six, and ten big white chrysanthemums on shorter stems. I was starting on the ferns when Libby came and silently led me back into the room.

A week later I went to live with Aunt Laura and Uncle Jeff. Libby told me it was "by court order."

"Aren't you going to adopt me?" I asked.

"I can't," she said. "They've appointed your aunt legal guardian."

"I hate her!" I said. "I don't want to live with her. I want to stay here with you!"

Libby looked away from me. "Don't hate her. She's your mother's sister. That makes her mighty fine."

She helped pack my clothes and games, and let me pick whatever I wanted from Momma's things. I took her dress watch and a big green sweater with eight buttons that she always wore.

"Will you come visit me?" I asked as she fixed me an egg salad sandwich on the last day.

"I want to, but I can't. Court order." She put her arm around me, and we stared out the sliding-glass door at the picnic table and the brick barbecue and, behind them, the fence that we'd painted bright yellow the summer before. I'd gotten paint all over me, under my fingernails and in my hair. "I'll miss you so much, Summer, you don't know," Libby said so softly I almost didn't hear.

"What?" I asked, so she'd have to say it again.

It's the end of October now. I'm getting sort of used to Aunt Laura and Uncle Jeff, and they're getting used to me. My new school is okay and I've made a couple of friends.

Last week Aunt Laura and I were working on my Halloween costume. I got to thinking about the year before when I was a bag of jelly beans, and Momma, Libby and I had blown up so many little balloons that we were gasping for breath, and then we started laughing, which made it even worse.

"Can I call up Libby?" I asked Aunt Laura.

She told me no, the judge had forbid it. Anyway, she said, she'd heard that Libby had rented out the house and moved away, she didn't know where. I ran to the phone and dialed. A recording told me that the number had been disconnected, and to be sure I had the right one. As if I wouldn't know the number that had been my own for more than two years!

I ran to my new room and sat for a long time on the edge of my new bed, thinking about everything that used to be—Momma and Libby and our house and our yard. Our yellow fence that had one hundred and fifty-four pickets and fifteen posts, including one where Libby had carved as soon as the paint was dry, the words:

LIBBY

+

THERESA

+

SUMMER

TOGETHER FOREVER

 Anne Seale has four adult children. She writes and performs songs, stories, poems, and plays. Her short stories are included in several recent anthologies and periodicals. She divides her time between Arizona and New York.

Thirty Years Past

I released your souls before I knew
how life would be divided
From tender kisses and playful coos
which fell silent as worlds collided
Inside my womb you were punished
by parents too young to see
Consumed by confusion and anger,
we were questing to be free
Enduring angst for you, my sons,
I learned to live in fear
The life I anticipated turned
delight into a tear
Cherishing, protecting and loving you
was what I suffered for
Six months later, our bond was snapped
as love traveled out the door
My world crashed hard that fateful day
as my sons became displaced
To another world filled with hope
they left without a trace
Thirty years past and here I sit
searching for a clue
Where are you, my grown-up boys?
Are your eyes green or blue?
Love isn't stilled by distance
nor time passed on the clock
It's a void within my saddened soul
where my heart's transformed to rock
Your picture sits atop my desk
I envision you every day
If I pass you in crowded mall
will two heads turn my way?
I'll recognize you by your smiles,
you'll know me by my need
Questing for your acquaintance
is an end I'll never heed.

Happy 30th Birthday 7-29-96

Lynn Ellyn Rausin Sheldon

Lynn Ellyn Rausin Sheldon was born in Upland, California. She has written hundreds of poems but not for publication. At sixteen, she gave birth to twin sons Steven and Michael. After six months, she realized that she could not provide adequate care for them and gave them up for adoption the day after Christmas 1966. Later she had another son. Lynn recently made a successful search for Steven and Michael and learned that right after they were placed in an adoptive home, they were diagnosed with a potentially fatal lung disease. In retrospect, Lynn realizes that she was too young to recognize their illness and that their placement perhaps saved their lives. With the gracious cooperation from their loving parents and the curiosity of genetics, Lynn and her sons discovered they have many things in common. At this writing Lynn has not actually met her sons but will in the near future.

Postscript: Lynn Rausin Sheldon met her sons on May 16, 1998. She writes, "Our journey has been an incredible experience and our love is truly special."

Little Girl Little Boy

little girl with corn rows
and dark eyes
and tongue at a mischievous slant
that's what I want

tied for first place though
is a boy with that same tongue
same eyes
in a pair of old jeans
and a yellow slicker
running to school

tell ya what
I'll take both

John Sherman

"Little Girl Little Boy" appeared in the Poetry on the Buses program in the Indianapolis METRO (bus system), 1989.

For David Who is Only at This Point a Photo

to me now
you are but a photo
given me by our social worker
with lots of talk
and lots of big words
we don't yet understand
and a promise of delivery
two weeks from friday
should we still want you

should we still want you:
do we want the sun to rise

I said the other night:
I have a son
and tears came to my eyes
and I opened my mouth
and made a gasp
and inhaled quickly
and exhaled quickly
and your mother leaned over
and hugged me
and asked me why I was crying
as if she did not know

since I was ten years old
I have been planning on you
and the gasping realization
that you are finally born
and ready for me
is almost too much to believe
despite the reports
the phone calls
the photo
we stare at every hour
in between our discussions
of fixing up the crib once again
and getting a new high chair
and worrying about your sister
and her sudden sharing
the social worker said
you will cry in the night
because it will all be new and strange
and that will make your sister cry

as you will suddenly make it all
new and strange to her
and we will have rushing second thoughts

and we will probably cry too
sitting up
hugging each other
in a sobbing foursome
at three a.m.
wondering if the world were meant
to be one after all
and deciding at three fifteen
that it probably is
(and having only a tiny relapse
when the alarm screams us semi awake
three hours later)

we are ready for that
almost anxious
so we can get beyond it
and into a foursome
that will spill food at
cheaper restaurants
and take off for the woods
to walk and talk
about what families find to talk about

when I was ten years old
I knew about you
you won't have to wait so long
to get to know me
you can start two weeks from Friday
when I grasp you in your snow suit
bring you close to my teary face
say your name out loud
pull your chest
close to my chest
your cheek close to mine
and hug you for the first
of a thousand times

my first son
following my first daughter
two children sitting together
singing on the rug
making faces at us
in the world

of their generation
clapping hands
in a child's game
absorbing our stares
of amazement that
the rug has any life on it at all
let alone two of our own children
one from our loins literally
and one from our loins so to speak

John Sherman

John Sherman has published two
volumes of poetry. His poems have
appeared in many literary and small
magazines around the country. He was a
finalist in the Walt Whitman Award
competition, sponsored by the Academy
of American Poets, for his book-length
collection of poems on growing up in the
1940s and 1950s on a small Indiana
farm. When he lived in Santa Fe,
Sherman also authored two pictorial
history books on Santa Fe and Taos,
New Mexico. He is the owner of a public
relations firm in Indianapolis.

Emi-Mama
Joan I. Siegel

I became a mother some nine months before my 50th birthday. I didn't have one of those late-life pregnancies or a miracle of IVF technology. Instead, motherhood began when the two-year-old Chinese orphan my husband and I were to adopt was placed in my arms by one of her foster mothers from the Yi Wu Welfare Institute in southeastern China.

Prior to this moment, despite my longing for a child and our repeated failure at adoption, I argued against parenthood. We were already too old, I lamented. We would be sixty when our daughter turned ten, seventy when she was only twenty and probably dead by the time she reached thirty. We would have to continue working for the next twenty years as English teachers at the community college where we already felt burned out. How would we fit in with the parents of her friends, people twenty and thirty years younger, people with different interests and a lot more energy. We were accustomed to a life spent writing, listening to music, reading, walking on the country roads near our home. How could we counter the materialism and crassness around us and succeed in raising a gentle child with a love for nature, and books, and Bach?

These arguments ceased the moment Emily was placed in my arms and I felt the full weight of her twenty-two pounds and the dampness of her body as she struggled for the foster mothers she called *Mama*. That moment alone gave birth to my motherhood. Every instinct surged through me to protect and comfort her, to make her pain go away, to have her reach for me and say, "Mama." In the weeks following, I watched her wrestle with her loss. Her own mother had abandoned her in a railway station when she was fourteen months. As Emily saw it, her foster mothers had abandoned her as well. And now this stranger who spoke a language she didn't understand was carrying her away to a place she didn't recognize, a place where even the air had a different smell. How could I convince her that I would never leave her? How to make her feel loved as my own flesh and blood?

But the truth is I didn't. Though I loved her from the beginning, it was what anyone would feel for a suffering creature—pity, compassion, the desire to heal. Yet in these nine months, that feeling has evolved into something I have never known before, a love both joyous and heavy with longing and grief. This mother love makes me giddy with pleasure when she comes running into my arms and makes me hurt with everything that has ever hurt her in the past and that will hurt her yet. When I lie with her at night until she falls asleep, she often cups my face in her tiny hands and repeats a litany—part confirmation of our relationship and part prayer. "Mama. Emi-Mama," she says. She is terrified when I leave the house. She stands at the door with my husband, points her finger, and says as both reprimand and reassurance, "Mama home! Mama home!"

I hug her, saying, "I love you. I will come back. Mama will never leave Emi," Yet even as I speak these words, I know their falseness. For she doesn't know about death. Or maybe she does. Still, though I accept the necessity of dying at some indeterminate time later, I do not accept it for the present. I worry that she might lose me, that I might get killed in a car accident, get cancer and die. For the first time in my life, I must keep myself safe for someone else, for her sake.

And for my sake, as well as for hers, I must keep her safe. Violence erupts in me when I imagine anyone hurting her. The death of children has assumed a new reality and my mind reels when I think about losing her. I worry about serious illness and about being rear-ended on the highway while she sits in her car seat behind me. I read with sickening fright about child molesters, kidnappers, madmen like the one in Dunblane, Scotland, who killed a gymnasium full of children. Even when she is gone from the house for a few hours, a peculiar sadness edges around me. The rooms shrink and darken and the silence rebounds with her imagined laughter. I stand in her room where time has stopped with the dolls perched at tea, the pile of buttons purloined from my sewing box, the configuration of blocks under the bed.

With the pain, the joys of motherhood make the old questions pale. In these nine months, we've had 170 tea parties, watched 400 hours of Barney and Sesame Street videos, strolled 540 miles, scrambled 200 eggs, baked 300 muffins, washed 75 loads of laundry, taken 300 baths and 10 showers, read 75 books, some of them 75 times, and planted a spring garden. Yes, I am much older than the mothers of Emily's friends. And yes, I have less energy than they. But when my little girl comes running across the lawn with a fist full of dandelions for me and shouting, "Mama," I wouldn't care if I were 150.

And yes, she . . . loves music too and has found room in her heart for both Big Bird and Bach.

Telling the Story

Of all the stories on your bookshelf
the ones with sadistic step-mothers
and wicked giants
the one I fear most is the story
you will ask me to tell again and again
the story whose beginning I don't know
the one without an ending. What do I tell you
that you will believe
the way you believe the part about fairy godmothers
and kind woodsmen. Should I begin: *Once upon a time*
there was a beautiful Chinese girl. She grew up and
married and had a beautiful baby she loved
more than the world. She named her Peach Girl.
One day the evil prince made her leave the baby
on a hillside shrouded in mist. She cried and
cried for a hundred days and a hundred nights until
she drowned in a river of tears and floated out to sea.
Or should I say: You were luckier than most. Your mother
loved you 14 months before she left you on the roadside. I
don't know what happened to her. *When the mist cleared*
wild cranes dropped from the sky and carried the baby girl
to a far away land where a man and woman dreaming
of the child they could not have
opened their eyes to the sound of wild cranes
and cried for joy when they saw Peach Girl. They lifted her
in their arms and loved her
forever and ever.

Joan I. Siegel

Answer

You want to know who made you
I can't say
I planted you inside me
like morning glories
we put in the garden last spring
you grew in another garden
not mine
but long ago
you had a sister
a blind fish
snagged on a root
who made way for you
here is the mark on my belly
a seam crooked as a riverbed

Joan I. Siegel

Second Father of Our Daughter
for Joel

In the middle of the night
her cry pierces your dreams
and you kick off blankets
weighty as sleep and
rush to her room
where I hear you speak
in a language I never thought you knew:
those murmuring sounds
that rock a baby to safety in the dark
when furniture and stuffed bears
prowl the room with other beasts.

The next morning
you kneel with her in the snow
among bare trees
filling her tiny hands
with seeds for hungry nuthatches.
Her cheeks are red as apples.
I watch her pick up sticks for the wood stove
and put them in your hands.
I wonder about the first father of our daughter:
has he gathered enough winter kindling?

Joan I. Siegel

Joan I. Siegel's poetry has appeared, or is forthcoming, in *The American Scholar, Yankee, Commonweal, Cumberland Poetry Review, The Amicus Journal, The Southern Poetry Review, New Letters, The Bridge, Nightsun, The Journal of the American Medical Association, The Literary Review, Wilderness, River Oak Review, Liberty Hill Poetry Review, Interim, San Jose Studies, Poet & Critic, Plainsong, Poem, Poet Lore, The Hampden-Sydney Poetry Review, Tennessee Quarterly, Free Lunch, The Wisconsin Review,* and *Kalliope.* Her poems are also anthologized in *Beyond Lament,* Northwestern University Press, and *American Visions,* Mayfield. She is an Associate Professor of English at Orange County Community College in Middletown, New York.

The Wings of the Wind
Floyd Skloot

He came swiftly upon the wings
of the wind.
He made darkness his covering around him.
Psalm 18

My son Isaac, adopted at twelve weeks of age, turned twenty on September 15. That day, he measured exactly seven feet five and three-quarter inches tall. When he was home last summer, I stood beside him posing for a photograph and my head came up to about his pancreas.

Isaac outgrew Loretta when he was eight and me when he was ten. But until he was sixteen or so, he loved to walk between us holding hands, towering over us like a spike on a graph. He would giggle at our reflections in shop windows and at the looks on the faces of passers-by. Isaac weighs exactly what my wife and I do combined, 290 pounds. And as you will see, I'm accustomed to using precise numbers when I speak of my son.

Loretta and I got him from an orphanage in The People's Republic of Romania at the zenith of Ceausescu's power. All we knew was that he had been born near Sibiu, a small industrial city north of the Transylvania Alps, his mother had been a textile worker, and he had such raging impetigo around his nose and mouth when we first saw him that it looked as though someone had drawn on a bright red clown's face.

We named him Isaac after my father, but the name would have had a nice resonance for us anyway. According to Genesis, the biblical Isaac was born when his parents were quite old and thought themselves well beyond child-bearing age. Same as us. He was also the fulfillment of a promise, which felt right in our case as well, a kind of entitlement due to a couple who loved as deeply as we did. Then what does God do after giving Sarah and Abraham their son? Right. No wonder Loretta and I were overprotective, despite our Isaac's size.

He was virtually silent during the entire plane trip from Bucharest to New York. He slept for long periods, waking with a soft whimper wanting to be fed, then sitting in his carrier with his eyes wide open, hands moving vaguely in front of his face as though warding off something strange and unpleasant. His smiles seemed wholly inward, prompted less by anything he saw than by forces going on inside his body.

Probably you've heard of him. Isaac Berg, the great basketball star. Most people call him Ike and the press dubbed him The Ikeberg, a huge mass afloat in the middle of the lane. They say he may be the best collegiate center since either Wilt Chamberlain or Kareem Abdul-Jabbar or Bill Walton or Shaquille O'Neal— depending on your era—and maybe the best big man ever. In his freshman year at the University of Oregon, Isaac averaged twenty-six points, fourteen rebounds and six blocked shots a game, leading the Ducks to the NCAA Final Four where absolutely no one had expected them to be and where they had never been before.

People in and around the game thought he would leave school then and make himself eligible for the pro draft, but he stayed on and had an even better sophomore year. In a press conference last spring, to stop all the speculation, he announced that he was staying in school for his final two years. He wanted to get his degree, help the team to its third straight Final Four appearance, and play in the Olympics as a true amateur before basketball became a job for him.

I hope you got to see my Isaac during that press conference. Except for his size, everything about him said Gentle Scholar, said Books, said Soulful. For the first time, his nickname seemed to make sense, to reflect the truth that so much of Isaac was hidden below the surface regardless of how much there was above it. After every question, he looked down as though to collect his thoughts, smiling shyly, humble, unwilling to seem the smart-ass like so many other young athletes. It was the proudest moment for me, prouder than all his on-court honors, prouder than the night he scored 67 points and grabbed 28 rebounds against U.C.L.A.

The name Isaac Berg, I would be the first to admit, fits a little strangely on him now. We had him circumcised when he was an infant, brought him up within the Reform movement as a moderately observant Jew, and kept telling him that he, of all people, was truly one of the Chosen. Of course, he looks about as Jewish as Vlad the Impaler, but who knew that when he was six months old? He was a dark infant, had huge hands and feet, a mop of curly black hair and deep-set eyes that followed me everywhere I moved, and while I didn't think he was necessarily of Jewish parentage, I didn't imagine he would look quite so gentile either. His features became enormous, everything growing at an accelerated pace, and, with his basso profundo voice thrown in, my son could be quite terrifying to encounter. This is so ironic, since I believe it worries him to box opponents out for a rebound lest he accidentally crush someone.

At his Bar Mitzvah, Isaac stood six foot five and towered over the rabbi. Most thirteen-year-olds have to stand on a stool to see over the podium when they read their Bar Mitzvah portions to the congregation. Isaac, clean-shaven but heavily shadowed with stubble by 10:00 A.M., had to stoop so that Rabbi Herschorn didn't hurt his neck looking up to bless him. As Isaac carried the Torah in a slow march through the congregation, some of the little old men reaching up to touch the scroll with the hems of their prayer shawls suddenly backed away, as though seeing a Cossack on horseback. But he was oblivious, blissful at being a newly consecrated member of the tribe, his face literally glowing as he passed into light that poured through the stained glass window at the rear of the sanctuary. That night, at home after his party, Isaac could not stop talking about feeling hugged by God—those were his exact words. He had been embraced in that light, taken over, and felt himself to be loved and protected forever. It was a feeling I have never had myself, even at his age, and I remember hoping that whatever caused him to lose it would not be too great for him to bear.

Like so many extremely tall young people, Isaac had his social difficulties, especially as an adolescent. He didn't join clubs, didn't have any close male friends, didn't date much. The first time, near the end of his sophomore year, he asked me to drive him and the young girl, a foreign exchange student from Paris named Laura Quost, to the downtown cinema where a French film was showing.

I dropped them off, went by myself to another film in a theater across the river, then picked them up four hours later at the Metro on Broadway, where they had gone for snacks and sparkling water. Isaac's relief when he saw me walk through the restaurant's doors was so palpable that I felt like crying for him.

He knew he was strange looking and, I think, secretly agreed when kids called him Frankenstein, Moonman, Geek or Bronto. But that all changed halfway through his junior year in high school, when Isaac's talent as a basketball player asserted itself and he became a hero over the course of one frigid Portland winter.

I will never forget the silence that fell over the gym the first time Isaac's rage was expressed on the court. The silence only lasted for two seconds, a kind of collective stoppage of breath, before turning into something like joy as the fans erupted in whistles and wild cheers. But it was those two seconds I will never forget. Isaac had been taunted by the opposing fans and, worse, by players on the other team, throughout the first half of the season's opening game. As the game progressed, he had played mildly, passing the ball off whenever he got it, sticking up his arms but not moving aggressively to block any shots, reaching for rebounds but not boxing out or jumping. It seemed as though he was afraid to stumble and look awkward, though I knew it had more to do with his fear of causing harm. As the third quarter was drawing to a close, I saw his eyes narrow and his nostrils flare and I felt that something had snapped in Isaac. After all those years of being razzed, of trying to act small, denying his essential isolation, he had finally grasped some essential truth about his situation and reached an instantaneous decision. He moved into position at the top of the key and raised his arms, calling for the ball. The point guard bounced the pass to him. Isaac planted his feet, spun to his left and took one incredibly long step toward the basket. With the ball securely stuck in his right palm, he threw down a slam dunk in one great windmilling motion. The ball tore through the net and bounced back up off the floor so high that time seemed to stand still as everyone watched it reach its apogee before reacting to what they had seen. Isaac had dunked from the foul line, moving through the air with such power, authority and grace that he looked like a seasoned professional—or a prehistoric bird riding a zephyr. Back on the ground, he stood there glaring into the middle distance while the gym filled with noise. Then his eyes changed again, found me where I sat at mid-court as he trotted back on defense, and the expression on my son's face was a terrifying mix of triumph and grief.

Believe me, there was never a spoken plan. However, Loretta and I understood that Isaac intended to buy us a new home on Lake Oswego as soon as he signed his first professional contract. He thought we might also like matching leather recliners for the new living room, a big screen television on which to watch his games, a dark green Lexus, a summer trip to Israel after the basketball season. Where he came up with Israel, I don't know; my fantasy has always been a month on the beach in Rio.

This idea of Isaac's was something we knew from hints and suggestions he would drop into conversations. We'd be sitting in the living room after dinner, all three of us immersed in our books, and Isaac would suddenly wonder if it would be nice to listen to some Mozart right about now, maybe that Piano Concerto in C Major that we all went to hear last year in downtown Portland, be nice to savor the crystal clear sound one of those new CD players is capable of. Then furniture and electronics catalogues started to arrive for us in the mail after his freshman season at Oregon. We were suddenly on the mailing lists for travel agencies and fancy automobile dealerships. Taking care of us in this way was probably the only thing that made Isaac hesitate to turn down the professional inducements and stay in school till he graduated. I'm glad he did.

These dreams on our behalf were pure American dreams; they certainly weren't Romanian ones. So equating personal success with waterfront homes or luxury cars is not in our genes after all! Tay-Sachs disease is in our genes, a hundred times more than in anybody else's, but not the need for a big screen television. Excuse me. I've been a bit emotional lately.

Although Isaac's dreams for us were as contagious as airborne viruses, and we couldn't help talking from time to time about when we would be living on the lake, I would have been happy—and I'm confident Loretta would have been happy too—just to see Isaac at ease in this world we had brought him to, see him pleased with his achievements in it and smiling as he looked it in the eye. Of course, I'd also like to have a view of water. But so would my friend Henry Ah Sing, who owns a Szechuan restaurant in Old Town and is far more likely to get such a view than I am.

Because three months, one week and two days ago, on a typically dark, windy December night in eastern Washington, I watched Isaac follow his own missed sky-hook shot with a brilliant rebound and slam dunk over the seven foot Nigerian center who plays for Washington State, turn to head back down court, come to a complete stop while everyone ran by him, raise his arms a few inches toward his breastbone, and crumple to the court as though he'd been shot. He hit the wood floor so hard that I could hear the sound of it over the wildly beating drum that Cougar fans were using to whip themselves into a frenzy as they urged their team on. I swear I could feel it through my toes.

The team doctor rushed onto the court. He threw himself onto his knees and skidded to a stop beside Isaac, jerking open a bag as he reached toward my son's chest. Almost instantly, they were surrounded by members of the team, all of them too tall to see past.

The image that stayed before my eyes was of Isaac's utter stillness there. He lay sprawled across the top of the key, his face down and twisted slightly to the left in a position exactly like the one he always slept in as an infant. My first thought, odd and unbeckoned, was that I was glad Loretta's arthritis was acting up so that she had decided against coming to Pullman with me.

I got up to run onto the court but was restrained by some people sitting nearby. Their collective grip on my arms and shoulders—part embrace, part shackles—felt as though it was cutting off my air supply. I shook myself free and ran onto the court. The videotapes appearing over and over on the news, especially the one on ESPN, show my mouth opening and closing as if I am screaming, but nothing is coming out. To me, it looks like I am trying to breathe for Isaac.

Technically, he was already dead when he hit the floor. But I didn't need to be told that. As I watched him fall, I swear I glimpsed a faint spray like the sweat that comes off a boxer's face when you see a slow-motion film of him taking an uppercut to the jaw. I understood that this was the spirit rising out of Isaac, a soft blue incandescence, it seemed to me, the actual formation of an aura around his collapsing form. When I knelt beside him, Isaac's gigantic body seemed vacated and when I touched the center of his limp palm—his most ticklish spot—there was nothing.

Marius DePino, the west coast's premier heart surgeon was in the crowd. Dr. DePino had come from Seattle to tour the campus with his youngest son, who wanted to become a veterinarian. When they'd heard that Oregon would be playing at Washington State, they stayed to see the great Isaac Berg in person. Dr. DePino quickly made his way down from the stands and trotted onto the court, working through the circle around Isaac's form until he was beside my son. His hand brushed my shoulder gently, asking me to step aside.

Marius DePino brought my son back and kept him here, turning the visitors' locker room into an emergency room (while getting me to scribble a waiver of liability on the back of a Cougars-Ducks souvenir program) and working on my son's heart before my eyes. The inventor of the Depino Procedure for correcting mitral valve prolapse and of the DePino Technique for grafting veins in bypass surgeries, the author of two cardiology textbooks and a popular novel about the mystical bond between a heart transplant recipient and his donor's daughter, the man was both brilliant and bold. I don't remember anything after seeing DePino's hands begin moving toward Isaac's chest. The team doctor got to work on me while DePino worked on my son.

There was more surgery later, after he was stable, to correct Isaac's hypertrophic cardiomyopathy, a thickening of the inner wall of his heart's pumping chamber. Usually, this disease can only be discovered after its young victim has died a sudden death. This is why I'm suppose to regard Isaac as lucky. They put a small electronic defibrillator behind his stomach muscles to shock his heart back into rhythm whenever it goes haywire on him.

Isaac always wondered how to get closer to God. To me now, it feels like he is—the Lord's hand present in tiny heartshocks emanating from Isaac's belly. But what it feels like to me is not what it feels like to my son.

You see film clips on the news all the time. These very tall young men in the greatest physical condition imaginable, these invincible kids on the brink of vast fortunes, suddenly collapse on the court. One minute, they slam dunk and make the whole backboard shake or they swat a shot into the fourth row; the next minute, they're dead. Hank Gathers of Loyola Marymount, dead. Reggie Lewis of the Boston Celtics, dead. Marcus Camby of Massachusetts, prostrate on the court, out of action for a few weeks, then coming back to play and no doubt terrifying his parents. It even happens to women athletes, always the long and lanky ones, basketball or volleyball stars, the ones with slender fingers curling under toward their wrists, great specimens, dead. Marfan's Syndrome, a hole in the heart, a faulty valve, a heart too large, a heart hiding its flaws until the sudden failure.

There were three hospital beds turned sideways and pushed together with their side-bars down to accommodate Isaac's body. His first coherent post-operative words were spoken in a raspy whisper five days after his heart had stopped.

"Dad, I'm sorry."

"And I'm overjoyed, Isaac. You're still with us." I let go of his hand and stroked the side of his face. "Now let me go outside and get your mother."

"Wait." He squeezed my arm. In the past, he could bruise me with such pressure but now his grip was weak, child-like. "It's all over. They made that clear yesterday. No more basketball. No running. A very quiet life. What, I'm suddenly going to become a physicist? Everything we planned for is out the window."

"I never planned for any of that stuff."

He closed his eyes and seemed to drift off. I shifted my weight to get up and leave the room, but he squeezed my arm again. "The house, the car, the trips, all out the window. I can't believe it."

"It doesn't matter, Isaac. Look," I pointed to his right, "all that's out the window this morning is sunlight." I couldn't believe that these were his primary thoughts after all he'd been through, after all he'd lost for himself.

His hand fell back to the bed. He swallowed dryly. "What good is a seven-and-a-half-foot tall non-basketball player? I've never done anything else. Never even thought about it."

"Don't exaggerate."

He blinked and looked at me closely, as though seeing me there for the first time. "I don't think I am, Dad. This is serious, what happened to me."

"Well I think you're exaggerating. You're only seven-feet-five and three-quarters. Now let me go get your mother. She'll want to hear your voice."

When I brought Loretta back into the room, Isaac was asleep again. She looked at him, then back at me, her face filled with questions and worry. I bent over the bed and stroked Isaac's brow.

"What?" he whispered, opening his eyes.

"Nothing. You were dreaming, I think."

He moved his eyes back and forth. "He was here, it wasn't a dream."

I started to shake my head, contradicting him, but Isaac grew more agitated. It worried me and I thought about going out to fetch a nurse, but Loretta held me in place.

"I think I may be getting nearer to God," Isaac whispered.

"He's gotten near enough."

"I don't think so." He reached vaguely in my direction and I handed him the cup of water. "Just the outskirts, where the light turned me around."

"You can remember that?"

He nodded. "And a sound, something like a windstorm in the darkness, but filtered through a long stand of trees. I don't know." He sipped and handed back the cup. "This is something I can tell people about."

"Sure. When you're ready, maybe we can set up some kind of speaking tour."

He blinked. "I think maybe this is what I'm supposed to do, you know? Maybe it's why I'm so tall, to be closer to Him than most people."

Loretta nodded. But I didn't get what Isaac meant. He was so tall, we'd learned, because of a combination of genes and a pituitary disorder.

"Maybe," I said. "But you need to rest. You need to heal for a while before you even think about what to do next."

"This has to have happened for a reason," he whispered, closing his eyes.

"You were born with a thick wall in your heart. The pump was bad, that's the reason. You should get some sleep, there's plenty of time to talk about what you'll do."

"Nothing happens by accident," Isaac whispered. "Do you think Marius DePino was there by coincidence?"

"Yes," I said. "We're lucky his son didn't want to be an electrical engineer or they might have been watching the Gonzaga game instead."

Isaac closed his eyes. A faint hiss came from the machinery beside the bed.

Out in the hallway, Loretta took my arm and gently led me toward the waiting room at the end of the hall. We plopped down together on the brown plastic couch, sighing as one, relieved to have him talking but, I believed, a little shaken at what he was saying.

Loretta patted my arm, always a bad sign, and announced, "Well, you handled that about as badly as a man could, I would think."

"I'm not even sure someone who's a Jew by adoption can become a rabbi."

"We're Reformed Jews," Loretta said. "So almost anything is possible."

I looked out the waiting room window into a parking lot where cars all neatly fitted into their diagonal slots gleamed in winter light. It seemed possible to rearrange their pattern, to shift them so they faced the other way, noses to the street instead of noses to the hospital wall, just by fluttering my eyes or twitching my pinkie.

"For some reason, I just don't like it. The idea makes me squirm."

"Who says you have to like it?" Loretta asked. Her tone wasn't particularly challenging, just curious, a gentle questioning. "I never much liked the idea of his being an athlete, myself."

"You're kidding me."

She shook her head. "So I didn't come to very many of his games. Big deal. You could skip his services, or start going to the Conservative temple, whatever." She paused; I could hear her swallow. "The point is, George, you don't have to like what Isaac does."

I nodded, but a person would have to be looking closely to tell. Of course she was right, I should just be glad he was still here to do anything. "Tell me something." I paused, still looking down at the cars, picking one long Lincoln and changing the angle of my head so that the reflected sun pinged off the fender like a shot. I got lost in the game of it.

"All right. But first you have to ask it."

I turned to face her, "Why do you think I'm uncomfortable with this?"

"Beats me." She got up and came over to me, putting her arms around me from behind and hugging me to her. "No it doesn't. You're terrified, my love. You're in shock. You want everything to go back to where it was two weeks ago."

I nodded, leaning back into her. "Probably right."

"And you've had enough God for a while, I think. You don't want Isaac inviting him back into our lives any time soon."

"What if it's something else?"

"Well, then it's something else. Now why don't we go for a walk and let him sleep."

"In a minute."

"Ok, George, what is it?"

"The new house, the recliner, the trip to Rio?"

"You hate the beach."

When we brought Isaac home two weeks later, the house immediately seemed tawdry to me. It felt too small to contain him, though he'd lived there with us all his life, and our furnishings looked shabby in a way I'd never seen before.

I've worked hard for thirty-one years now, and this is all I have to show for it? Three decades selling people insurance, eventually opening my own office, making nice money, and I live in a house I'm secretly embarrassed to own? We haven't had friends over to dinner in years—I always thought it was because we were too busy, too involved following Isaac's career or with our little projects, our routines. Now I realized it was out of shame; who wants to bring people in here, with the faded wallpaper and dull paint and threadbare carpet? It was as if we had stopped tending to the place five years ago, almost exactly when Isaac's potential as a basketball player revealed itself. Every place there was wood there were chipped surfaces, as though the house had been subject to airborne abrasion. Posters of flowers and vegetables were wavy and sagging behind their glass, windows whose seals had busted were all blurred with contained moisture, there was noise everywhere from appliances that labored to keep up. All of a sudden, I could see the place for what it was, for what it had become—an abandoned home.

While Loretta tended to Isaac upstairs, I found myself sitting in my old easy chair staring out the window. The view, what I could see of it, was east toward a commercial section of Portland. A flickering neon sign with two letters out told people driving on the below-grade freeway that home furnishings were for sale. CAREYS FURN URE. Across the freeway, a new medical center loomed. The day seemed unnaturally dark. I turned back and listened for the sounds of my wife and son, his deep murmuring voice, her high breathy melody of comfort and devotion.

The doctors had told us that Isaac had a very good chance for a satisfactory outcome, whatever that might mean. His heart was essentially good, which I could have told them without holding it in my hands, though slightly enlarged by years of extra pumping action. His circulation and respiration were all good. He was in great condition, under the circumstances. It was just that he couldn't play basketball again, or engage in strenuous activity, or do much of anything he'd always done and always dreamed of doing.

Perhaps what bothered me more than all this was Isaac's reaction. He seemed happy, relieved. He was still tormented by the feeling that he had let us down, broken his promises, but with help he was getting beyond that. He seemed, in fact, gradually to have grown joyous about the new direction his life would take.

What, did I want him to be depressed? To be immobilized by despair over his losses, to be so angry that he jeopardized his recovery? No, of course not; but giddy, as though he'd been let off the hook? It was all very confusing to me.

We had made inquiries about how Isaac could begin studying for the rabbinate because that's what he asked us to do. I'm sorry to admit that if Loretta hadn't taken over, it might not have gotten done. Neither of us—nor Isaac—had realized how many credits in philosophy and religion he'd already accumulated. Still, it would be a good five more years, provided his recovery continued apace, before he was likely to stand before a congregation of his own.

I turned back again toward the window and began to drowse. A glimmer of color erupted outside the window. At first I thought it was just the Carey Furniture sign blinking, but then it came back, a small bird darting quicker than any point guard I'd seen on the basketball court. It was the most outrageously bright yellow, with hints of black on the wings and tail, a brilliant red head, and it zoomed across my field of vision like a flash of sunlight bright enough to cut through the barrier of the cloudy window. I thought I could even hear its hoarse call, its *pit-ik pit-ik* over the traffic sounds and the voice of the refrigerator cycling on in the kitchen. What's a western tanager doing a half-mile from the Banfield Freeway, I thought. What's it doing with a red head in winter?

Then, jerking up with a start, I realized that was where I really wished we were, the three of us, where the bird was. We should be in a small house in the woods, in springtime. One of those yurts maybe that come pre-designed so you can assemble them yourself in the middle of your acreage. Not by an urban lake in a big house paid for by my son, but a cozy little place without many walls, located halfway between the city and the shore, precisely the kind of home I'd always dreamed of having. I had five years left for selling insurance before I was ready to retire. By then, Isaac would be finished with his studies. Could he find a congregation for himself in rural Oregon?

I stood and went over to the window. Nothing. At least, nothing in the way of yellow birds. Still, it would be nice, I thought, and turned to head upstairs to see what Loretta and Isaac might think about my dream.

Floyd Skloot has published three novels, two books of poetry and a collection of essays about the illness experience. His work has appeared in *The Atlantic Monthly, Harper's, Poetry, Southern Review, Sewanee Review, Hudson Review,* and *Commonweal.* He had an essay published in *The Best American Essays of 1993.* "The Wings of the Wind" originally appeared in *Virginia Quarterly Review,* Volume 73, Number 2, Spring 1997. He lives in Amity, Oregon, with his wife Beverly.

Ocean Roads Home
B.A. St. Andrews

Dragon moray, moon jellies, pudding wife, peacock flounder. The quiet couple wandered through the aquarium viewing fish as magical as their names. The fish swam in wide looping circles; the walkers moved in circles, too. The currents directing them were fashioned by architects who led visitors carefully around and through the shoals of various exhibits.

The man's face was a study in brown with deep-set eyes flashing gold that gleamed from some fire within. He stopped where a flashlight fish only recently plucked from the sea's midnight tapped out an S.O.S. "This is not," the dots and dashes noted urgently, "not the ocean's floor."

The man's finger absently tapped out a response which the woman beside him could not decipher. She studied his fingers as the strange phosphorescence flashed on and off. Her sea-green eyes narrowed with concentration, then frustration.

She wanted to know, to understand everything. What he could say and what he could not find words for. She wanted to move her fingers across that small crease between his brows and read the Braille there, the record of each mysterious unutterable truth shining beneath his surface.

In their eight years, he had never been harder to read. "I have tried, but I cannot," her heart ticked its warning, "I cannot decipher this," it repeated, tolling solemnly back and forth like a buoy in a deep fog.

Turning from indecipherable code toward the huge central tank, she singled out one fish. Sailing along, it seemed to move effortlessly despite its heavy armor. Chain mail, she thought, that could belong to Gawain and all the other green knights lumbering under the surface of things.

And here she was, standing on the other side of glass, surrounded by the whole Round Table both armed and armored. She gestured. "Tom," pointing as if not to startle the fish. In the mirroring glass, she saw the sleek shining armor reflected against her husband's chest. He came up beside her, silent and shining.

"Tom," she repeated silently inside as his armor glistened against the glass. Like that fish, he could never remove it, not in all the days and all the nights she had reached for him. That steel sometimes chaffed against her skin, but he had never intended her any harm.

It was, he explained long ago, an invisible covering, a second kind of skin. A pediatrician facing the life and death of infants and children, he needed it. For all of them as well as himself. For the parents fulfilled or suddenly and terribly bereft, he needed it; for the grandparents and the great aunts and the trembling jovial uncles, he needed it. For the suffering.

He found her staring at or through him and his heart contracted. He lifted the corners of his mouth because the beauty shining exactly where she stood always made him hope for and believe in what had no name. He lifted her hand as if to check her pulse and bent over it, brushing his thumb back and forth, back and forth across the blue veins there and there.

"Emma," he whispered to the blue blood running through those fragile banks. "Emma."

She studied his head, finding the small new-minted coin where the years of care were wearing away his youth. The bald spot bothered him, she knew, but she was tender of it. There. Right there. Her hand rose to touch it.

The little fountain. Fontanelle. The soft spot where the three bones of his baby skull had fused. Against any conscious intention, her lips touched it. They were statues filled with heartbeat.

Shouts. Her head jerked up with his. A group of second graders plowed jubilantly into one another and tumbled like acrobats and clowns toward the central tank.

Tom turned back to her, as surprised as she by emotion. "Perfect timing," he laughed, catching her arm playfully and peering down like a stern instructor. "A public display, Counselor? Better watch that."

In the tumult of children suddenly flowing around them, he saw emotions shifting in her face, equal parts of consternation, love, anguish, loss, and fear.

"We're only talking about living with one," he said hurriedly. "Not a whole school of them, remember." He tried to keep his tone light.

Her shoulder moved eloquently, but she kept her face turned from him. He walked to a viewing area some distance away, wanting her to have time to compose herself. Better than anyone, he understood the paralysis caused by parenting: the dread, the expectation, the fear of it happening, the fear of it not happening.

She felt him move off; she felt the children streaming noisily around her. Surrounded by them, she thought her legs would crumble like clay cliffs, but the little ones left as suddenly as they had appeared.

In their wake, muddled and disembodied words rushed through her mind with the force of spring rains: fertility and infertility, insemination and adoption, risk and responsibility. Zygote. Mitosis. "Blood of my blood." Biological clocks. Alarms. Hysteria. Womb-suffering.

She badly needed his shelter; she needed to be harbored in him, but he was part of this storm they had brewed up together. An insistent staccato jerked her from this reverie. Her eyes searched him out after the sound did. He was pushing the beeper back inside his jacket and turning to find her as she approached.

"Probably Marian Drayton," he smiled tiredly.

"Number three?" She tried to keep her voice even, no jealousy and no judgment.

"Number four," he corrected, his mouth set.

Finding themselves alone for the moment in an unpopular exhibit about how flushing toilets upset the eco-balances, she leaned against his sleeve. She breathed in the fragrant bark of him, the autumn leaves and leather books and clean sheets and antiseptic hand soap and strong coffee and British wool. She inhaled the safety, the strength.

"Destined never to talk," he said huskily.

"Tonight."

"No sense rushing this," he said hurriedly. He went on, his voice tense with emotion, "I mean . . . have you . . . Did Gayle say we had to let them know this weekend? I mean, we don't need to . . ."

Even as he spoke, he was turning away. They could both feel the sense of urgency. For one, the decision about adoption had to be made soon and with finality. For another, the gravitation pull of the delivery room was real. She could feel his excitement for Marian. He was concerned, and that concern was forcing him away from Emma. Even now. Now, when their own deliverance was hanging in the balance.

"Back home?" he called over his shoulder.

"I'll take the T," she assured him, smiling. "I'm stopping downtown to check on some records for court tomorrow."

"We almost had a full morning off," he added, smiling lopsidedly.

"It's fine," she soothed him. "It's all fine." Neither hand nor voice betrayed her. She walked swiftly up to him, smoothed the jacket across his shoulders, and watched him until even the darkest waters could not mirror his retreating back.

She returned to the depths and tried puzzling out the oceanic code. "Decide," she said to no one. "Decide," she repeated to the great and the small, the armored and the vulnerable denizens of this water world.

She was aware of standing alone in this aquarium, this haven for tourists and harried schoolteachers. Yet she was neither. She was left standing there by a husband who earned his living from babies, yet he had none. This was a seascape and an escape, yet she was not this powerful, mysterious element. This was a world of underwater life as strange to her, finally, as Tom's world of births and deaths and generations. In both, she was the misfit, the foreign organism, the odd woman out.

She turned toward the stairway and made her way slowly to the top of the tank. What a perfect metaphor it was, this aquatic world as unknowable as Tom and Emma and their shared longing. This terrible longing. This miserable longing—perfectly named—that had lasted so long and that could not be satisfied without some third, mysterious presence. A presence their own bodies—his sperm, her eggs—were allowed neither to create nor to sustain.

The wind at the top of the stairs stole her breath. It gusted, filled with salt and smoke from the busy center of the harbor. Few viewers lingered today above the enormous cylinder to watch the turtles lift their impossible heaviness toward the weighty air.

She was not aware of time or of herself until a pale white flag fluttered beside her lowered eyes. Startled, Emma took the tattered Kleenex, blowing her nose vigorously and turning simultaneously to see who had witnessed her complete and utter disintegration.

"The soot up here is so bad some days I can hardly see my own hand," came a peevish voice. "Not like the old days in paradise. And the wind nearly lifted me and my contraption right into the water yesterday."

The old woman dwarfed her wheel chair. She wore a pink velour running suit and seemed to speak into her leather reticule, all the while pulling vigorously at a small packet of wipes that tore at her every attempt.

310

"Hankies, dear. Remember them? Hankies." She looked up, her rheumy eyes an astonishing shade of aquamarine.

What the old woman saw up close verified what she had been watching from the corner of the roof: a slender woman in her thirties, her delicate features distorted. "Stark-naked emotional suffering" was what Ollie actually diagnosed. Maybe suicidal, probably not, but Ollie had started over toward the alarm system just in case.

Aloud she snorted, "It's all Kleenex to youngsters." She stuffed the jumbled contents back into a gigantic sack that was half purse, half file cabinet and did so with a greater force than needed. She tried to make her voice sing-song, wanting the young woman to think her less perceptive than she actually was.

This young woman was no fool. Emma knelt beside the old woman, one hand grasping the cold metallic armrest. "I really am all right; I hope I haven't upset you."

"Upset me?" the old woman clicked her enormous bag shut. "You've upset me enough that I demand a cup of tea." She saw Emma's eyes widen and added forcefully, "Name's Ollie McNair. Don't worry. I'm no head case, either. I wonder, could you help me?" She wanted a nod and received it. "We both need a cup. Roll me over there." She pointed to a wall and did so imperiously.

Emma did exactly as she was told. At a push from an old bony finger, half the wall slid open. They rolled onto the freight elevator. "I'm a marine biologist. Older than that two hundred-year-old turtle you nearly drowned with tears."

Emma coughed and laughed simultaneously; it seemed to clear her head. The doors opened; she heard a high droning sound like bees in a June meadow and hurried after Ollie McSomething's rapidly moving chair. They passed through double doors, slid down a windowless corridor, and entered through a green door bearing the plaque "Dr. Olivia McNair, Professor Emeritus."

"That's you?" Emma managed.

"Part of me," the old woman laughed, plugging in an electric pot. "Worked at the university thirty-seven years or so; helped start the whole oceanographic thing in the islands." She pulled two mugs from their hooks. "Earl Grey or Darjeeling? None of that herbal sissy stuff around here."

The room was small and crowded with manuscripts and maps; a conference table overflowed with starfish, stones, sea grasses, blasted bits of glass, cod skulls, and one huge, perfectly preserved horseshoe crab. Emma walked around in silence while Dr. McNair found a box of Girl Scout cookies and poured out the tea.

"Ever see these?" Ollie demanded, pointing to a map while setting a mug down in front of a battered, blue-cushioned easy chair. Emma studied the lines, shaking her head and blowing into the mug. Warmth and life were surging into her.

"Sea roads," Dr. McNair snorted. "Huge highways. Big enough for right whales . . . herds of them. Makes the four lane part of the Mass Pike look like a country footpath, my girl."

Emma looked closer, amazed at charts of a world she thought uncharted and unchartable.

"So," Ollie sipped noisily. "Speak."

Emma's natural reserve spoke eloquently; her back stiffened and her full lips attempted to form a straight and solemn line.

"What do you do?" the old woman insisted. "How's that for starters?"

"Law. I practice law. Trusts and codicils, estates and wills."

"Doesn't sound bad," Ollie mused into her cup. "You find that work upsetting?" She took another sip. "I thought it was about a fight. Maybe with the man in the herringbone jacket. Or with your mother," Ollie barked like a seal. "Or did you lose your job or your car keys or forget where you put the children?"

Emma sat up suddenly, hands so tightly around the mug that her knuckles whitened. Dr. McNair thought over the nouns, studied Emma intently, and decided on lost lover and lost child or both. The professor nodded suddenly and fell back into the arms of her leather wheelchair, wiping her eyes wearily.

"Know who I really am, Ms. Whoever You Are? I'm the stranger on the elevator. I'm the secret sharer, the sea cove you'll only visit once. I'm the safe place, the one to talk to Ms . . . Mrs . . ."

"Taylor. Emma Taylor." Emma looked into those old eyes and decided to say it all. Out loud. Just once. Clearly and without embarrassment or dread.

"The man," she began, "was . . . is . . . my husband Tom. We've been trying . . . in expensive and ungainly ways . . . to have what is clinically termed a biological child." She blew out a breath. "Nothing. So, a year or so ago we put in with an agency. My friend Gayle at work just found out from her friend at the Texas clinic a baby's coming up. It's ear-marked. Everything fits. It's ours. If we still want it."

She stopped. The silence stretched like a cord. She couldn't breathe waiting for this strange little confessor to decide. Decide? About her, about Tom. About the baby. The fit.

Could everything finally really fit?

"Never had any children myself." Ollie leaned over a chart and followed a road with her fingertip. "No interest. Crustaceans. Gills. Evolution. Coral reefs. Sea roads. Now all that got to me." She looked up slowly, her eyes steadying Emma. "You want this child?"

Emma's heart twisted. "Yes. I'm no romantic. I want the pain of it. The thanklessness." She looked into the strange face but could not discern the features. "The daily miracles."

Dr. McNair leaned over her mug and closed her eyes in meditation. Emma felt as if she were sitting beside a mountain, powerful and still. The stillness gave her more language.

"More than anything," she volunteered. "If he still wants it." Her fist curled and rested beside the mug. "We're finally here. At the edge of this." She lifted both hands and opened them in a spilling motion. She seemed unconsciously to be weighing air or shifting water back and forth between two vessels.

"I can't tell if he thinks I do but he doesn't. Or he thinks I don't but he does." Emma reached automatically for a Kleenex, then found she had no need of it. She was not crying. She felt calm. "We're all made for each other. I just know it."

Now that she'd said it, she smiled at how simple it seemed. Simple and absolutely correct.

During Emma's revelations, the old woman looked through half-closed eyes as if not to startle the speaker. Now she sat bolt upright, rubbing her hands thoughtfully. Then she softly thumped the table in a quiet tattoo.

"You know, it's strange, Emma Taylor." She grabbed the pot and topped off their cups.

Emma waited. So many things qualified as strange: meeting this old woman, the children at the aquarium, the timing. It was all strange.

"Odd, really. Talking about this." Her knobby finger traced a sea lane. "I'm adopted myself. Two fine people—best I've known—shared their lives with me." Dr. McNair looked down down into the depths of that other sea. "A strange porpoise like me," her voice lifted. But not her eyes.

Emma leaned forward, not aware of holding her breath.

Dr. McNair lowered her great beluga-white head and studied her hands. "Odd, our speaking so plainly."

With the grace and power of a grey whale, Emma startled from her chair and swam all eight sea lanes to Dr. McNair.

B.A. St. Andrews teaches medical humanities and creative writing at the SUNY/Health Science Center in Syracuse, New York. Her writings appear in *The Paris Review, Carolina Quarterly, Yankee Magazine,* and *The Gettysbury Review.*

One of Hypermnestra's Sisters
J.J. Steinfeld

She heard The McGuire Sisters singing "Sincerely," the words coming over the radio softly. Then the crackling static started again. She turned up the volume and "Sincerely" blared through the hospital ward. The floor nurse rushed in and pulled out the cord, waving her finger at the girl, "Shame, shame . . ."

"Sincerely" was her memory song: softly romantic, with static, blaring, summoning the outraged nurse and the memories. "Sin-cere-ly . . ." It was on the radio so much then.

The forty-two-year-old woman hummed "Sincerely" as she sat at a small, round table, recalling the first time she had read the letter from her daughter. She had run out of her suddenly confining house and rushed around the block, passing without notice the elegant Rockcliffe residences that ordinarily so comforted her. Occasionally she stopped, read a fragment or precious word and nearly collapsed with joy. The letter was now in her purse, along with three others, but she did not need to remove them. All the letters were known by heart, their words imprinted deep within her.

Glancing at her watch, the woman scolded herself for arriving so early. She was almost through her first vodka and orange juice. "Marjorie, Marjorie," she whispered and drifted back through time. Twenty-six years evaporated; long-forgotten days sprang forth with clarity. One memory or thought ignited another.

There was no doubt that she had learned to live without Marjorie, but the thought of her was never far away, at times a bayonet to the heart, more often the stirrer of longing and loss. The waitress seemed to pounce upon her, crashing through the shuffling memories.

"Another," the woman said automatically. She wondered where Marjorie was now, driving toward her through the strange texture of miles and years. Twenty-six years of thoughts and imaginings were in jeopardy. The mind stories of the child growing, maturing, developing like all other girls: first steps, vaccinations, middle-of-the-night coughs, the start of school, a new bicycle, first date, first kiss, first love. Through all the exotic and banal settings there was Marjorie.

Her husband argued against meeting Marjorie. Tony, finally earning the six figures he had strived after for so long, thrived on order and predictability. "Nineteen good years of marriage is nothing to tamper with," he had said when she informed him of the letter—a full month after its arrival. Then he flew into the first of his many rages when she insisted she wanted to meet Marjorie. "What if she's psychopathic or vengeful?" he asked, assuming his controlled courtroom manner. "What if she wants money?" She struck him for the only time during their long years of polite marriage.

Marjorie was a dark spectre in their relationship, an apparition from the past *he* had no control over. When the woman had taken up painting, in an effort to relieve the stress of teaching, the paintings were exclusively of Marjorie: from infancy to womanhood, the colours rich, the details intricate. Her husband advised her, as if counselling a client, to seek therapy, and even compiled a list of psychologists and psychiatrists, claiming her obsession with Marjorie was unhealthy.

Now she told her husband to relax, assuring him that the meeting would puncture the obsession he complained about. Tony left for a week to frighten his wife but returned penitently—confessing he missed her, needed her—yet she would not waver. The mind stories, the paintings, the dreams and nightmares would finally be illuminated.

She drank but did not taste, rotating her swizzle stick without any thought. An attractive man at a nearby table was attempting to catch her attention, going through an odd assortment of smiles and gestures, but she only absently deflected his advances.

On each of Marjorie's last twenty birthdays, the woman had gotten drunk. Stinking, falling-down drunk. She was not much of a drinker—the obligatory social imbibing, the infrequent celebration. She had watched too many of her friends dissolve their lives with drink. Her own father took the lovable drunken Irishman joke too far and saw a brilliant journalism career reduced to hack reporting. Once a year, defying good sense, she drank until memory was crushed. For three days she would leave Tony, against his complaints; one day for the ritualistic drinking and two to recover. Then she would resume her marriage and sober career. She always took a room near the hospital in which she had given birth to Marjorie. Expiation? Exorcism? Self-punishment? The preservation of sanity? The reasons or motives were unknown to her, only that the once-a-year binge was necessary.

Ten more minutes. What measurement do you give to an eternity? Marjorie would be punctual, the waiting woman believed, as if she knew the absent woman intimately. *Didn't she though?* She had not glimpsed Marjorie for twenty-six years. Sitting in the cozy lounge, the woman reflected: Were people given a second chance? Was there really a benevolent force overseeing the jumbled universe? *Try again, old girl; make amends.*

The waitress reappeared and the woman ordered another drink. She told herself to nurse this drink carefully, to wait for dear Marjorie. Nothing must interfere with this meeting, with the reclamation. The gentleman from the nearby table stood above her. She broke out of her reverie and momentarily lost hold of Marjorie.

"May I join you?"

Any other time she would have been tempted. A playful, flirtatious evening would be pleasant, rejuvenating. Tony had been distant and unsupportive since she had disclosed the letter. She enjoyed putting on a mask, exploring, romanticizing. Around her friends or Tony or the children at school, she was never able to let herself go, to pretend even slightly. There were so few havens left for romantics.

"I'm waiting for my daughter," she said almost boastfully, as if announcing a momentous achievement.

"Then tomorrow?" he asked in a rich baritone. His manner was self-assured and a neat Vandyke beard provided a pleasing touch. He appeared to have stepped out of a magazine ad for an expensive liqueur.

She considered making an assignation with the handsome stranger, guessing him to be a high-level civil servant or well-connected judge. Maybe Tony had even faced him in the courtroom. The possibilities were inviting.

"Let us put ourselves in fate's hands," she said with a sly wink, knowing that on Monday she would be back in the classroom, bereft of any romantic persona.

He walked away, perplexed. She noticed a few moments later that he had approached a young woman at the bar and engaged her in rapt conversation. The woman shook her head knowingly. Men, she thought, I give them too much credit sometimes.

The piano player arrived, welcomed people to the lounge's Happy Hour and began playing an upbeat rendition of "The Shadow of Your Smile." It was five o'clock. Manny at the Keyboard initiating the Friday evening's liquid festivities. She hadn't been in this lounge since she and Tony celebrated their wedding anniversary six months ago, yet Manny started with the same introduction and song. Marjorie was driving in from Toronto, but the woman kept expecting her to be on time. She blamed the traffic, drifted back to 1955 and began to drink her third vodka and orange juice, imagining that Manny at the Keyboard was playing "Sincerely" for her and Marjorie.

By 5:30 two more men had approached her table, one a smiling giant with all the urbanity of a cave man, the other young enough to be her son. Ah men, they're all boys, she thought unsympathetically. She feared Marjorie would not come. Accident? Change of heart? A cruel hoax from the start? Several young women entered the lounge but she knew they were not Marjorie. A mother knows. She would recognize her baby immediately. Beyond the rigours of science, beyond the constraints of rationality, there were a mother's impeccable instincts. For a defenceless moment she allowed herself to think that Marjorie was sitting disguised in the now crowded lounge, observing her, afraid to approach her mother.

She had not smoked for nearly a year, but she craved a cigarette. She didn't want to move, to risk going to the cigarette machine and missing a single second with Marjorie. Twenty-six years made each second sacred. She straightened her corsage. She had written to Marjorie—after getting her to agree to this meeting—and told her she would be wearing a purple corsage and yellow print dress. The silky dress Tony thought was sexy. Maybe she should have dressed in a more motherly fashion. But she wanted her daughter to see her as youthful, unscathed. She had even sent a photograph of herself with one of her classes; she reasoned that it was a safe picture. Marjorie had refused to send a photograph or even talk on the phone—she needed time to prepare, to establish her emotional equilibrium—and finally wrote that she would be the one with the befuddled smile and twenty-six-year-old diapers. My daughter has a sense of humour, the mother had thought, pleased, refusing to read any bitterness into the statement. She always had to strain to think of anything humorous to say.

Conversations clattered everywhere; smoke drifted as from some effete volcano and Manny at the Keyboard finished "Chattanooga Choo-Choo," then offered a few jokes about the Ottawa political scene.

At 6:10 she still did not think of leaving. Marjorie was an hour and ten minutes late. It was her own fault that she had come so early. Traffic can be ensnarling; a wrong turn, a mechanical problem. She had almost choked on the thought that Marjorie had never been to Ottawa. *Marjorie was born in Ottawa.* The lawyers, civil servants and stylish secretaries were occupied in a raging concert, indecipherable words bouncing off the ceiling and walls and alcoholic identities. The faces were changing; bodies shifted and clamoured. She finished her drink and fought back the start of tears and regrets. When she was sixteen she cried easily; her imaginary heroines could cry with great élan. She had thought herself dried up and greeted the incipient tears with mixed feelings. Once she could even cry when "Sincerely" played on the radio. In her mind she heard a baby cry reproachfully.

A young woman, her dusty brown hair shoulder-length, frizzed and uncombed, walked toward the table, confidently swinging an oversized denim bag, carefully avoiding the swaying crowd as Manny at the Keyboard hoarsely sang "Them There Eyes." In a room of many beautiful and smartly attired women, the young woman's cool indifference and facial radiance were startling, her almost floor-length man's blue coat incongruous. Eyes tried to seize her, but she flowed toward the table where the purple-corsaged woman sat.

All memory crumbled before the fresh vision; an unexpected fear crashed through the years of resolve and preparation. "Marjorie," the woman barely whispered. She thought, How could someone so beautiful come from me? She searched for her own features in the young woman's face and discovered only the brown eyes and the memory of her hair colour before the trickery of age and frequent visits to beauty parlours. There was so much of him in her face that she could no longer blot out his image. She almost forgave the bastard when she saw her daughter's beauty.

"You must be Mrs. Andover," the beautiful young woman said firmly, offering a long and slender hand.

"Marjorie," the woman moaned in reflex. Then, realizing her unsteadiness, repeated the magical name twice more, each time forcing the uncooperative syllables forward. She was uneasy being called "Mrs. Andover," wanted to say "Betty, please," but only stared in amazement as the young woman dropped her bag and sat down.

"I'd appreciate it if you called me Greer. Marjorie was your choice. My mom called me Eloise, but I've taken to calling myself Greer lately. Professionally."

Marjorie/Eloise/Greer spun through the woman's head. She squeezed her empty glass and after twenty-six years of preparation groped for something to say. The conversations in unguarded daydreams, alone in rooms or hidden on a Sunday afternoon in the Gatineau Hills, meant nothing now, were all compressed into a hideous inarticulateness.

"Professionally?"

"A Scotch and soda," the young woman said to the ubiquitous waitress. The older woman shook her head to indicate no more; she thought she would drown with another drop.

"Eloise Oberheim seemed so untheatrical, so it's Greer Montague on the perilous road to fame and fortune.

The woman was bewildered, as much by the young woman's presence as the casualness of her revelation. She wanted to begin over, to greet Marjorie with an endless embrace. Questions and answers, rigid chronology, objective detail, would be much more manageable. Instead her mind was swirling, encased in a whirling, unnavigable time machine.

"I would have been on time, I was even figuring on being early, but this morning's rehearsal went on forever. *Actors . . .*"

The older woman reviewed the letters. Her daughter had been careful not to reveal anything substantial. Now she thought it might have been intentional. No, not her daughter; the mother refused to attribute any contrivance or subterfuge to this lovely child. She had been open in her own letters, even to the point of disclosing her turbulent feelings about Tony. It was only the identity of Marjorie's natural father that she disguised.

"So you're an actress," the woman said, regaining some of her balance.

"Former actress. Currently a playwright and director par excellence."

My goodness, what a busy talent." She wanted to tell her daughter of her teaching, the incredible progress she could sometimes make with mentally retarded children others had given up on, but the storm-tossed bridge between her thoughts and utterance was impassable.

"After a few hundred too many plays, I found myself complaining like a witch about good new roles for women—you can only play Tennessee Williams or old Ibsen so many times—so I decided I'd better try creating for myself. Complaining depresses me. After the required suffering and lack of recognition, now I have a play that's three nights from opening. Knock on wood, knock on piles of lumber." With a single forefinger the young woman rapped at the table.

"I'd love to see it."

"Just a small production, but it is a start." The young woman drank quickly—all her movements were brisk, like an excited bird fluttering—with no apparent effect. The older woman sat silently, despite the younger woman expecting her to say something. So energetic, the young woman was intolerant of any lull in conversation.

"To be honest, I'm nervous as can be . . . Did you bring the pictures?"

The older woman could not hold back a groan. She grasped her purse, as if it were an unruly child intent on mischief and flight. She did not want to open the purse. "Yes," she said faintly.

"Marvellous. Obviously, I can see you and that takes care of half the puzzle. You're a great-looking lady, Mrs. Andover. You've got a lot of Colleen Dewhurst in your features. Dewhurst is one of my favourite actresses."

"You're so beautiful, my dear . . ." *My child, my daughter . . .*

The older woman offered an uneasy smile, little more than a forced parting of the lips. Viewing her daughter's naturalness, she now regretted applying so much makeup.

318

"May I see, please," the young woman said, her hand already extended.

The older woman handed her a plain white envelope and as the young woman eagerly opened it, said to her: "I could only find three photographs. I don't know why in the world I kept them."

"I'm certainly glad you did. They're great." The young woman studied the old photographs, as if contemplating delicately mounted butterflies. "How much do you want for them?"

"Oh no," the older woman said in genuine horror. "It's the very least—"

"Thanks. But you don't owe me a thing, really."

"I was only sixteen."

"Hey, forget it. You apologized enough in your letters. It was no one's fault. Life's full of bumps and nasty curves, especially for women . . . No problem. I learned to be philosophical pretty young."

"I'm still learning." They both smiled, but the young woman's lacked sincerity or warmth; the older woman's smile was forlorn, tremulous.

"I imagined him different, you know. He looks a little like a cross between Al Pacino and a young Tyrone Power, if you know what I mean. Do you ever see him?"

"No! Never!" the older woman nearly shouted. It was her first direct lie to her daughter. He was now a local TV personality and she could see him any time she wished to stay home from school and switch on her television. During vacations she sometimes watched his show for a few minutes and offered silent curses. He could have stood by her.

"It's okay, Mrs. Andover. I'm not here to open old wounds. The photos are great. I think meeting you and these pictures will definitely help me creatively. A few nagging ghosts laid to rest."

"How did you select Greer Montague for a name?" the woman asked, desperate not to break down and begin an unextinguishable scream, feeling cheated that her daughter was not calling herself Marjorie.

"Quite simply, I'm a fanatic about old flicks. Just always was crazy over Greer Garson. I can play Mrs. Miniver in my sleep . . ."

The woman smiled, thinking of Greer Garson playing Eleanor Roosevelt in *Sunrise at Campobello*. Tony and she had seen it on one of their first dates.

"One summer I was with an acting troupe and we played P.E.I. Our bus broke down in this place called Montague, east of Charlottetown. It made me think of the Montagues in *Romeo and Juliet*. Lucky I didn't like ZaSu Pitts and we were travelling through Mississauga. Can you just see ZaSu Mississauga on the marquee?"

The older woman forced a laugh. "Quite a combination—old movies and a bit of Canadian geography."

"Contradictions, irony, juxtaposing the expected and the unexpected, all that appeals to me. My friends tell me I have a somewhat perverse world view. My play is just loaded with contradictions and ironies."

"What is your play called?"

The young woman paused, as if waiting for a cue, then formed an expression of delight. "*One of Hypermnestra's Sisters*. Three acts of pure anguish." She grabbed her heart theatrically. *"Oy vay iz mir!* as my dear friend Jackie says each time the world bumps her."

The older woman looked confused. "Hy-perm-nes-tra?"

"Perfect. It's tough to pronounce right off, but you got it beautifully."

"Not a city in P.E.I., I assume."

The young woman laughed and heartily clapped her hands. "Hey, with lines like that you should be writing . . . I was first exposed to Hypermnestra and her sisters when I made my acting debut in the chorus of Aeschylus' Suppliant Maidens. Then I went through a Greek mythology phase. I found all the human emotions and significant experiences there in the myths. But it was the one myth that totally captured my imagination. I read everything I could find on Hypermnestra and her sisters. Two years ago, I finally started to write my play. I've modernized the myth however."

"Hypermnestra? *One of Hypermnestra's Sisters?*"

"You should be an elocution coach, Mrs. Andover."

"It sounds so mysterious and esoteric."

"Not really. Pretty basic stuff once you know the myth's outline. You see, this outrageous character, Danaus, had fifty daughters—"

"Before the pill, no doubt."

"Before Margaret Sanger was even conceived . . . Danaus' fifty daughters marry the fifty sons of his brother, Aegyptus. Yenta the Matchmaker would have had a coronary . . . It does get a bit confusing at first, maybe I should draw a diagram," the young woman said, opening a napkin and starting to search for a pencil in her coat pockets.

"You're doing wonderfully. I love listening to you speak."

"Well then, speaking on, Danaus' fifty daughters marry Aegyptus' fifty horny sons. I'll tell you, the plot thickens—revenge, vindictiveness, blood-feud, the whole bloody shebang—and all the daughters, except darling Hypermnestra, kill their husbands on their wedding night. Talk about *oy vay iz mir!*"

"How brutal."

"Mythology penetrates right to the core of emotions and passions and that's what life is all about, at least in my perverse world view . . . Well, to make a long story short, Hypermnestra does not bump off her hubby, Lynceus. The forty-nine murderous wives get saddled with ultimate domesticity in Hell—really Hades— drawing water eternally through a sieve. Can you picture it? No plumbing or dishwashers; Sisyphus in spades."

"Pre-women's lib."

"You got it."

The woman watched her daughter's animation and thought about her own outward passivity. Tony complained about her lack of emotion, the way that she corralled things inside herself. She remembered that before the adoption she was lively, the class clown—then, all of life was overflowing with girlish mischief, one continuous prank.

"I set the play in rural Ontario in the Thirties. Emotions are emotions, pain is pain, if you know what I mean."

The woman nodded in agreement.

"It's five daughters and five sons and there are only two murders. A little Agatha Christie mixed in with Aeschylus. Three more days . . ."

The older woman wanted personal details from her daughter but felt helpless to extract them. The young woman ordered a coffee, complaining that she couldn't hold her liquor, and repeated that she was nervous about the play. Shaking her hands for effect, she said, "Imagine, I feel like a blushing virgin."

Once again the young woman looked at the photographs, spread them out side by side on the table in front of her, sighed dramatically, then put them away in her bag. "Maybe even a bit of Ernest Borgnine," she added, smirking.

"Twenty-six years—"

"Please, Mrs. Andover, don't worry. I'm happy with my life. In three days my first play—"

"I've always felt so guilty."

"That's completely understandable. Listen, Oedipus ripped out his eyes when the guilt got too heavy. When I found out that I was adopted, I was a real mess. There I was, a pimply, self-conscious teenager, still trying not to smile because of a mouth full of braces." The young woman smiled and displayed brilliantly white, straight teeth. "But I got philosophical. My mom and dad were great . . ."

I'm your mother, the woman thought, realizing her jealousy and sense of being betrayed were unwarranted.

The young woman, declaring that it was getting warm, stood and began to remove her long blue coat. "It took me forever to get this coat. A friend of mine wore it in *Uncle Vanya* and just didn't want to part with it."

"It's a lovely coat."

"He found it at the Goodwill store."

Then the older woman, just when she was beginning to relax, to fend off the demons and confusion, trembled as if a cruel voltage had been sent through her body. She wanted to scream, to embrace her daughter. The voltage increased. The young woman remained standing for a few gripping seconds, rubbed once the swollen curve of her belly, then sat down and resumed her animated talk.

"I figured it was now or never, meeting you and getting the photos of my father. I'm so involved with my work. In a few years I plan to be on Broadway. I can taste it."

The older woman could not speak. She was in the hospital, feeling the pain, the contractions punishing, the radio blaring "Sincerely" as she waited for Marjorie to be born.

"I've received great feedback from important theatre people in Toronto. I've been told I just might have a hit on my hands. I like writing better than acting. I was always playing such sluts or weak women. *Abused* women, *the other* woman, *the fallen* woman, *the bright scarlet* woman. I was getting schizoid. I found myself wanting to walk down Jarvis Street and make a few extra bucks. With writing you have some control. *One of Hypermnestra's Sisters* is my creation . . ."

Suddenly the young woman stopped and looked at the woman across the table. The older woman's face was stretched into a ghastly pallor, her posture one of submission and pure mortification. The young woman had witnessed the transformation but made no attempt to comfort the older woman. Now the change was too much, as unavoidable as a stricken woman lying in the middle of a street.

"You feeling ill? Maybe you should have some tea."

The older woman weakly shook her head and offered a languid smile.

"This meeting must be very traumatic for you. Motherhood does peculiar things to a woman."

"You're so beautiful," the older woman said, the colour slowly returning to her face.

The young woman pointed emphatically to her head. "This is what counts. I was a model for a year and believe me, you get sick of beauty, of people seeing your exterior and not giving a damn about your insides."

The social worker and nurse and priest and her father—the beautiful playwright's grandfather—were all there, confusing her, stealing her lovely baby, rearranging her future. Her mother would not even visit until her daughter had signed the papers giving up the child. Her hand trembling, crying so hard she could barely see, she signed the papers.

"Creativity is everything, as far as I'm concerned. *One of Hypermnestra's Sisters,* you might say," the young woman said, leaning over her still untouched coffee, staring at her quivering mother, "is my offspring."

The young woman leaned back and placed her long, slender hands protectively on her belly. "I have to leave early in the morning. I want to be on the road by seven . . ."

"Stay . . ." *I won't give you up; I won't sign the papers.*

"I just had to meet you before the play opened. Now nothing can hold me back. Mrs. Andover, I am an ambitious woman. I want to be a force in the theatre. I need to make a statement—"

"I couldn't bring myself to have another child."

"You should have."

"I couldn't. I kept thinking Tony would leave me too. And he really doesn't like children."

"Ironic, I guess, you being a teacher and all that. Motherhood is transforming . . . It's incredibly creative."

The older woman couldn't stop staring at her daughter's life-enfolding stomach. She couldn't extricate her mind from the past or stabilize herself in the treacherous present.

"I think we should go somewhere and gorge ourselves silly," the young woman suggested, standing, her exuberance in no way diminished. "I could eat a dozen pepperoni and anchovy pizzas right now. You like pizza?"

The older woman nodded but couldn't get up. She was affixed to the past, "Sincerely" becoming louder and louder.

"Maybe you should lie down, Mrs. Andover."

"No, no . . ." She was speaking to the social worker and nurse and priest and her father . . .

"I hate my mother," the older woman confessed, the long-buried secret unearthed.

"I don't hate anyone except lousy actors who show up late and drunk for rehearsal."

Trying to grasp a lifeline, the older woman reached out a hand, but the young woman did not take it. She put on her man's long coat and lifted her large denim bag. "Hmmm, 'Moon River.' That's from *Breakfast at Tiffany's*. I like most of Capote's work—"

"A pizza would be fine."

"It's your city. You'll have to lead the way." As the older woman stood, the young woman carefully helped her on with her coat. The older woman grabbed her daughter's hand and squeezed, desperately and lovingly.

"There's a nice spot in the Byward Market," the woman said, feeling her baby's soft hand, performing a lifetime of motherly functions in an instant. Then, shakily, the words escaped: "Are you married?"

"I'm about as monogamous as Mae West was. I have an aversion to artificial commitments." The young woman pulled her hand free and helped the older woman steady herself. They looked directly at each other, only twenty-six years making any difference in their soft brown eyes, peering across the chasm that emotions and an inhospitable world sometimes create.

The older woman began to cry, the flow of the sixteen-year-old, and the younger woman embraced her, no longer able to sustain her performance, starting to cry also. The two women held each other as everyone in the lounge watched them.

"Don't worry, I'm going to keep the baby, Mom . . ."

Arm in arm they went off to have their pizza, the ghosts and demons just a little weakened, mother and daughter on the way to their reunion.

J.J. Steinfeld is a Canadian writer, living in Charlottetown, Prince Edward Island. He was born in Munich, Germany, of Polish Jewish parents, grew up in the United States, and has lived most of his adult life in Canada. Steinfeld has published seven short story collections: *The Apostate's Tattoo,* Ragweed Press. 1983; *Forms of Captivity and Escape,* Thistledown Press. 1988; *Unmapped Dreams,* Crossed Keys Publishing. 1989; *The Miraculous Hand and Other Stories,* Ragweed Press. 1991; *Dancing at the Club Holocaust,* Ragweed Press. 1993; *Disturbing Identities,* Ekstasis Editions. 1997; *Should the Word Hell Be Capitalized?* Gaspereau Press. 1999; and a novel, *Our Hero in the Cradle of Confederation,* Pottersfield Press. 1987.

323

Awareness

                    alone

        born   into this

        emptiness of warmth   you

nowhere   can't see you, touch feel you

        search faces for   myself

        my reflection

                    missing

Jill Stengel

Naming Rebecca

rocking rocking rocking
trying to be talking

mmma mmma mmma mmmmaaa
mma mm mm mmm

    I know what others
        call you   I do not know my name
        for you   don't know
    what calling for you sounds like

mm mm mmma
mm aa aa
umma umma ma um um ma
mm

    How can I mourn   what I cannot pronounce
    How can I pronounce what I cannot name

    first warmth   first embrace

    This baby's a woman
    This baby's soul is an ocean

mmm mmma mm mmma

I want to name you
I want your name

Jill Stengel

Jill Stengel lives in San Francisco with her husband Andy Hilliard and their dog Pupusa. She is completing her MFA and M.A. in Poetics and Writing at New College of California, where she also teaches poetry. Additionally, Jill publishes a+bend press and coordinates an occasional reading series. Recent work appears in *WOOD, Prosodia,* and *Art/Life;* and her new book is *History, Possibilities:*.

September 2
for my daughter

You entered my life on a sunny
September afternoon.
You hid behind your hair,
> clinging to anger to numb your pain,
> daring me to reach you.
I hid behind the stars in my eyes,
> clinging with determination to empty promises,
> not daring to see what my life had become.
Our journey began with talks of earthquakes and Ethiopia.

On the way, it led us through an Alternate Reality Oz,
> where the Cowardly Tin Man hid behind the curtain
> before he staggered off with the Wicked Witch of the North.
We have met villains and heroes that Dorothy never knew . . .

We were befriended by M'Lynn and Ouizer and Truvy and Clairee.
There were times that we were mostly dead all day.
We examined our premises and learned from each other
> that we don't have to believe the reflections from a warped mirror
> that life isn't fair, but that's just the way it is
> and that we never had to take any of it seriously, did we?

God has quite a sense of humor.
What else could explain pairing Sid Vicious and Pollyanna
to guide each other through the apocalypse?

Karen Taggart

Adopting My Daughter
Karen J. Taggart

In 1983, my house evolved into the unofficial Teen Center for our area. My son was in high school and many of his friends just "hung out" here. In the spring of 85, one of those kids, a seven-teen-year old girl named Raven, was kicked out of her house by her stepfather. She lived with me during her senior year in high school. At the beginning of that school year, she brought home a fifteen-year-old girl named Sutton. Sutton was very quiet, which I took as a mixture of shyness and teenage angst. As time went on, Sutton began spending time here even when the other kids were gone. Little by little, I learned about some problems she was dealing with at home. At the time, however, I was only seeing the tip of the iceberg.

About a year later as she was leaving for a week at an artists' retreat, she asked when I was going to adopt her. I thought she was kidding and popped back that she needed to file a petition for adoption. A few days later in the mail was a hand-written *Petition for Adoption*. It was such a naked cry for help that it gave me chills.

The next year when she was again leaving for the artists' retreat, her biological mother told her not to come home when the retreat was over. She wrote to ask if she could stay with me until she found someplace to live. I suggested she stay through the next school year until she graduated.

While all of this was going on, my first marriage was coming to an ungraceful end. When it did, I changed beneficiaries on my insurance to include Sutton. In the process, I learned that if she was not legally related to me, she would have large tax consequences. This put the first thought of adoption into my mind, but the real reason for going through with it was more emotional than financial. All her life Sutton had lived with many types of abandonment. Once I had the idea, I realized adoption could be a public declaration of my commitment to and love for her.

In the last few years, Sutton has overcome many physical and emotional problems brought on by the abuse she received growing up. God brought several wonderful healers into our lives—most notably, a truly gifted and compassionate counselor and an exceptional medical doctor, who detected serious physical problems previously overlooked by several other MDs.

Sutton's physical and emotion problems coupled with financial problems of my first husband's bankruptcy made things pretty rocky. For several years, she seemed determined to find some way to make me and others in my family abandon her too. This may have been a conscious or unconscious effort to prove what she was taught to believe—that she really wasn't worth being loved.

Thank God things are better. I've seen remarkable changes in her during the last six years. Those changes have accelerated even more during the last eighteen months. In August 1997, her biological mother, who she calls the egg donor, showed up again. I witnessed first-hand a taste of the physical abuse as she lunged at Sutton with her fingers curled like claws and screamed, "I've never laid a hand on you!" At this moment, something broke in Sutton and triggered extraordinary healing. Though tough for both of us, it has definitely been worth it.

Karen Taggart and her second husband own B & K Software Solutions, where they develop programs for small and medium-sized businesses in Oklahoma. She also teaches software classes to adults using curriculum she developed. She has a son John and her daughter Sutton, plus two granddaughters. She writes, "A long-time-believer in the extended family and communal living, I have a big ninety-one-year-old house a block away from a university. At the moment, all six bedrooms are full." She loves to cook and has an on-line cookbook: www.cartag.com.

Shining
for Dann

There was a picture in the paper
A baby crying his eyes out
Pudgy face gray in print all smushed up
Dark fuzz glued flat on his head
A white nurse dressed in white holding
Infant Boy Found on Doorstep of City Church
If the dogs had come he might have been killed
the janitor said when he found him early Sunday morning
Baby's just hours old
Told Dad We have to go get that baby
We did we picked you up cried for joy
Tears flowed baptized you warm and wet
Made your skin shine like caramel
Exalted in you oh the blessing of you
She loved you to leave you
Trusted God at his very door
Trusted us

Loving so loving you are
Fingertips with eyes seeing and reaching
You make your life to love children
Finding your way bound tight solid
Driftwood soul floating on waves
But you are your lighthouse home
Now shining everywhere light on everyone
Even left some at the church
Handsome so handsome you are
Tall strong lean bronze body finely chiseled face
Girls falling all over themselves trying to get you
I am privileged so privileged grateful blessed
To call you my brother and
She would be so proud
Made your skin shine like caramel
Exalted in you oh the blessing of you
She loved you to leave you
Trusted God at his very door
Trusted us

Loving so loving you are
Fingertips with eyes seeing and reaching
You make your life to love children
Finding your way bound tight solid
Driftwood soul floating on waves

But you are your lighthouse home
Now shining everywhere light on everyone
Even left some at the church
Handsome so handsome you are
Tall strong lean bronze body finely chiseled face
Girls falling all over themselves trying to get you
I am privileged so privileged grateful blessed
To call you my brother and
She would be so proud

Beth Thompson

Baby Brother
for David

We were going to pick up my new baby brother
First time an arrival was announced with passion
Didn't question the contradiction of Mom's flat belly
Dressed up polished for a good first impression
We went

Found you in a stark magic room my new baby brother
Chunky piece of sweet toffee dipped in creamy chocolate
Milk skin so smooth I wanted to lick it
Bib eyes holding up a cap of thick shiny black hair
We cried

Never knew you were anything by my new baby brother
Till fat man came over said no niggers on the block
Mom screamed told him to leave
Went over to his house screamed some more
Mom screamed

Didn't know your blood came from Africa my baby brother
How that blood had cried so I did when I understood
Flashed your smile too big for your face too many teeth too
So they all loved you could help it
Loved you

Grew braids long and proud around your strong face
A grounding brown angel right down among us
Your spirit is original earth calm peace
My sanity when I call you screaming about injustice
My baby brother

Beth Thompson

The eldest of six children, Beth Thompson was born and raised in Minnesota. Two of her brothers are African-Americans. They were adopted as infants in the mid-1960s. They grew up in an all-white suburb and later an all-white rural community. The family overwhelmingly experienced love and acceptance among family, friends, and community members. They learned about prejudice and discrimination through the infrequent words and acts of the racially intolerant. This only reinforced what they already knew—they were blessed to see love in color. Beth Thompson holds a B.A. from Hamline University in St. Paul and attends The Loft Literary Center in Minneapolis. She resides in St. Paul with her husband and two children.

The Death of a Gadfly

Somewhere, in night's empty spaces,
A wanderer sleeps at last—
By the river, in the thrift motel,
Received by the arms of a gentle maiden.

Sleep this night.

She appears to him in dream,
A naked child in the garden,
Where lambs graze on the eternal green,
Calling him back to play.

So many nights.

Into the wooded expanses,
Now as mother at the opening gates,
Holding forth hope—
A blazing torch, a rose.

Sleep this night.

In the field of battle,
Appearing among the dead
As the wrinkled face of an angel,
Bestowing at last a piteous rest.

Gentle sleep, tender sleep.

Song is in the distance,
Calling the wanderer home
The maiden holds him to her breast,
And from the void they pass.

Sleep this night, my child.

John N. Wright

Into the Void

In the beginning an angel carried me
through the water's warm,
out a fissure grown larger in approach.
Early in our flight
Through the fissures folds
The bond was torn asunder,
As the break of the flaxen harp string,
Fleshy tethers loosened, cast me away,
Down into the void.

Emptiness was quick to fill my lungs,
And color no longer was.
Phantom talons sought my form to clutch,
Gales of sorrow swept me further into the abyss
Beholding there a mirror,
And in the mirror a serpent.
I hid my face in the angel's robe,
Fearing to see, daring to weep.

The angel, holding me to the glass,
Revealed there a youthful face
A laugh to fill with song,
A smile to fill with light.
There, in the glass,
Were the lamb, the tiger, and the silly old bear,
So I asked,
And she replied, "It is so."

Wings soon grew weak;
The angel lay me down softly, sadly.
Placing the mirror then upon a great anvil,
Taking to it a mighty hammer,
Sheered off a piece, gave it unto me,
Placed within my tiny heart.
Turning then, I believe in tears,
She flew away, into the void.

Now, some sixteen years later,
My face pressed once again to the glass,
I can see you looking back
Through tears, sweat,
In the reflections of my heart
I can feel you smiling.

John N. Wright

Sons of Adam

a boy sits on a bench,
watching the husky shells of men
passing before him.
the boy's mother died at birth,
and he is fatherless;
he is my son—yours.
somewhere a baby is crying.
somewhere.
the boy thinks of the days when he,
as I, would watch a boy on a bench—

His son, my son—yours.

John N. Wright

Born in Lake Forest, Illinois, to a single mother, John Wright was adopted at three months. He was placed in a secure, loving home with two parents and a younger sister, also adopted. Wright writes fiction and poetry on many themes, including his own adoption experience. His adoptive parents and sister will forever be family. However, he realizes a natural and tender bond will always exist between biological mother and child. Severing this bond elicits primal emotions that simple prose often fails to capture. Wright draws upon the raw essence of verse to express the consciousness of a young adoptee.

the sun was redder than before

The sun was redder than before
that moonless night the years had made,
and as I traveled swiftly to my time
up the coast of wishes
by the sometimes saddening sea,
and as dark lay down
upon my journey home,
I held the son I had not kissed
since cradled in my arms.
His cries became my sounds
in that hour so long ago
when running reckless in my ways
and blindly reaching for the sky,
I fell to earth, childless in my pain.

Now years of listening for his voice
to speak my name
and vindicate the blood-made bond
of father to a son,
I pray to bind the wounds
the years have cut
and hope to heal the severed knot
of love's remaining hours.
Do not believe my thoughts are gone
of he who bears my blood,
for every day and sleepless night
I watch the sun and moon
reflect his raging eyes
and see the face that through the years
becomes the mirror of my soul.

W. David Wright

W. David Wright came of age in the sixties—for him an era of restlessness, exploration, and experimentation. His marriage produced a son and then fell victim to the unstable times. After he and his wife divorced, his wife remarried. Her new husband wanted to adopt David's son as well as to eliminate any contact between them. Eventually this all came to be and David's later efforts to have the adoption reversed were unsuccessful. The son, now an adult, and David are rebuilding a relationship. The poem the "sun was redder than before" was written a few years ago after a visit with his son.

The Parenting Obsession

"Want to find your birth parents?"
we ask our son, now thirty-three
and our daughter, thirty-eight.
"Not me," he says. "Who cares?" says she.

When first we cradled them in our arms,
each a few weeks old,
we believed they would be our
creation. We'd shape the mold

in which they became like us—
neurotic, of course, but literate and pure.
Intellectual, devotees of the arts.
But who knows what's nature, or nurture?

Today, our children tower over us.
He became a hockey bum, she dropped out.
The razor's edge of their revolt, each crisis,
slashed our illusion, filling us with doubt.

In the insomnia of small hours, I'd explore
the urge to parent, concluding
it's a species of madness, an unfathomable
need, whose traumas are not amusing.

But we survived. Our children walked
into their lives, eccentricities similar
to ours. They became loving brother
and sister, our family quarrels the mortar

bonding us. Their mates long ceased
to wonder how our hugging-love grew
so stubborn, our grandchildren mirrors
of our kids, not us—a lucky virtue.

David Zeiger

David Zeiger lives in New York where he taught English at the Fashion Institute of Technology in NYC for many decades. Recently his poetry collection *Life on My Breath* was published. He is the winner of several awards and his poetry has appeared in *College English, The Literary Review, Blue Unicorn, Manhattan Poetry Review, Confrontation, Free Lunch, Minnesota Review, Verve, Slant, Milkweed Editions,* and *Ashland Poetry Press.*

Photo Credits:

Ellen Bass: Joan Boskoff, Berkeley, California

Dina Ben-Lev: Dirk Stratton

Jody Brady: Bill Brady

Nicole Burton: Carol Clayton

Esther Cohen: Staci Rodriguez

Christopher Fahy: Beth Gwinn, Nashville, Tennessee

Emilie G. Gillis: Cascade Photographics

Floyd Skloot: Beverly Hallberg

Penny Partridge: Pam Hasegawa

Judith Minty: Robert Turney, East Lansing, Michigan

Eliza Monroe: Lynn Brady

Ehren Robinson *(cover picture):* Westmont School, Chester, New Jersey

Ehren Robinson *(older picture):* Hagiwara

Mac & Nancy Robinson: Royal Phillips

J.J. Steinfeld: Brenda Whiteway

Ordering
Touched by Adoption

🍂

Additional copies of *Touched by Adoption* may be obtained by:

Post: Green River Press, P.O. Box 6454, Santa Barbara, California 93260, include check or money order, and name and address where order is to be shipped.

Sales Tax: Add 7.75% for books shipped to California addresses.

Shipping: $4.00 for the first book and $2.00 for each additional book sent to the same address.